The Great Stink of London

Sir Joseph Bazalgette and the Cleansing of the Victorian Capital

STEPHEN HALLIDAY

Foreword by

ADAM HART-DAVIS

SUTTON PUBLISHING

First published in 1999 by
Sutton Publishing Limited · Phoenix Mill
Thrupp · Stroud · Gloucestershire · GL5 2BU

Reprinted 2000

British Library Cataloguing in Publication Data
A catalogue record for this book is available from the British Library.

ISBN 0-7509-1975-2

Typeset in 11/14 Garamond.
Typesetting and origination by
Sutton Publishing Limited.
Printed in Great Britain by
Butler & Tanner, Frome, Somerset.

Contents

Sir Joseph Bazalgette, about 1880; from a picture in the possession of Rear-Admiral Derek Bazalgette, CB.
(Derek Bazalgette)

Acknowledgements

Writing this book has been, for me, a labour of love but in the process I have incurred many debts. First, my family: my wife Jane, my daughter Faye and son Simon have tolerated, without complaint, my frequent references to Victorian waste disposal arrangements, often in front of their friends. The same is true of my colleagues, particularly the two who share my office, Jane Fletcher and Christiane Hermann-Duthie, who for over a year allowed me to decorate the walls with pictures of Victorian sewers and their contents. Christiane also found for me, and translated, information about the life and work of Justus von Liebig and Robert Koch which would otherwise have been inaccessible to me. Joyce Speller typed up the notes from which the book was written, learning more than she ever expected or wanted to learn about Victorian sewage.

My employers, Buckinghamshire Business School, allowed me the time to do the research and the staff at Guildhall Library, the Metropolitan Archives, the British Newspaper Library at Colindale, the Wellcome Trust and the Institution of Civil Engineers demonstrated the tact and patience which is a necessary quality of librarians who are required to deal with hapless and technologically incompetent academics. One hardly ever learns the names of librarians but two that I came to know well were Michael Chrimes and Carol Arrowsmith at the Institution of Civil Engineers, where they take good care of Sir Joseph Bazalgette's archive material. Regrettably this does not include a diary or other personal papers, a fact which may be attributable to the sheer volume of professional work that left him, in the words of his great-grandson Rear Admiral Derek Bazalgette, 'time only to produce children and work on London'.* Professor Roderick Floud and Dr John Sheldrake, of London Guildhall University, who supervised the PhD which was the pretext for the research, often pointed me in directions which would not have occurred to me if I had been left to my own devices.

Bazalgette had 'time only to produce children and work on London'

---

*   Sir Joseph and Lady Bazalgette had ten children. Derek Bazalgette's comment was recorded in the Newcomen Society's *Transactions*, vol. 58, 1986–7.

I have been privileged to meet many of Sir Joseph's descendants who have given me all the help and encouragement I could have wished in completing this work, particularly his great-grandson Paul Bazalgette, whose exertions have been well beyond the call of duty. Thames Water PLC, who now operate the system that Sir Joseph built, have a fine collection of contemporary illustrations which they kindly made available to me and it is through the generosity of the company chairman, Sir Robert Clarke, that the colour illustrations have been included. I am especially indebted to Robin Winters who spent many hours on my behalf searching the company's archives at Abbey Mills.

Finally, I acknowledge the help and encouragement given to me in the early stages of the research by my good friend the distinguished engineer Dr Edmund Hambly. In 1994 he was elected President of the Institution of Civil Engineers, an office that Sir Joseph Bazalgette himself held in 1883–4. Edmund's unexpected and untimely death in March 1995, only four months into his Presidency, deprived the world of an individual whose distinction as an engineer was outweighed only by his qualities as a man. He is greatly missed by his family and by his many friends.

To his memory this work is dedicated.

Stephen Halliday, 1998

Foreword

by Adam Hart-Davis

Throughout human history, the number one cause of death has been contamination of water supplies. During the 1830s the infant mortality rate in British towns was close to 50 per cent; that is, of all the babies who were born, only half reached their fifth birthdays. The unlucky ones died of diarrhoea, dysentery, typhoid, and the newly imported and horrifying disease cholera – but basically they died because the sewage was not separated from the drinking water, so that one person infected with cholera could easily start an epidemic. This is still a major cause of death in some parts of the developing world, but in England we no longer have a problem. Why? Because of the sewers built against much political and other resistance by Joseph Bazalgette.

By 1850 the rapidly expanding population of London had reached two million. As Stephen Halliday describes in graphic detail, the sewage overflowed and leaked from the limited number of cesspools, and seeped through inadequate sewers into the Thames, where it slopped up and down with the tides, slowly decomposing on the gently sloping mud banks. Matters came to a head in the long hot summer of 1858, when the great stink resulting from this rotting sewage was debated in Parliament, where it got right up the noses of the Members, who could no longer ignore the pestilent filth.

After a careful account of the labyrinthine complexities of the political red tape that had to be cut, this book tells the dramatic intertwined stories of the Great Stink, the dreaded cholera and the arguments about what caused it, the construction of the Victoria, Albert, and Chelsea embankments, and above all how the sewers were built and cholera epidemics eliminated from London.

For thirty-three years Joseph Bazalgette was Chief Engineer to the Metropolitan Board of Works. His primary and most important task was to design and build the great system of intercepting sewers which have ever since taken London's sewage away from the city, but in order to do this he also had to construct the vast embankments, which reclaimed more than 50 acres of land from the river and provided accommodation not only for his low-level sewers but also for underground trains and other services, and roads and parks on the surface. Bazalgette built or restored several of the major bridges across the river, and also laid out some of the great roads in the metropolis, including Shaftesbury Avenue and Charing Cross Road, not to mention Battersea Park, Clapham Common, and various other parks. The shape of London as we know it today owes much to his design and foresight.

I enjoyed all the technical information, and was particularly intrigued to find out how Bazalgette championed the use of the new-fangled Portland Cement, set up rigorous tests for quality control, and eventually used it without bricks for miles of sewers.

While reading the epic stories in this book I was delighted by the little boxes with potted biographies, which helped to paint many of the characters into the scene; such people as Marc Brunel and W.H. Smith surprised me when they turned up, and I was glad to have a succinct account of their lives and work. And the main narrative of the book is dotted with such delightful little stories as the restoration of Leicester Square, and the meanness of Gladstone, which, coupled with the wonderful pictures, provide a vivid picture of Victorian London.

Adam Hart-Davis
March 1999

Preface

What a pity it is that the thermometer fell ten degrees yesterday. Parliament was all but compelled to legislate upon the great London nuisance by the force of sheer stench. The intense heat had driven our legislators from those portions of their buildings which overlook the river. A few members, indeed, bent upon investigating the matter to its very depth, ventured into the library, but they were instantaneously driven to retreat, each man with a handkerchief to his nose. We are heartily glad of it. (The Times, 18 June 1858)

The condition of the River Thames described in *The Times* during the hot summer of 1858 was echoed both in the Chamber of the House of Commons itself and in the columns of other publications. *Punch*, the *Illustrated London News* and the *Observer* carried columns of indignant correspondence on the subject and editorial theories on what should be done about it. The sober, scholarly *Journal of Public Health and Sanitary Review* reported 'stories flying of men struck down with the stench, and of all kinds of fatal diseases, upspringing on the river's banks'. Benjamin Disraeli was seen fleeing from the Chamber, handkerchief to nose, complaining loudly about the 'Stygian Pool' that the Thames had become, as an ever-increasing volume of metropolitan sewage flowed into the river through underground rivers and proceeded to be borne endlessly up and down the tidal stretch of the river as far as Teddington. Since much of the capital's drinking water was drawn from the river the citizens of the metropolis were literally drinking one another's sewage but this was of less immediate concern than were the foul smells that arose from the tide of sewage that swirled around the most heavily populated areas near the river.

'stories flying of men struck down with the stench, and of all kinds of fatal diseases, upspringing on the river's banks'

This was not the first occasion that the state of the river had aroused concern among men of influence. The problem reached one of its many climaxes in 1855 when *The Times* published the following letter from the distinguished and celebrated scientist, Michael Faraday:

Sir, I traversed this day, by steam boat, the space between London and Hungerford Bridges, between half past one and two o'clock; it was low water and I think the tide must have been near the turn. The appearance

Michael Faraday presenting
his card to Father Thames;
Punch, July, 1855; the picture
followed Faraday's letter to
The Times describing the
horrors of a journey by boat
along the stinking river.
(*Punch*)

and the smell of the water forced themselves at once upon my attention.
The whole of the river was an opaque, pale brown fluid. In order to test
the degree of opacity, I tore up some white card into pieces, moistened
them so as to make them sink easily below the surface and then dropped
some of these pieces into the water at every pier the boat came to; before
they had sunk an inch below the surface they were indistinguishable,
though the sun shone brightly at the time, and when the pieces fell
edgeways the lower part was hidden from sight before the upper was
under water. This happened at St Paul's Wharf, Blackfriars Bridge,
Temple Wharf, Southwark Bridge and Hungerford Bridge; and I have no
doubt would have occurred further up and down the river. Near the
bridges the feculence rolled up in clouds so dense that they were visible at
the surface, even in water of this kind.

The smell was very bad, and common to the whole of the water; it was
the same as that which now comes up from the gulley holes in the streets;
the whole river was for the time a real sewer. Having just returned from

out of the country air, I was, perhaps, more affected by it than others; but I do not think I could have gone on to Lambeth or Chelsea, and I was glad to enter the streets for an atmosphere which, except near the sink holes, I found much sweeter than that on the river. I have thought it a duty to record these facts that they may be brought to the attention of those who exercise power or have responsibility in relation to the condition of our river; there is nothing figurative in the words I have employed or any approach to exaggeration: they are the simple truth. If there be sufficient authority to remove a putrescent pond from the neighbourhood of a few simple dwellings, surely the river which flows so many miles through London, ought not to be allowed to become a fermenting sewer.

The condition in which I saw the Thames may, perhaps, be considered as exceptional but it ought to be an impossible state, instead of which, I fear, it is rapidly becoming the general condition. If we neglect this subject, we cannot expect to do so with impunity, nor ought we to be surprised if, ere many years are over, a hot season gives us sad proof of the folly of our carelessness.

I am sir, your obedient servant

M. Faraday, Royal Institution July 7th, 1855[1]

In 1855 the condition of the Thames appalled the eminent scientist but three years later, in 1858, the hottest summer on record reduced it to a state in which it offended a more influential body: the politicians whose recently rebuilt Houses of Parliament stood upon its banks. This proximity to the source of the stench concentrated their attention on its causes in a way that many years of argument and campaigning had failed to do and prompted them to authorise actions which they had previously shunned. In particular, it gave to the great Victorian engineer whose achievements are the subject of this book the authority to create a sanitation system of unprecedented scale and complexity which changed London forever and turned the Thames from the filthiest to the cleanest metropolitan river in the world, which it remains. He was Sir Joseph Bazalgette and at his death in 1891 he bequeathed to London a sanitation system which remains in use to this day. Bazalgette has many other achievements to his name. He created many of London's best-known thoroughfares, its embankments and major bridges as well as parks and open spaces which changed the Victorian metropolis above as well as below ground, and place him, with Sir Christopher Wren, in the front rank of the creators of London. His twentieth-century successor, Dr Steve Walker, Engineering Director of Thames Water, has recorded that he is 'in awe of the vision and scale of engineering achievement which Bazalgette conceived and managed'.[2] This book is an account of that achievement, of its consequences for nineteenth-century London and of the benefits which remain with the capital as it approaches the twenty-first century.

He turned the Thames from the filthiest to the cleanest metropolitan river in the world, which it remains

Chronology

1859	Work begins on the system; Bazalgette specifies Portland cement; draconian quality control system introduced
1864	Metropolitan Board accepts the Hope-Napier scheme to convey London's sewage to Maplin sands
1865	MP proposes that £6,000 bonus be paid to Bazalgette for his work; Crossness pumping station opened by Prince of Wales (April); Southern system in operation; construction of Hope-Napier scheme begins
1866	Cholera epidemic ravages the East End of London which is not yet connected to Bazalgette's system; remainder of the Metropolis escapes; the theory that cholera is water-borne starts to become more widely accepted as a result of the East End epidemic
1867	Hope-Napier scheme in abeyance; never to be revived
1868	Abbey Mills pumping station opens; Northern system in operation
1869	Albert Embankment opens; Bazalgette designs drainage system for Budapest and Port Louis, Mauritius
1870	Victoria Embankment opens
1871	Native Guano Company starts to manufacture manure at Crossness
1873	Native Guano Company's process pronounced a failure
1874	Chelsea Embankment opens; Bazalgette knighted; newly landscaped Leicester Square opens
1875	Western drainage system in operation
1876	Northumberland Avenue opens
1878	Bazalgette installs London's first electric light on the Victoria Embankment; *Princess Alice* disaster; pollution of Thames estuary criticised; Waterloo bridge freed from tolls; Bazalgette proposes a new bridge at the Tower, a tunnel at Blackwall and a ferry at Woolwich
1879	Lambeth, Battersea, Chelsea, Albert and Vauxhall bridges freed from tolls
1880	Wandsworth, Putney and Hammersmith bridges freed from tolls; (Hammersmith later substantially rebuilt by Bazalgette)
1883	Robert Koch discovers the cholera bacillus in polluted water in India
1884	Bazalgette President of the Institution of Civil Engineers; Royal Commission criticises pollution of Thames Estuary
1886	Bazalgette's new Putney bridge opened
1887	Discharge of sewage to Thames ceases; practice of dumping at sea begins
1889	Metropolitan Board of Works replaced by London County Council; Bazalgette retires
1890	Bazalgette's new Battersea bridge opened
1891	15 March: death of Sir Joseph Bazalgette
1892	Hamburg ravaged by cholera; London escapes owing to Bazalgette's system
1998	Dumping of sewage at sea ends; incineration of sewage begins

Introduction: who was Joseph Bazalgette?

'The engineers have always been the real sanitary reformers, as the originators of all onward movement; all their labours tend to the amelioration of their fellow men'.

(Sir William Cubitt, January 1850).[1]

In 1997 the Highways Agency announced that Hammersmith flyover, at the London end of the M4 motorway, would be closed for urgent repairs. Thirty years of traffic had worn out some of its concrete supports and the closure was likely to be for a long period. At the same time it was announced that the nearby Hammersmith suspension bridge, reopened in 1887 after it had been strengthened to convey horses, carts and pedestrians across the Thames, long before the days of heavy goods vehicles, would also have to be closed for repairs. The Victorian engineer's design had lasted almost four times as long as had that of his twentieth-century successor, bearing traffic whose weight and volume he could not possibly have imagined. In the same year, 1997, Thames Water PLC started to commission a huge incinerator at the company's Barking sewage treatment works, the largest in Europe. The treatment works was built by the same engineer who designed Hammersmith bridge. The new incinerator would, in 1998, finally replace the sewage treatment system bequeathed to London County Council when that engineer retired over a century before, in 1889.

To find a monument to this distinguished Victorian you will have to make a thorough search of the Victoria Embankment, another of his great works, which runs beside the Thames between Westminster Bridge and Blackfriars. The monument lies in a hidden corner beneath the railway bridge at Charing Cross, at the foot of Northumberland Avenue, which the same engineer created after a long dispute with the Duke of Northumberland whose London home was demolished to make way for it. The engineer was Sir Joseph Bazalgette (1819–91), Chief Engineer to the Metropolitan Board of

The Victorian engineer's design had lasted almost four times as long as had that of his twentieth-century successor

Somerset House in 1820; before Bazalgette built the Victoria Embankment this prominent London landmark stood in the Thames. (By courtesy of the Guildhall Library, Corporation of London)

Works which was London's first Metropolitan government between 1856 and 1889, when it was replaced by the London County Council. Bazalgette's monument is to be found in the Embankment wall and takes the form of a bust unveiled in 1901 showing a bewhiskered figure, framed in a circle. Underneath is the Latin text *Flumini Vincula Posuit* ('He placed chains on the river').

The inscription and the circle in which the monument is framed modestly represent the achievement for which his fellow citizens were most grateful. The circle symbolises the sewers which he designed and built and which lie beneath the feet of the few who stop to look at the monument and wonder who Bazalgette was. The Victoria, Albert and Chelsea Embankments, on each side of the river, were built to house a small part of the system of intercepting sewers which he designed to prevent London's sewage from running into and polluting the Thames: hence the Latin reference on his monument to 'the chain on the river'. His numerous other responsibilities included over twelve million pounds worth of London street improvements, of which the best known are Garrick Street, Queen Victoria Street, Northumberland Avenue, Shaftesbury Avenue, Southwark Street and Charing Cross Road. Twelve bridges across the Thames were acquired and freed from tolls; all were strengthened under Bazalgette's supervision and three were rebuilt to his designs: Putney, Hammersmith and Battersea. He instituted the Woolwich Free Ferry and in October 1878 he persuaded the Metropolitan Board to experiment with electric lighting on the Victoria Embankment. He even submitted a design for Tower Bridge, though not the one that was chosen.[2] In addition to his responsibilities for London Bazalgette

The opening of the Victoria
Embankment, July 1870;
Somerset House is to the left of
the picture, now firmly
situated on dry land.
(*Illustrated London News*)

found time to design or advise on sanitation systems for numerous other British cities as well as for foreign and colonial communities including Budapest and Port Louis, Mauritius.

In his book *The Living Thames: the Restoration of a Great Tidal River*, the author John Doxat described Bazalgette in these terms: 'Though perhaps less remembered than his contemporary, Isambard Kingdom Brunel, this superb and far sighted engineer probably did more good, and saved more lives, than any single Victorian public official.'[3] That Bazalgette is less well remembered than Brunel, his friend and colleague, is uncontroversial. Brunel is perhaps the most celebrated of all engineers, the subject of many biographies, his name associated with railways, bridges, tunnels, stations, steamships and numerous other achievements of the early Victorian period. Brunel's statue is a prominent feature of Paddington Station, the London terminus of the Great Western Railway which he designed, and he even has a university named after him. Paradoxically, a further statue of Brunel is a prominent feature of the Victoria Embankment, close to Somerset House. The Embankment was designed and built by Joseph Bazalgette, yet Bazalgette's own monument nearby is easily overlooked. A more recent historian of London has also noted Bazalgette's contribution to its fabric in appreciative terms. In writing of Wren's work in the reconstruction of London after the fire of 1666 Roy Porter writes that 'thanks to Wren the reborn City was left more attractive. Alongside Nash and Bazalgette, he stands as one of London's noblest builders.'[4] Brunel and Wren are celebrated. By contrast, no biography of Bazalgette has ever been written though the infrastructure that he built for London has long outlived Brunel's broad-gauge railway, and the streets, bridges and embankments that he designed for the capital are certainly of the same magnitude as Wren's works.

Although he is now sometimes forgotten, Bazalgette was celebrated in his lifetime. While the system of intercepting sewers was being constructed he was a major public figure and there are numerous references to him and his work in *The Times*, the *Illustrated London News*, *The Builder* and other contemporary publications. Another indication of his stature may be gained by examining biographical dictionaries of the period. From 1865 until his death in 1891 Bazalgette has a regular entry in George Routledge's *Men of the Time*. The entry ranges in length from about one to one-and-a-half columns. This is comparable with the entries for Matthew Arnold and Cardinals Manning and Newman, rather longer than that of W.S. Gilbert and a little shorter than the entries for Florence Nightingale and Charles Babbage. The entry for Charles Dickens ran to three columns while Gladstone, at the height of his power, qualified for seven.

He 'saved more lives than any single Victorian public official'.

Bazalgette's contemporaries might well have agreed with Doxat's flattering assessment that he 'saved more lives than any single Victorian public official'. In August 1890, less than a year before his death in March 1891, Bazalgette was interviewed at his home in Wimbledon for Cassell's *Saturday Journal*, one of a series of sketches of 'Representative Men at Home'. The writer of the profile began his article by referring to the fact that the construction of London's system of main intercepting sewers had ended the scourges of cholera, typhoid and other water-borne diseases which had carried off tens of thousands of citizens during the terrible epidemics of the mid-nineteenth century. The opening sentence of the article reads: 'If the malignant spirits whom we moderns call cholera, typhus and smallpox, were one day to set out in quest of the man who had been, within the past thirty or forty years their deadliest foe in all London, they would probably make their way to St Mary's, Wimbledon.'[5] In the same interview, Bazalgette himself described the problem which his employers, the Metropolitan Board of Works, had been called upon to solve forty years earlier.

At that time, the river at Westminster was in such an abominable condition that they were obliged to close the windows of the Houses of

Parliament and there was a talk of Parliament having to shift to other quarters altogether. What was the cause of it? The drains of London were pouring down their filth into the river at low water. There was no outflow from them at high water. The tide kept the sewage up the drains then; but when the tide had been running out for hours and the water in the river began to run low, then the drains began to pour out their sewage and of course when the tide came in again it was all swept up by the stream. When the tide ebbed it all came down and so it kept oscillating up and down the river, while more filth was continuously adding to it until the Thames became absolutely pestilential.[6]

Bazalgette's death was widely reported both in the national press and in engineering publications. The *Illustrated London News* in March 1891 began its obituary notice:

Londoners who can remember the state of London and of the Thames about thirty-five years ago, before those vast undertakings of the Metropolitan Board of Works, the system of main drainage and the magnificent Thames Embankment, which have contributed so much to sanitary improvement and to the convenience and stateliness of this immense City, will regret the death of the able official chief engineer, Sir Joseph Bazalgette.

The Institution of Civil Engineers, of which Bazalgette had been President, entered a resolution in the Minutes of Proceedings[7] which recorded that: 'His life had been given to considerations affecting public health and welfare in all the large cities of the world, and his works, as the engineer for many years of the Metropolitan Board of Works, will ever remain as monuments of his skill and professional ability.'

Celebrated and honoured in his own lifetime, almost forgotten since: Doxat's claim that Bazalgette was 'Perhaps less remembered' than Brunel is an understatement. The qualified claim that he 'Probably did more good, and saved more lives, than any single Victorian public official' is more controversial. Indeed the claim is astounding when one reflects that the category of public official certainly includes Florence Nightingale, Lord Shaftesbury and Edwin Chadwick. It may not be possible to quantify with any precision the right of these and others to qualify for such a title. Nevertheless the claim that Bazalgette's work was of this order of importance in improving the health and welfare of his fellow citizens is a useful starting point from which to begin an examination of the significance of the great projects he executed on behalf of the Metropolitan Board: a significance reflected in the quotation which opens this chapter, from William Cubitt's presidential address to the Institution of Civil Engineers.

Who was Joseph Bazalgette?

Joseph Bazalgette, like several other prominent Victorian figures, including Marc Brunel and his son Isambard, was of French extraction. His grandfather, Jean-Louis Bazalgette, was born in the small town of Ispagnac, Lozère, near Mende, on 5 October 1750.[8] Lozère, at the heart of France in the Massif Central, is the most sparsely inhabited of France's Departments. A village on the moorland nearby, now desolate, is called La Bazalgette, its existence being recorded as early as 1270 in an official document held at the departmental archives in Mende.[9] The name is unusual even in France and several explanations have been offered of its origins, none of which has been proved beyond doubt. One account claims that the name derives from the Sultan Bajazet who defeated the last crusaders at Nicopolis in 1396. Another suggests that the name was brought to France in the late eighth century by a Spaniard fighting in the army of Charlemagne and that this ancestor settled in the Gévaudan area at this time, just north-west of Ispagnac. By the thirteenth century the family had acquired a coat of arms, Pierre Bazalgette being appointed a judge in Ispagnac by King Philip the Fair in 1298 while another member of the family was commemorated in the church of Aigues Mortes, in the Camargue, as having accompanied Louis IX (Saint Louis) on crusade in 1270. In 1604 a Martin de Bazalgette is found further east in the Vivarais, near Montélimar, on the patrimony of his new wife. They lived in the château de Charnève, near the town of Bourg St Andéol, on the Rhône just south of Montélimar, where a substantial residence L'Hôtel de Bazalgette de Charnève is still to be found. Raymond Bazalgette de Charnève was among the noblemen nominated to the Estates-General which precipitated the French Revolution in 1789. Other members of the family remained in the Ispagnac area where the name is still found. One of them, Antoine Bazalgette, was appointed to the office of consul (magistrate) in 1663[10] and in about 1770 his great-grandson, Jean-Louis, aged twenty, left France for the Americas, an act which may, according to an account in the local chronicle, the *Almanach Cévenol*, have been prompted by a desire to escape conscription into the French Army. What is certain is that he acquired property in Jamaica.[11]

Jean-Louis later claimed to have arrived in England in 1775 though the first definite record of his presence is his marriage to Katherine Metivier on 14 August 1779 at St George's, Hanover Square. At this time, according to contemporary rate books, he was living in South Moulton Street. Jean-Louis prospered. By 1789 he had established himself as a merchant in Little Grosvenor Street (now

One account claims that the name derives from the Sultan Bajazet who defeated the last crusaders at Nicopolis in 1396

SIR MARC BRUNEL, 1769–1849

The father of Isambard Kingdom Brunel, Marc was taught by the French mathematician Gaspard Monge who became secretary to the French navy under Napoleon. Marc joined the French navy but his royalist sympathies prompted him to flee to New York in 1793 where he became the city engineer. He came to England in 1799 and invented a process for making ships' blocks, thousands of which were required to guide the ropes which hoisted the sails on a man o' war. The process was adopted by the Admiralty as it expanded the Royal Navy to meet the threat from Napoleon and in this way Marc contributed to Nelson's destruction of the service for which his former tutor, Monge, was responsible. Marc also invented an early typewriter, a cotton winding machine, a knitting machine and a boot-making machine. He built the floating docks at Liverpool. He showed little commercial acumen in exploiting his inventions and in 1821 spent several months in a debtors' prison from which he was rescued by a £5,000 payment from a belatedly grateful government. His greatest achievement was the Thames Tunnel, the first tunnel ever constructed beneath a river. For this he invented the tunnelling shield whose design still underpins tunnelling methods. Work began in 1825 and, following many vicissitudes, was completed in 1843. It was designed as a foot tunnel but now carries the London underground railway from Wapping to Rotherhithe.

Marc Brunel: father of Isambard and designer of the Thames tunnel; like Jean-Louis Bazalgette he was born in France.
(By courtesy of the National Portrait Gallery, London)

Grosvenor Street) in an area where there had been a substantial number of French émigré merchants, including many tailors, for almost a century.[12] By this time he was a very wealthy man. His ability to accumulate a substantial fortune was matched only by the imprudence with which he advanced loans to some very doubtful debtors, possibly in an attempt to secure social acceptance in his new country. On 11 May 1787 the Prince of Wales (later George IV), writing to William Pitt about his debts, disclosed that he owed £16,744 3*s* 2*d* to Bazalgette, whom he described as a tailor.[13] The debt was paid off by May 1788. Jean-Louis did not learn much from his experience of granting credit to the Prince. An examination of the archives of Coutts Bank, of which Jean-Louis had become a client, reveals that from 1794 onwards he continued to advance substantial loans to prominent members of the royal family including the Prince of Wales and the Prince's brothers the Dukes of York, Clarence[14] and Kent, the last being the father of the future Queen Victoria.[15] He also loaned money to friends of the Prince, including the playwright Richard Brinsley Sheridan, whose capacity for spending other people's money almost matched that of the Prince himself.

In 1795 Parliamentary Commissioners were appointed by George III with the task of examining the Prince of Wales's financial affairs and 'for the payment of any debts that may be due from His Royal Highness and for preventing the accumulation of debts in future'.[16] Jean-Louis, one of the larger creditors among a host of clockmakers, horsedealers and other unwise tradesmen informed the Commissioners that he had made loans to the value of £22,134. He later returned to the Commissioners to inform that there was also a tailor's bill outstanding for £3,086 7s 6d. Presumably, in his anxiety to recover the loan, he had overlooked the trifling matter of a three-thousand-pound tailor's bill.[17] The bill was largely settled by the Commissioners but some portion of the debt remained outstanding according to a plaintive letter written by Jean-Louis twenty-eight years later. In May 1823 he wrote to Sir William Knighton, the private secretary of his debtor (who was by now George IV), complaining that: [18]

The Prince Regent, later George IV, to whom Jean Louis Bazalgette unwisely loaned over £22,000. (By courtesy of the National Portrait Gallery, London)

> When the Commissioners, under the direction of Parliament (in the year 1795) took arrangements for paying the Debts of his present Majesty, then Prince of Wales, my Bill was examined and found to be a just one but I was told that ten per cent must be reduced from every Creditor's Bill and that I must submit to share the same fate with all the other creditors . . . During more than thirty-two years that I served his present Majesty I never made application to His Majesty for the debt he owed me. I do therefore solicit you Sir, to represent to His Majesty the facts above stated and I humbly hope that he will take my case into consideration, and give orders that I may be paid.
> Your ever humble servant
> Louis Bazalgette

On 18 October 1792 Jean-Louis had been 'denizened' (acquired British citizenship)[19] and in 1809 he purchased the estate of Eastwick Park near Great Bookham in Surrey, later adding the Lordship of the Manor of Great Bookham. Eastwick Park was a substantial, sixteen-room property which became a school before being demolished in the 1950s to make way for a housing estate. In Jean-Louis' lifetime it was the home of the Surrey Union Foxhounds and, in addition to the parkland surrounding the house itself, exercised rights over 2,280 acres of cultivated land and 785 acres of Bookham and Ranmore Commons.[20] When Jean-Louis died in 1830 his will bequeathed not only these estates but 'also the manors and other hereditaments and real estate whatsoever and wheresoever situate in Great Britain, Ireland, Jamaica and elsewhere'.[21]

By his first marriage Jean-Louis had three children. One of them was a son, Joseph William, born in 1783. He entered the Royal Navy in 1796 and was promoted to sub-lieutenant on 15 October 1805, six days before the battle of Trafalgar. He attended Nelson's funeral. In March 1809 he was wounded and lamed for life in an engagement off the Spanish coast, for which misfortune Parliament granted him a lifetime pension of £150. He retired from the Navy in July 1814 with the rank of commander, went on to work for the Naval and Military Bible Society and died in 1849.[22] This Joseph William was the father of the engineer, his only son, who was born on 28 March 1819 at Enfield and privately educated. At the age of seventeen Joseph the younger became an articled pupil of (later Sir) John MacNeill, formerly one of Telford's principal assistants in road and bridge building. He was employed by MacNeill as a resident engineer on land drainage and reclamation works in Northern Ireland, for which purpose he visited Holland,[23] and these works were the subject of his first paper to the Institution of Civil Engineers[24] of which he had become a graduate member on 6 March 1838, MacNeill acting as his proposer.[25] He became a full member of the Institution on 17 February 1846 when he had, according to his membership certificate, 'Served a regular period of pupillage under Sir J. MacNeill, was for 2 years Resident Engineer on works in Ireland, 1 year laying out lines for the Railway Commissioners and has been upwards of 2 years in business for himself as a civil engineer'.[26] He was to become President of the Institution in 1884.

In 1842, aged twenty-three, Joseph had set up his own civil engineering practice and by 1845, the year in which he married Maria Kough of Wexford, he was leasing an office for the purpose at 24 Great George Street, close to the headquarters of the Institution of Civil Engineers itself. This part of London was the 'Harley Street' of the engineering profession and Bazalgette's office had itself previously been occupied both by the Stephensons and by George Hudson, the railway entrepreneur whose disastrous bankruptcy shortly afterwards caused a temporary slump in the railway construction boom. Indeed in 1847 Bazalgette suffered a complete breakdown in his health which was attributed in a short account written during his lifetime to his involvement in the 'railway mania' of the previous two years:

'Served a regular period of pupillage under Sir J. MacNeill, was for 2 years Resident Engineer on works in Ireland, 1 year laying out lines for the Railway Commissioners and has been upwards of 2 years in business for himself as a civil engineer'

In November of the year in which the railway mania began [1845] he found himself at the head of a large staff of engineering assistants, designing and laying out schemes for railways, ship canals and other engineering works in various parts of the United Kingdom and preparing the surveys and plans for Parliamentary deposit, which had to be accomplished by the last day of November. While his remarkable success was most encouraging, its effects soon began to tell upon his health, which completely gave way in 1847; he was compelled to retire from business and go into the country, where a year of perfect rest restored him to health.[27]

The experience that he gained in preparing plans under the pressure of deadlines and in dealing with Parliamentary requirements during this testing period was to be invaluable in his later work as Chief Engineer to the Metropolitan Board of Works. He was certainly well connected within the engineering profession and apparently well regarded by some of its most distinguished practitioners. His applications for employment were supported by referees whose names include the most distinguished engineers of the nineteenth century: Robert Stephenson, Member of Parliament, co-designer with his father George of *The Rocket* and builder of the London to Birmingham railway; Sir William Cubitt, consulting engineer to the Great Northern Railway, and builder of the South-Eastern Railway; and Isambard Kingdom Brunel himself.[28]

Very little is known about the personality of the man who was to have such a decisive influence on the sanitation of Victorian London and the health of its inhabitants. One of his pupils, H.P. Boulnois, who became Bazalgette's pupil at the Metropolitan Board on 1 January 1865, gives the impression in his few references to Bazalgette that he was, above all, meticulous, with a sharp eye for detail. Bazalgette had specified the use of Portland cement in the construction of the intercepting sewers, the first large-scale public work in which it was used. He adopted it because it was stronger than other kinds of cement owing to the vitrification process that occurred during manufacture but, if over-heated, it was liable to fail.[29] Bazalgette, though adventurous in the use of the new material, was aware of these dangers and was a cautious man so he instituted an elaborate quality control procedure which ensured that defective batches were rejected. Boulnois was required, with other engineers and pupils, to carry out tests on each delivery of Portland cement to ensure that it was sufficiently strong. Boulnois also records that Bazalgette complimented him on a drawing he had prepared but criticised its lettering on the grounds that 'an engineer should be able to do his own lettering and printing in a neat manner, even if it

Bazalgette was meticulous, with a sharp eye for detail

were only block printing'.[30] It was commonplace at this time for established engineers to take as articled pupils young men who wished to gain entry to the profession by working under the guidance of an experienced master. Bazalgette had learned his trade in the same way as a pupil of MacNeill and seven of Bazalgette's pupils eventually passed into the service of the Metropolitan Board of Works, two of them being graduates and one of them being Bazalgette's son, Edward. Each articled pupil paid a fee of several hundred pounds, Boulnois paying £420.[31] Bazalgette's salary upon appointment was £1,000 (later increased to £2,000) so the fees thus received represented a significant source of additional income. As he became a celebrated public figure Bazalgette's income from consultancy in Britain and abroad rose rapidly and after his death his estate was valued at £184,431, a colossal sum at the time.[32]

Photographs of Bazalgette show that he was a small man, and his great-grandson, Rear-Admiral Derek Bazalgette, recorded that he suffered from asthma.[33] His published correspondence on the main drainage, notably in *The Times*, and the doggedness with which he confronted the numerous interest groups and other obstacles that stood in the way of the completion of the intercepting sewers suggest that he was a man of heroic patience and exemplary persistence in the face of frustrations and opposition which many would have found daunting and which had in fact brought about the early death of one of his predecessors, Frank Forster.[34] He certainly made a strong impression on a young man who joined the Board of Works in 1882 and later became Comptroller of the Board's successor, the London County Council. In an account written after his retirement Sir Harry Haward, commenting on the people working at the Board in the year he joined, wrote that: 'The most prominent figure among the officers of the Board was the distinguished Chief Engineer, Sir Joseph Bazalgette, the designer of the main drainage system of London and of the Victoria Embankment – two monumental works entitling him to a niche in the temple of fame.'[35]

A man of heroic patience and exemplary persistence in the face of frustrations

Bazalgette as Consultant

Besides his work in London Bazalgette was active as an engineer in other spheres and his reputation ensured that his services were frequently called upon by other communities in Britain and overseas. The *Proceedings of the Institution of Civil Engineers* record over one hundred contributions by Bazalgette either in the form of his own papers or in discussions of papers given by others.[36] The former include a paper printed in the first volume of the Institution's *Proceedings*[37] on the subject of land reclamation from the sea, based upon his early experience in Northern Ireland, as well as his paper on London's intercepting system and his presidential address on the same subject.[38] His contributions to discussions on papers given by others range from familiar territory such as sewage treatment processes (fifteen contributions) to comments on the water supply to the fountains in Trafalgar Square, the adoption of novel mechanical devices for dredging and the geological problems of constructing a tunnel between Dover and Calais.[39] However, an examination of the archives of the Institution of Civil Engineers suggests that he was most frequently engaged either as an expert witness in a dispute involving proposed construction work or as a consultant in the preparation of drainage plans for towns and cities outside the metropolis. Sometimes Bazalgette himself prepared the plans and sometimes he was called in for a second opinion on plans devised by others.

Bazalgette's Plans for Cambridge, Norwich, Budapest and Mauritius

On 6 February 1866 the town surveyor for Cambridge invited Bazalgette to visit the town and advise on a scheme to divert sewage from the River Cam.[40] This followed a resolution by the town council's Cam Purification Committee that 'to discharge sewage matter into the Cam between Mill Lane and Jesus Green is to convert the River into an elongated cesspool', words which echoed the ordeals of London in the previous decade. Bazalgette visited Cambridge on 16 March, charging the substantial fee of one hundred guineas, and prepared a scheme which involved intercepting the sewage before it reached the river and conducting it to a point 2 miles downstream where it would be stored and pumped out to irrigate an 800 acre field at Chesterton. He estimated the cost as £27,059. The council was evidently reluctant to spend this sum, and twelve years later Bazalgette's advice was again sought, the explanation being given that the Public Health Act of 1875 now allowed the council greater powers to implement such a scheme than they had possessed at the earlier date.[41] Bazalgette, together with a firm of engineers called Law and Chatterton, devised a modified scheme which extended the drainage area to Newnham. The drawings, signed by Bazalgette, and somewhat battered after more than a century of use, remain in the city engineer's department to this day.[42] He devised a similar scheme for Norwich in 1865, also involving sewage irrigation downstream of the City.

More surprisingly, in the midst of all his other responsibilities, Bazalgette found time in 1869 to visit Budapest[43] in response to a request from the Burgomeister and Sir Samuel Morton Peto whose

'to discharge sewage matter into the Cam between Mill Lane and Jesus Green is to convert the River into an elongated cesspool'

SIR SAMUEL MORTON PETO, 1809–89

Morton Peto was an apprentice bricklayer before he inherited his uncle's building business and turned it into one of Britain's largest contractors. He built many of London's clubs, including the Reform Club and the Oxford and Cambridge Club in Pall Mall; parts of the Great Western, Great Eastern and South Western railways; much of London's docks; railways in Argentina, Australia, Russia, Algeria, Canada and Norway; part of the new Houses of Parliament; and, most notably, Nelson's column. He became a Member of Parliament in 1847 and served on many Parliamentary committees.

Samuel Morton Peto. (By courtesy of the National Portrait Gallery, London)

civil engineering and contracting firm had been advising the City Council on how to clean up the River Danube.[44] Bazalgette recommended a system of three intercepting sewers and one outfall to the river downstream of the City and estimated the cost as £204,646 if executed by Morton Peto. He emphasised the beneficial effects of the scheme on the health of the inhabitants of the City, then numbering two hundred thousand:

> Having carefully examined the city and studied the levels and other data connected with the drainage of Pest which have been placed in my hands, I have now the honour to submit for your consideration a plan, section and estimate of a scheme which I have prepared for its improved drainage . . . No-one can calculate how great the saving of life may be in case the city should be visited by Cholera and Fever.[45]

Pest City Council seem to have been unwilling to spend the money required, and five years later they consulted Bazalgette again who replied, on 18 May 1874, that, before offering further advice, he would like them to pay him the £1,208 fee due 'in payment for my time and thought in preparing the plans . . . after the use that has been made of my ideas by the city authorities, and their recognition of the soundness of the principles laid down by me'.

His advice was sought even further afield when the Crown Agents asked him to devise a plan for the drainage of Port Louis, Mauritius, in 1869 but on this occasion he sent his son Edward to carry out the field work. The town was at that time dependent upon the removal of sewage by carts at night (hence the expression 'nightsoil') but Bazalgette dismissed this as a long-term solution by citing the experience of Paris where, despite 'removing all nightsoil by carts . . . with all the precision and discipline of a military nation', the River Seine was frequently polluted. Bazalgette again devised a system of intercepting pipe sewers, to be made in England, shipped to Mauritius and assembled there at an estimated cost of £204,616.

The Master of the Horse

In February 1868, while Bazalgette was heavily engaged on the problems of metropolitan drainage, he was asked to devise a solution for an embarrassing problem which was arising at Hampton Court. The Thames conservators, who were charged with maintaining the cleanliness of the river, complained to the Chief Commissioner of Works, who was responsible for Crown property, that sewage from Hampton Court Palace was polluting the river. Bazalgette devised a plan to divert the sewage through a pipe which ran past the Royal Tennis Court and the celebrated Hampton Court vine to 12 acres of grassland where the horses from the Royal Mews grazed. The Master of the Horse was alarmed at this prospect, despite Bazalgette's assurances that the resulting crop would be of the highest quality. He objected that the odour would affect a nearby 'place of recreation and amusement to hundreds of the poorer inhabitants of Hampton Wick' and added, for good measure, that 'the Roman Catholic church which is frequently attended by the [exiled] French Royal Family is just the other side of the river'. The Chief Commissioner of Works remained steadfast in his support of Bazalgette's scheme so the Master of the Horse appealed to Queen Victoria, who rarely used Hampton Court. Unsurprisingly Her Majesty did not wish to become involved in a dispute on such a base, if sensitive, matter since the reply from her secretary was not reassuring: 'The Queen has expressed no opinion whatever as to the general merits of the scheme.'[46]

Her Majesty did not wish to become involved in a dispute on such a base, if sensitive, matter

Bazalgette as Expert Witness

Besides his work in designing drainage schemes for communities outside the metropolis, Bazalgette was frequently called in as an expert witness to testify to the suitability or otherwise of projects designed by others. This work continued after his retirement from the post of Chief Engineer to the Board. Drainage schemes devised by British engineers for St Petersburg and Berlin were sent to Bazalgette for his opinion. The plans for Berlin had been criticised by a consultant called Baldwin Latham as 'the most contemptible thing as a proposition for the drainage of a town which I have ever witnessed'. The engineer who devised the scheme, understandably aggrieved by this judgement, wrote to Bazalgette 'I ask you candidly for your opinion on my project for the drainage of Berlin', and invited him to condemn Latham's insult.[47]

'I ask you candidly for your opinion on my project for the drainage of Berlin'

In more conventional circumstances he was called upon by parties engaged in legal disputes. In 1874 he was asked by J.F. Bateman, a fellow civil engineer and resident of Moor Park near Farnham, Surrey, to give his opinion on the causes of pollution of the River Wey. Bazalgette wrote to him reporting that 'I examined the River Wey from Moor Park to the neighbourhood of the Gostrey Meadow, Farnham' and giving his opinion that the pollution was caused by Farnham's sewers.[48] Bazalgette's intervention did not resolve the dispute since the matter went to Aldershot County Court as Bateman vs. Farnham Local Board in January 1883. A similar case arose in Birmingham in the years 1872 and 1874 when a group of citizens proceeded against the Borough Council over the pollution of the River Tame. Bazalgette swore an affidavit for the plaintiffs to the effect that the storm waters which were the cause of the pollution could be purified to a degree which would solve the problem.

He was also called as an expert witness to oppose schemes proposed by developers of railways, tramways and other facilities which met with the disapproval of local authorities. In May 1889, shortly after his retirement, he appeared as a witness for the London County Council (successors to the Metropolitan Board), which was concerned that the proposed Central underground railway (the Central Line) would damage the middle level intercepting sewer. Having expressed his scepticism about the need for the railway, Bazalgette testified to the Committee considering the London Central (Subway) Bill that its construction would damage the sewer in the vicinity of Shoe Lane and proposed that the railway company be required to deposit a bond of £25,000 as surety for the cost of repairs to the sewer should the need arise.[49] In the same month he appeared again as a witness for the LCC in hearings concerning the Shortlands and Nunhead Railway Bill, in opposition to the company's plans to build its line across a recreation ground which Bazalgette had been involved in designing when he was Chief Engineer. Bazalgette's evidence on this occasion resonates with later concerns: 'There is always a tendency in all parts of London for railway companies to take open spaces, because they can be more economically acquired, and, if there was not a public body to watch those open spaces, they would be very soon all absorbed and destroyed.'[50]

In the chapters that follow it will be argued that Bazalgette's achievements at every level entitle him to a place in the front rank of great Victorian engineers. The scale and complexity of the task that confronted him in cleansing the largest city in the world of filth and pestilence had defeated his predecessors. The technical and political problems that accompanied his work demanded immense patience and novel materials. The changes he made to the face of London in the form of new bridges, parks and streets, and the railways and sewers which run below them, have remained to the present day. Indeed, as observed at the beginning of this chapter in the comparison between the relative longevity of Hammersmith flyover and Hammersmith Bridge, we may regret that his methods, as well as his structures, did not survive into the present century.

Bazalgette's achievements at every level entitle him to a place in the front rank of great Victorian engineers

CHAPTER ONE

London's Sanitation before 1850

The flood is now, below London Bridge, bad as poetical descriptions of the Stygian Lake, while the London Dock is black as Acheron . . . where are ye, ye civil engineers? Ye can remove mountains, bridge seas and fill rivers . . . can ye not purify the Thames, and so render your own city habitable?

('Quondam', 1853)[1]

From Complacency to Panic

In 1844 the influential contemporary journal *The Builder* published a pompous but reassuring letter from a Professor of Chemistry. Professor Booth wrote: 'The free currents of air which are necessarily in constant circulation from their proximity to the majestic Thames . . . have been considered (and not improperly) as a great cause of the salubrity of the metropolis.'[2] This claim is significant for two reasons. First, it is a clear statement of the 'miasmic' theory of disease which was prevalent at the time and which held that good and bad health were caused primarily, if not exclusively, by the properties of the air inhaled by the lungs. In the same passage Booth expressed a more extravagant version of the theory: 'From inhaling the odour of beef the butcher's wife obtains her obesity.' The theory long survived the discovery that diseases like cholera were transmitted through water rather than air and Florence Nightingale, who died in 1910, went to her grave firmly believing in the miasmic theory. The theory bedevilled many attempts by reformers to secure improvements in the water supply and sanitation of London, as will be seen in later chapters.

However, the greater reason for the significance for Booth's claim about the 'salubrity' of London lies in its complacent view of the waters of the Thames. Fourteen years after Booth made this claim, in the hot summer of 1858, the drapes of the Houses of Parliament were being soaked in chloride of lime to act as a barrier, albeit an

'From inhaling the odour of beef the butcher's wife obtains her obesity'

ineffective one, against the foul odours arising from the river. Despite
these precautions the leader of the House and Chancellor of the
Exchequer, Disraeli, was seen fleeing from the chamber, his
handkerchief to his nose and, as Bazalgette observed in his interview
with the *Saturday Journal*, there was even talk of moving Parliament
elsewhere. Henley upon Thames was considered.

Professor Booth's flattering assessment of the quality of London's
air and the condition of its river was not unique in the eighteenth or
early nineteenth century. Charles Lucas, an Irishman who qualified as
a doctor in Paris, had written in 1756 that London's water
'undoubtedly is one of the principal causes why our capital is the
most healthful great city in the world',[3] and in 1818 another writer,
Samuel Leigh, claimed of the capital:

*London's water 'is one
of the principal causes
why our capital is the
most healthful great
city in the world'*

> Its healthfulness is equal to that of any other metropolis in existence;
> its plentiful supply of water which is furnished by different water
> companies, must also have an excellent effect on the cleanliness, and
> consequently on the health, of the inhabitants of London, while its
> system of sewers and drains . . . adds still more to the general causes
> which conduce to salubrity.[4]

In 1826 John Britton had written:

> With regard to the diseases and proportion of salubrity usually
> attaching to London, it is a satisfaction to state generally, that since
> the complete extinction of the Plague by the Great Fire of 1666, this
> metropolis has fully deserved to be considered as one of the most
> healthy on earth; and that in consequence of the open mode of
> building that now prevails, its increase to an almost indefinite extent
> is not likely to be attended with additional unwholesomeness.[5]

London's Water Supply

For many centuries the condition of London's water supply had been
a cause of some pride to its inhabitants. The Romans had laid clay
pipes throughout the City, conveying the waters of the Walbrook to
public conduits and baths like the ones discovered in Upper Thames
Street. During the medieval and Tudor periods water was drawn
from the Thames, from its tributaries and from the numerous natural
wells which are remembered in modern street and district names
such as Well Court, near St Paul's Cathedral; Wellclose Square, off
Cable Street; and the Clerks' Well, or Clerkenwell. Other important
wells were found at Holywell, near Blackfriars, and St Clement's
Well, close to St Clement's Inn. Most inhabitants drew and carried

their own supplies from these sources while wealthier citizens employed the services of water-carriers who in 1496 formed themselves into a guild of their own called 'The Brotherhood of St Cristofer [sic] of the Waterbearers'.[6] From the thirteenth century onwards civil engineering projects of increasing complexity were undertaken to supplement local supplies using pipes of clay, sandstone, lead and hollowed-out elm trees. Thus in 1237, during the reign of Henry III, Gilbert de Sandford granted to the City all the springs in his fief of Tyburn at Mary le Bourne (now Marylebone), the water from which was carried to the great conduit in Cheapside by lead pipes. The water was freely available to householders but some revenue had to be collected to maintain and repair the pipes so in 1312 certain citizens were appointed 'to faithfully collect the money assessed upon brewers, cooks and fishmongers at their discretion for the easement they enjoy

A medieval water-carrier; most families were dependent on such men before the advent of water piped direct to houses. (Thames Water plc)

Cheapside Cross, 1798, with Gilbert de Sandford's conduit of 1236 visible in the background. (By courtesy of the Guildhall Library, Corporation of London)

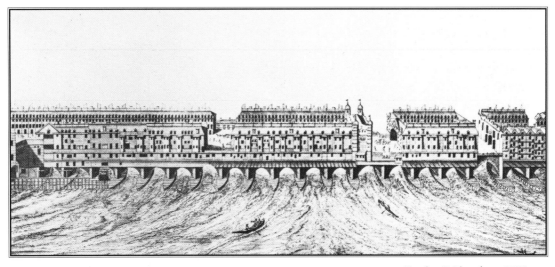

of the water of the conduit of Chepe, and to expend the same upon the repairs and maintenance of the said conduit'.

In the following century, in 1439, the abbot and monks of Westminster made a similar grant to the City, allowing them 'to erect a fountain-head with fountains, vents, cisterns and other works in the manor of Paddington' for the purpose of increasing the City's water supplies. In 1582 a Dutchman called Peter Morice leased from the City for £25 10*s* a year the first arch of London Bridge, within which he constructed a waterwheel which drew water from the Thames and piped it to premises in the City. This continued in use for 240 years until 1822 – seven years after house waste was permitted to be carried to the Thames via the sewers.

London Bridge about 1750; the waterwheel which drew drinking water from the river is visible to the left of the picture. (Thames Water plc)

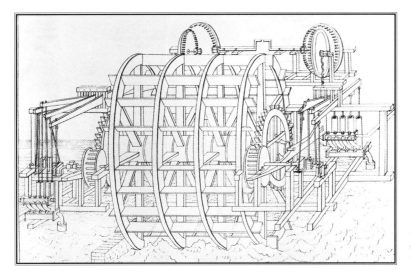

A diagram of the waterwheel on London Bridge. (Thames Water plc)

The most remarkable enterprise was that of Hugh Myddleton (or Middleton), a successful goldsmith, banker and cloth maker, and Member of Parliament for Denbigh. In 1613 he began to construct the New River which brought fresh water from a spring at Amwell in Hertfordshire to a point near Sadlers Wells, a distance of some 38 miles. Early difficulties in financing the project were overcome with the assistance of an investment by James I and for this successful enterprise Myddleton was made a baronet in 1622. The New River remains a source of London's water. A century later, in 1723, the Chelsea Water Company was established to draw water from the North Bank of the Thames, adopting the slogan 'water three times a week for three shillings a quarter' and over the following 122 years six other companies followed in drawing water from the river: the West Middlesex, Grand Junction, East London, South London, Lambeth and Southwark companies. By the time the last of these started, in 1845, thirty years had passed since house drains had been allowed to empty into the sewers. The consequences for the purity of the drinking water may be imagined, but these were overlooked by commentators such as Professor Booth and the other writers quoted at the beginning of this chapter.

Sir Hugh Myddleton (1560?–1631), builder of the New River which still supplies water to London. (Thames Water plc)

Not everyone shared Professor Booth's confidence in the purity of the Thames. In 1827 the pamphleteer John Wright had anonymously published *The Dolphin, or Grand Junction Nuisance, Proving that Several Thousand Families in Westminster and its Suburbs are Supplied with Water in a State Offensive to the Sight, Disgusting to the Imagination and Destructive to Health* which drew attention to the pollution of water supplies by industrial effluent and leakage from sewers. Copies of the pamphlet were distributed to houses in Westminster.[7] Wright had been an associate of William Cobbett and edited some of the old campaigner's works before his indignation at the quality of the water supplied to his house in Regent Street, and drawn from the Thames near the mouth of the Ranelagh sewer, led him to attack the Grand Junction Waterworks company which supplied it.[8] The pamphlet claimed that the company sent up 'to be used daily at the breakfast table . . . a fluid saturated with the impurities of fifty thousand homes – a dilute solution of animal and

New River Head waterworks, near Sadler's Wells, 1665; the medieval St Paul's Cathedral is visible in the background; it was destroyed the following year in the Great Fire of London. (Thames Water plc)

Sir Hugh Myddleton's New River at Sadler's Wells, approaching the waterworks at New River Head, about 1750. (Thames Water plc)

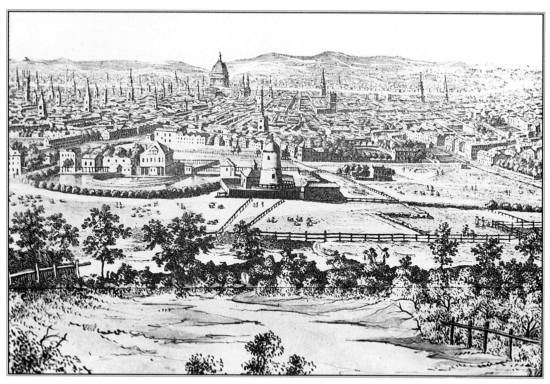

A view of the City, about 1750. The New River Head waterworks is visible in the foreground, while the spires of Wren's churches, built after the Great Fire, are clearly visible surrounding the newly built St Paul's. (Thames Water plc)

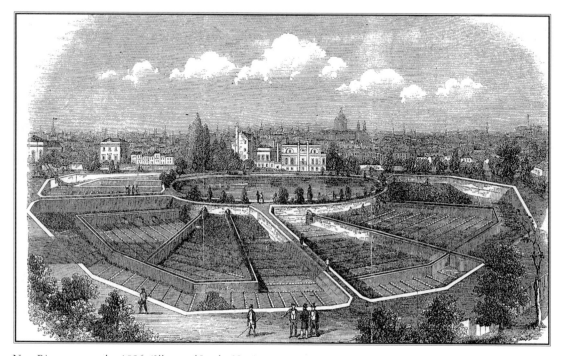

New River waterworks, 1856. (*Illustrated London News*)

vegetable substances in a state of putrefaction – alike offensive to the sight, disgusting to the imagination and destructive to the health'.[9]

Wright dedicated his pamphlet to the radical M.P. Sir Francis Burdett, who raised what a later Select Committee described as 'an alarm' which prompted the appointment of a Royal Commission in 1828. Its members concluded that 'the present state of the supply of water to the Metropolis is susceptible of and requires improvement; that many of the complaints respecting the quality of the water are well founded; and that it ought to be derived from other sources than those now resorted to'.[10]

The Commission's report was considered by a Select Committee upon whose recommendation Parliament appointed the ageing and distinguished engineer Thomas Telford 'to Survey and Report his Opinion as to the best Mode of Supplying the Metropolis with Pure Water'. His report recognised the pollution problems posed by the Thames and proposed to bring water supplies to London from three unpolluted sources. Aqueducts would bring water from the River Ver at Aldenham and from the Wandle at Beddington, while the New River company would augment its supplies by drawing on

'A Drop of London Water' as depicted by *Punch* in 1850, shortly after Charles Dickens had described the condition of the Grand Junction Waterworks at Kew in his journal *Household Words*. (*Punch*)

waters from the upper reaches of the Lee and from wells north of London. The cost was estimated with confident precision as £1,177,840 16*s* 5*d*. A further Select Committee was appointed to consider the matter further in 1834 following which no further steps were taken.

In April 1850, in his campaigning journal *Household Words* Charles Dickens gave an account of his visit to the works of the Grand Junction Water Company at Kew.[11] Dickens asked the engineer: 'How many companies take their supplies from the Thames, near to, and after it has received the contents of, the common sewers?' The engineer replied: 'No water is taken from the Thames below Chelsea, except that of the Lambeth Company, which is supplied from between Waterloo and Hungerford Bridges.' Dickens observed that, the Thames being a tidal river, any sewage entering the river was liable to be conveyed by the tidal flow above Chelsea but the engineer replied that many problems of water pollution were caused by dirt entering cisterns within houses. The engineer's complacency echoed that of a spokesman for the company, Dr Pearson, who, in his evidence to the Royal Commission on the Water Supply of the Metropolis twenty-two years earlier, had informed the Commissioners that: 'The impregnating ingredients of the Thames are as perfectly harmless as any spring water of the purest kind in common life: indeed, there is probably not a spring, with the exception of Malvern, and one or two more, which are so pure as Thames water.'[12]

Charles Dickens, whose account of his visit to the works of the Grand Junction Water Company in 1850 drew attention to the dangers lurking in London's water. (By courtesy of the National Portrait Gallery, London)

Early Filtration

The Chelsea company was not as complacent as the Grand Junction. In 1825 the quality of the company's water had been so poor that it prompted complaints from the royal palaces, and so in 1829 James Simpson, the company's engineer, introduced a process by which water was filtered through a bed of sand before being piped for consumption. This process remains the basis of water filtration to this day though it was sixty years before Pasteur's work revealed that the sand provided a biological as well as a physical barrier to impurities, as a result of which discovery further refinements to the process have been introduced.

A Stygian Lake

By 1853 London's drainage problem was being voiced in the columns of *The Builder*, the journal that had carried Professor Booth's complacent assessment only nine years earlier. A correspondent writing under the name 'Quondam' wrote the letter containing the complaint which opened this chapter: 'The flood . . . is now, below London Bridge, bad as poetical descriptions of the Stygian Lake, while the London Dock is black as Acheron . . . where are ye, ye civil engineers? Ye can remove mountains, bridge seas and fill rivers . . . can ye not purify the Thames, and so render your own city habitable?'[13]

'The flood is bad as poetical descriptions of the Stygian Lake, while the London Dock is black as Acheron'

Since this was written in mid-winter, when the river would have been relatively well supplied with winter floodwaters, and the temperature low, we may conclude that the condition of the river had markedly deteriorated since Booth's earlier claim. Within two years, in the summer of 1855, Faraday's famous letter, quoted in the preface, had drawn public attention to the condition of the Thames, while in the hot, dry summer of 1858 the 'Great Stink' was on the point of driving Parliament from London. The deterioration in the years since Professor Booth's flattering verdict on the qualities of the river can be explained by reference to changes in London's drainage system which occurred in the early nineteenth century and which represented a significant change from the arrangements which had prevailed at least since medieval times.

London's Natural Drainage System

In order to understand how London's drainage system developed it is important to grasp two principles. The first is that the drainage grew around London's system of natural watercourses, notably the following, shown on the map on the opposite page:

On the north side of the river, from west to east:

Stamford Brook:	Wormwood Scrubs to Chiswick
Counters Creek:	Wormwood Scrubs to Chelsea
Westbourne:	Hampstead to Chelsea via Hyde Park (and the Serpentine)
Tyburn:	Hampstead to Westminster (also called the Aye or Kings Scholars Pond)
Fleet:	Highgate and Hampstead to the City
Walbrook:	Islington to Cannon Street
Black Ditch:	Stepney to Poplar
Hackney Brook:	Hornsey to the River Lea

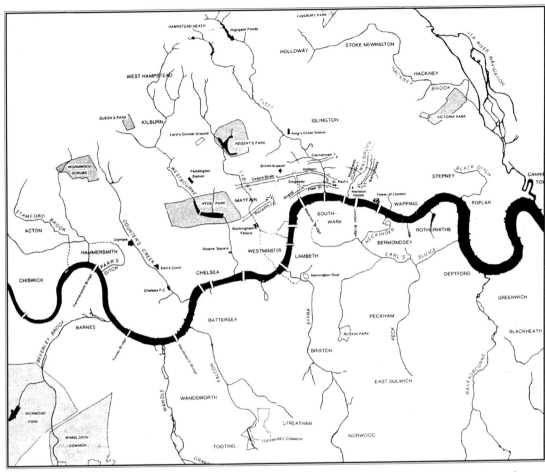

London's hidden rivers; they still flow, mostly concealed by streets, and freed from sewage by Bazalgette. (Thames Water plc)

On the south side, from west to east:

Beverley Brook:	Wimbledon to Barnes
Wandle:	Merton to Wandsworth
Falconbrook:	Tooting to Battersea
Effra:	Norwood to Vauxhall
Peck/Earls Sluice/	These originate in East Dulwich and enter the
Neckringer:	Thames at Bermondsey and Rotherhithe
Ravensbourne:	Bromley to Deptford

Originally, these were open streams and one of them, the Fleet, was a substantial river, navigable as far as Old Bourne (Holborn) and even harbouring pirates who emerged from the Fleet to attack a vessel carrying King Edward II in 1310. As London grew the streams were gradually covered over so that now only the Ravensbourne, Beverley Brook and the Wandle are still open streams for much of their length. The covering-over of the Walbrook began in 1463 and that of the Fleet in 1732.[14] In 1846 the foetid gases it contained caused it

Beulah Spa, Norwood, about
1825; source of the Effra.
(By courtesy of the Guildhall
Library, Corporation of
London)

to explode, disgorging a tide of sewage which swept away three poor
houses in Clerkenwell.[15] The remaining streams were mostly covered
over during the expansion of London's housing in the nineteenth
century, though part of the Tyburn near its junction with the
Thames remained open until the 1970s. The rivers still run beneath
London's streets. The Fleet, for example, is a substantial river
running beneath Farringdon Road and entering the Thames beneath
Blackfriars railway bridge. Occasionally, intrepid explorers journeyed
by boat along these subterranean passages. One of the most
enterprising was John Hollingshead, who, in 1862, published an
account of a voyage along the Tyburn, which at that date was still
conveying London's sewage into the Thames.[16] At one point his
guides stopped the boat and informed him that he was, at that very
moment, immediately beneath Buckingham Palace. His reaction was
all that a patriot could wish: 'Of course, my loyalty was at once
excited, and, taking off my fan-tailed cap, I led the way with the
National Anthem, insisting that my guides should join the chorus.'
     The second essential point that must be grasped about London's
early drainage system is that it was intended for surface water
drainage, as had been the case with Rome's 'Cloaca Maxima', built
between 800 and 735 BC. Foul sewage from buildings was diverted

Entrance to the Fleet River,
1756; the river still flows,
concealed beneath the
Farringdon Road, and enters
the Thames beneath
Blackfriars railway bridge.
(Thames Water plc)

into cesspools which were emptied, at irregular intervals, by
'nightsoil men'. Until 1815 it was illegal to discharge effluent from
buildings to the sewers. In the words of *The Builder*, written in 1884:

> At the commencement of the present century it was penal to discharge
> sewage or other offensive matter into the sewers, which were intended
> for surface drainage only. The sewage of the Metropolis was collected
> into cesspools which were emptied from time to time and their
> contents conveyed into the country for application to the land.[17]

Consequently, until this date London's streams, open or covered,
were supposedly performing little more than the function for which
nature intended them: carrying rainwater into the Thames, though
no doubt they were 'enriched' by some of the City's refuse, cast into
the streets or surreptitiously dumped in the sewers. The Thames
therefore remained a relatively clean river. As late as 1816, fourteen
salmon – the litmus test for the purity of river water – were caught
at Taplow, though only four years later, in 1820, no catches were
recorded.[18] By 1828 the Royal Commission on the Water Supply of
the Metropolis was drawing attention to 'an entire destruction of the
fishermen's trade between Putney Bridge and Greenwich' and
estimated that the number of fishermen working the river had been
halved since 1800. Moreover Metropolitan Brewers were seeking
their supplies from wells rather than from the polluted river.[19] The
last salmon to be taken from the river was caught in June 1833.[20]

The Drainage of Medieval London

This is not to claim that, before the nineteenth century, London had been without its waste disposal problems. It had been a matter of concern for the authorities in the City from medieval times. In 1189 the first Mayor of London, Henry Fitzalwyn, in an early attempt at building regulations, proclaimed that the 'necessary chamber [cesspool] should be at least 2½ ft from the neighbouring building if it was made of stone and at least 3½ ft if made of other materials'. The succeeding centuries provide abundant evidence of the need for this and similar measures. Edwin Chadwick in the *Report on the Sanitary Condition of the Labouring Population of Great Britain*, published in 1842, referred to numerous examples of petitions and decrees designed to deal with nuisances. In 1290 the Carmelite Friars of London 'petitioned Parliament to abate a nuisance (viz. a great stench) near them which they cannot endure and which prevents them from performing their religious duties'.[21] By 1300, according to John Stowe's *Survey of London*, Sherbourne Lane's Sweetwater Bourne had earned it the name Shiteburn Lane.

Henry Fitzalwyn (or Fitzalwine), first Lord Mayor of London, whose rules governing the construction of the 'necessary chamber', promulgated in 1189, were London's first building regulations. (By courtesy of the Guildhall Library, Corporation of London)

Edward III (1327–77), by ordinance, ordered the City to pay for twelve carts to remove sewage and refuse and he also ordered householders on the banks of the Walbrook to keep rakes with which to intercept refuse which had found its way into the stream. There is further evidence that, by the mid-fourteenth century, pollution of the streams, and thus of the Thames, had become a serious problem, judging by the number of times King Edward found it necessary to intervene in the matter. In 1354 he ordered the removal of waste on an appointed day each week by rakers, assistants to Ward Beadles who could levy fines on householders. In 1357 he addressed the mayor and sheriffs of the City in the following terms:

> Whereas now, when passing along the water of Thames, we have beheld dung and other filth accumulated in diverse places in the said City upon the bank of the river aforesaid and also perceived the fumes and other abominable stenches arriving therefrom . . . [we] do command you that you cause as well the banks of the said river, as the streets and lanes of the same City, and the suburbs thereof, to be cleaned of dung and other filth without delay and the same when cleaned to be so kept.[22]

RICHARD WHITTINGTON (d. 1423)

Richard Whittington was Lord Mayor of London three times (in 1397, 1406 and 1419) though the popular connection with the cat is more elusive, despite the fact that early portraits of him commonly include one. He probably came from the hamlet of Pauntley, near Gloucester and was a very wealthy mercer (cloth merchant). He advanced substantial loans to Henry IV and Henry V and so earned the confidence of the latter that Henry entrusted him with funds to rebuild the nave of Westminster Abbey and decreed that no building was to be demolished in the City without the permission of Whittington and two other citizens. He paid out of his own pocket for some improvements to the City's sewerage and water supply. In his will he left money for the rebuilding of Newgate prison; the repair of St Bartholomew's hospital; the restoration and enlargement of the Guildhall; and a hospital for 'thirteen poor men' which survived until it was dissolved by Henry VIII.

Richard II (1377–99), in a statute enacted during the time that Richard Whittington was Lord Mayor, decreed that: 'None shall cast any garbage or dung or filth into ditches, waters or other places within or near any city or town on pain of punishment by the Lord Chancellor at his discretion.' Latrines and public wash-houses were also built at this time.

The preferred method of disposing of foul sewage was to store it in cesspools (the 'necessary chambers' of Fitzalwyn's assize) whence it was removed by 'rakers' or 'gong-fermors' who, besides being well paid for their task, were able to dispose of it at a profit to farmers whose fields, in medieval times, were close to London's walls. In 1281 thirteen men took five nights to clear the cloaca of Newgate jail at a total cost of £4 7s 8d, each man being paid 6d a night, three times the normal rate. Accidents sometimes occurred: in 1326 Richard the Raker fell into a cesspit and drowned 'monstrously, in his own excrement'. In the sixteenth century a new market was found among saltpetre-men who extracted nitrogen from excrement for use in making gunpowder for the Spanish Wars. The Museum of London holds an advertisement for a 'chimney sweeper and night man' called Joseph Waller of Islington, who kept 'carts and horses for emptying bog houses, drains and cesspools'. Latrines did exist though from time to time it was found necessary to restrict their effects upon watercourses. In the reign of Henry III were constructed the first public latrine (and the first water pipes) since Roman times and in 1383 it was recorded that it cost £11 (about a year's wages for a skilled man) to build a latrine on London Bridge. In the same year, an Act ordered those with latrines over the Walbrook to pay the Lord Chamberlain two shillings a year for cleaning it, and another Act, in 1388, made it illegal to 'corrupt or pollute ditches, rivers, water and the air of London and elsewhere'. In 1477 an Act prohibited the construction of further privies over the Walbrook.[23]

By the fifteenth century, therefore, the pollution of tributaries had become a matter of frequent public concern and the condition of the Thames itself had attracted the critical attention of more than one monarch. Moreover there is evidence that the cesspools, which were supposed to hold the waste until it could be removed, were contributing to the problem. In 1328 William Sprot had complained to the Assizes that his neighbours, William and Adam Mere, had let their cloaca overflow his wall.[24] Three centuries later Samuel Pepys' diary entry for 20 October 1660 recorded: 'Going down to my cellar . . . I put my feet into a great heap of turds, by which I find that Mr. Turner's house of office is full and comes into my cellar'. Many cesspools regularly overflowed or leaked into nearby watercourses, thereby contributing to the pollution of the tributary streams and of the Thames itself, whose tidal reaches until the mid-nineteenth century were a major source of drinking water for the population of London.[25] Indeed most cesspools were not designed to retain liquid contents, which were expected to leak into the surrounding earth and hence into nearby wells – with fatal consequences during epidemics.

'Going down to my cellar . . . I put my feet into a great heap of turds'

Tudor and Stuart London: the Bill of Sewers and its Consequences

The 1531 Bill of Sewers (23 Henry VIII Cap. V) represented the first major attempt to regulate London's sewers in a systematic manner, though it also applied to other parts of the kingdom: 'Commissioners of Sewers shall be directed in all parts within this realm from time to time, where and when need shall require.' The Commissioners were to be nominated by the Lord Chancellor and one other official (the Lord Treasurer or the Lord Chief Justice). No further general statute concerning sewers was to be passed until three centuries later, in 1848. The 1531 Bill specified the qualifications of commissioners, assigned wages to them and gave them authority to survey walls, streams, ditches, banks, gutters, sewers, bridges, dams, weirs and other impediments to watercourses; to enquire into annoyances; to fine offenders; to appoint officers; and to enforce their orders. It established eight commissions to regulate London's system of sewers: The City; Westminster; Holborn and Finsbury; Tower Hamlets; Greenwich; St Katherine's; Poplar and Blackwall; and Surrey and Kent. Each commission was permitted to adopt its own practices concerning such matters as the size, shape and inclination of sewers, and the differences which resulted were to have serious consequences when the need arose for a unified system in the early nineteenth century.

The Bill of Sewers was followed by a number of local acts which amended or extended the powers it conferred, though the acts were not uniform in the authority that they conveyed. Thus the local acts for Westminster and Tower Hamlets did not empower their commissioners to build new sewers, though these powers were granted by Acts governing the City of London, Holborn and Finsbury, and Surrey and Kent. Most of the local Acts continued to envisage the sewers as intended for carrying away surface water and forbade the drainage of house waste into the system. In the words of John Thwaites, Bazalgette's chairman at the Metropolitan Board of Works: 'The earlier statutes did not in any way contemplate house drainage, and most of the local Acts prohibited its discharge into the sewers and enforced the construction of cesspools.'[26]

Inigo Jones; he was ordered by Charles I's Privy Council 'to arch over the Moor Ditch in order to eliminate a great annoyance' arising from the stench of its sewage.
(By courtesy of the National Portrait Gallery, London)

The inadequacy of the systems which were constructed following the Bill of Sewers is evident from the anxiety that continued to plague the authorities. Letters from Burleigh and Walsingham late in Elizabeth I's reign directed the Lord Mayor to clean up the City as a precaution against plague. On 10 April 1582 the Lords of the Council addressed the Lord Mayor, complaining that improvements to the sewer formed by the Fleet Ditch, made by Richard Matthew, Her Majesty's Cutler and Bailiff of London sewers, had fallen into disrepair through neglect.[27] The same source[28] contains evidence that the problem recurred in following reigns. A letter to the Lord Mayor from the Lords of the Council made known the wishes of Charles I:

> The king hath noticed that the ways in and about the City and liberties were very noisome and troublesome for passing, in consequences of breaches of the pavements and excessive quantities of filth lying in the streets. They require him, by the king's express command, to take effectual steps for the complete repair of the pavements and the removal of all filth, the fruits of which His Majesty expects to see on his return from Portsmouth.

The letter was dated 20 July 1628 and it is to be assumed that His Majesty was disappointed since a reminder was sent on 21 December. Six years later, on 11 June 1634,[29] an order in Council requested the 'Commissioners of Sewers of the City and Inigo Jones Esq. to arch over the Moor Ditch in order to eliminate a great annoyance'. Jones recommended a vaulted sewer 6 feet high by 4 feet wide, and this was authorised by the Council four days later, suggesting a degree of urgency in the matter. Half a century later, on 13 April 1678, Sir Christopher Wren proposed some modifications to the sewers of the Westminster Commission which would have improved their flushing by providing a readier supply of water from a natural watercourse.[30] This was part of a plan put forward by Wren and the diarist John Evelyn for a comprehensive redevelopment of the City's water supplies and sewerage following the great fire of 1666, Evelyn acting in his capacity as one of the City's Commissioners of Sewers. Nothing came of the plans and in the meantime the sewers generated their own industry to exploit their shortcomings: a community of 'toshers' who scavenged in the sewers, at considerable risk to their own health, for lost coins, discarded metal and anything else of value that could be salvaged from the filth. Despite the discomforts complained of by Charles I, Pepys and others, the inherent weaknesses of the system which had been substantially established by the Bill of Sewers in 1531 were contained while London's population was measured in hundreds of thousands and when fields were near at hand to receive the contents of the capital's cesspools.

A community of 'tossers' who scavenged in the sewers, at considerable risk to their own health

As demonstrated at the start of this chapter, many writers were describing the sanitary condition of London in complacent terms as late as 1844, though in the same year Joseph Quick, engineer to the Southwark Water Company, told the Royal Commission on the State of Large Towns that, by 1840, cesspools were being sunk as deep as the first stratum of sand, through which the liquid contents of the cesspools could flow into watercourses and wells. Quick reported that the deeper cesspools were preferred by householders since the release of their liquid contents into the sand (and thence into the water supply) left a smaller solid residue to be removed, thus reducing the cost of emptying the cesspools.[31] Consequently, he reported, well water was shunned by the local populace who preferred to be connected to the Southwark Company's supplies, though travellers passing through the area, unaware of the contents of the wells, continued to drink from them. However, the rapid growth of London's population after 1800 and an even greater increase in its use of water drew attention to shortcomings that had previously been tolerated or had passed unnoticed. Overcrowded slum tenements, poor workmanship, inconsistent standards and overflowing cesspools combined in the first few decades of the nineteenth century to precipitate a crisis which ensured that the drainage of the metropolis was a regular subject of critical debate in Parliament, the press and elsewhere for almost thirty years after 1840. These factors, and in particular the disastrous effects of the water-closet, will be examined in the chapters that follow.

CHAPTER TWO

The Water-closet: 'No filth in the sewers, all in the river'

Fifty years ago nearly all London had every house cleansed into a large cesspool . . . Now sewers having been very much improved, scarcely any person thinks of making a cesspool, but it is carried off at once into the river. The Thames is now made a great cesspool instead of each person having one of his own.

(Thomas Cubitt, 1840)[1]

This chapter will analyse the factors which, in the early decades of the nineteenth century, precipitated a crisis in London's drainage system which, only a few years earlier, had been a source of the satisfaction and pride that has been noted in Chapter One. It will examine the consequences that followed from the replacement of the traditional cesspool by the water-closet, and consider the further effects of London's rapid growth in population after 1800 and of the disproportionate increase in water consumption which accompanied the rising prosperity of the population. This will be followed by an account of the early legislative attempts to improve the living conditions of the urban population, dating from about 1839, and will describe the problems faced by the six Metropolitan Commissions of Sewers which held office from 1848 to 1855.

Edwin Chadwick and the Sanitary Movement

Anxiety about the condition of London's system of drainage must be seen in the context of the Sanitary Movement which became active from the 1840s onwards and in which Edwin Chadwick was one of

SIR EDWIN CHADWICK, 1800–90

C hadwick's energies as a campaigner for praiseworthy philanthropic causes were matched only by his ability to antagonise others who shared his aims. He was an active campaigner for reform of the Poor Law and became Secretary to the Poor Law Commission, a position he used with ruthless ingenuity to whip into line local Poor Law Guardians who did not approach their tasks with appropriate zeal. As a result of the antagonism aroused by his campaigning the Commission was dissolved. He turned his attention to the cause of sanitary reform and in 1848 became a member of the General Board of Health and of the Metropolitan Sewers Commission, both created in that year. In 1849 he (and his principal antagonist) were both removed by the Home Secretary from the Sewers Commission in order to restore harmony to that body. This left Chadwick more time to use his position as a member of the General Board of Health to interfere in the workings of local boards, and this was one of the factors that led to the abolition of the Board in 1854. Chadwick never held public office again. He tried unsuccessfully to enter Parliament and was knighted in 1889, the year before his death.

the most influential figures. For this reason it is appropriate to consider the origins of Chadwick's best-known work, the *Report on the Sanitary Condition of the Labouring Population of Great Britain*, and its main themes since these became major public issues at about the time that steps were being taken to improve London's drainage system. Chadwick's *Report* is also a valuable source of contemporary material not only on the condition of London's sewers but on the social and economic consequences of the deficiencies Chadwick described.

Edwin Chadwick was born in Manchester and trained as a barrister. He never practised the profession but the advocacy skills he learned were deployed in numerous causes during the nineteenth century and helped to earn him many enemies in his own country though his reputation as a sanitary reformer led to his being honoured in France, Belgium and Italy long before he received his knighthood in 1889, the year before his death.

Chadwick had been a friend and secretary to the Utilitarian philosopher Jeremy Bentham and attended upon him when he died in 1832. After Bentham's death Chadwick became an active campaigner for social reform and was associated with the new Poor Laws, establishing workhouses, which became effective in 1834. In the same year Chadwick was appointed secretary to the Poor Law Commission and this role led to his involvement in the enquiry upon which his *Report* was based. In 1838 government auditors queried the Poor Law unions' expenditure of public money on measures designed to remove 'nuisances' which the Poor Law Guardians believed to be the cause of diseases. Since the diseases, in turn, caused expenditure on Poor Law relief, the unions concerned may be judged to have acted prudently in adopting this early measure of preventive sanitation. It is possible that the Poor Law Guardians concerned were acting on Chadwick's instructions with a view to testing the government's attitude towards preventative public health measures.[2] The Home Secretary, Lord John Russell, contemplated the introduction of a bill amending the Poor Law legislation to permit such expenditure but he first sought an opinion on the matter from the Poor Law Commissioners.

The Commissioners immediately ordered small-scale enquiries in London into the relationship between urban sanitary conditions and disease, and the short, ten-page report was presented to the Home Secretary on 14 May 1838. A letter from Chadwick to Russell on 21 June 1838 reminded the Home Secretary of the evidence in the reports of the connection between insanitary conditions and disease and suggested 'it would be worthy of your Lordship to bring in a Bill for an Act . . . to regulate the future dwellings of the labouring classes, providing that none should be built without provision being made for proper drainage, and the width of streets'. Russell took no action so, in September 1839, Charles Blomfield, Bishop of London, moved in the House of Lords that an enquiry be made into the sanitary conditions of the labouring classes. Blomfield was a friend and admirer of Chadwick, and Sir John Simon, the City of London's first Medical Officer, later suggested that Blomfield had, like the Poor Law Guardians, been prompted to initiate the measure by Chadwick.[3] The motion was carried and the Sanitary Report was eventually published as a House of Lords paper.

Charles Blomfield moved that an enquiry be made into the sanitary conditions of the labouring classes

Chadwick made use of the machinery of the Poor Law administration to gather the materials required for his report. Letters were sent to Assistant Commissioners for the Poor Law in England, Wales and Scotland and the report itself contains evidence of Chadwick's extensive reading of continental and American works on sanitary questions, with particular attention to practice in France.[4] Chadwick's *Report* was published on 9 July 1842, under Chadwick's own name, since the three Poor Law Commissioners themselves declined to allow it to appear over their signatures on account of its controversial character. Copies were sent to every Board of Guardians and Chadwick claimed in July 1842, shortly after its publication, that 'upwards of twenty thousand copies of the *Report* have been sold'. It was extensively and generously reviewed in leading newspapers including *The Times* and the *Morning Chronicle* as well as in influential quarterlies like the *Quarterly Review* and Tait's *Edinburgh Magazine*.

The *Report* was principally concerned with establishing four major themes. The first was the relationship between insanitary living conditions and disease. The second was the economic effects of poor living conditions as manifested in the creation of 'cholera widows', orphans and those rendered by disease incapable of work, all of whom had to be supported by the Poor Rates. The third theme concerned the social effects of poor living conditions – intemperance and immorality as well as disease – under such headings as 'Domestic Mismanagement' and 'The Want of Separate Apartments'. Chadwick's fourth theme was the need for new systems of administration to bring about a reform of the appalling conditions to which the *Report* bore witness. This last theme reflects Chadwick's distrust of local bodies, operating under Acts which varied from place to place according to the whims of local citizens and often competing with other local bodies which exercised overlapping jurisdictions. He argued that:

> Whatever additional force may be needed for the protection of the public health it would everywhere be obtained more economically with unity, and efficiency, and promptitude, by a single securely-qualified and well-appointed responsible local officer than by any new establishment applied in the creation of new local boards.[5]

This was to become a recurring theme as Chadwick campaigned for strong executive bodies, appointed rather than elected and furnished with the authority and the money required to undertake the massive task of sanitary reform. It made him many enemies but earned him admirers among those who shared his authoritarian tendencies, including the French emperor Napoleon III whom Chadwick visited in Paris in 1864, while Haussmann was reconstructing the French capital in accordance with the emperor's instructions. Chadwick's sensitive and experienced nose had detected deficiencies in the French capital's drainage system so he offered some advice to the emperor: 'Sire, they say that Augustus found Rome a city of brick and left it a city of marble. If your majesty, finding Paris stinking, will leave it sweet, you will more than rival the first emperor of Rome.' Napoleon III's reaction to this is not recorded.

Chadwick's sensitive and experienced nose had detected deficiencies in the French capital's drainage system

Problems of Workmanship and Consistency

The standards of workmanship which applied in the laying of sewers often left much to be desired. In his *Report* Chadwick was very critical of the qualities of local surveyors, referring in particular to a recent experience of the Holborn and Finsbury Commission:

> When the Commission advertised for a person to act as surveyor to the works who understood the use of the spirit level, the candidates, who were nearly all common house builders, were greatly surprised at the

novel demand, and several of them began to learn the use of the instrument, in order to qualify for the appointment.[6]

Further evidence came from Henry Austin, consulting engineer to the First Metropolitan Sewers Commission, who was asked to conduct a survey of the sewers. It was the practice in many areas to construct egg-shaped sewers with the narrow end downwards so that, when the flow was small (for example at night or in dry weather) the liquid would be concentrated in a narrow area and thus speed the flow. However, on 16 September 1848 Austin reported to the Commission that the sewer beneath Cumberland Street in Chelsea was 'egg-shaped, with the broad end down'. In the circumstances Chadwick's verdict on the condition of London's sewers is not surprising:

> The sewerage of the Metropolis, though it is a frequent subject of boast to those who have not examined its operations or effects, will be found to be a vast monument of defective administration, of lavish expenditure and extremely defective execution.[7]

Problems of poor workmanship were compounded by the district surveyors' limited authority to correct faults. Two years after the publication of Chadwick's *Report*, John Roe, surveyor of the Holborn and Finsbury Sewers Commission, in his evidence to the Commissioners for Inquiring into the State of Large Towns and Populous Districts (The 'Health of Towns Commission', 1844), explained the difficulties he faced. While he had the authority to forbid builders to connect defective drains to public sewers he had no power to require them to make connections.[8] He gave an account of a case in which a house drain was laid so that it flowed towards the house.[9] In this case, his authority allowed him only to prohibit a connection but fortunately this coercive measure was sufficient to make the builder re-lay the drain.

He gave an account of a case in which a house drain was laid so that it flowed towards the house

More difficulties arose from the widely differing powers assumed by different commissions of sewers, operating as they did under different Acts of Parliament in London and the other fifty urban areas to which the Health of Towns Commission directed its enquiries. A further problem arose from the fact that Commissioners responsible for one district were under no obligation to coordinate their activities with those of the other seven. In the words of R.C. Middlemass, one of Bazalgette's successors as Chief Engineer to Thames Water:

> While some useful work was carried out, there was little co-ordination, and drainage work was executed regardless of the effect upon neighbouring systems. Levels and sizes were not compatible – for

example egg-shaped sewers with point downward met neighbours with point upward. Moreover the outlets to the river were at about low tide level and in consequence solids settled out in the lower sections of the sewers so that, when a storm coincided with a high tide, serious flooding of the low-lying levels occurred.[10]

Nevertheless, the condition of London's sewers and of the Thames continued to be tolerated and was even the source of considerable complacency as late as 1844. London sewage continued to be collected in cesspools, numbering some two hundred thousand in 1810 for a population of more than one million.

Cesspools and their Consequences

Edwin Chadwick in his *Report* drew attention to some of the consequences of London's two hundred thousand cesspools. He noted that the cost of emptying a cesspool was about one shilling (at a time when three shillings was a good day's wage for a workman) and 'with a population generally in debt at the end of the week, and whose rents are collected weekly, such an outlay may be considered as practically impossible'.[11] He went on to quote a report by a civil engineer called Howell, who, in his capacity as a surveyor for the metropolis, had inspected two houses about to undergo repairs:

> Upon visiting the latter, I found whole areas of the cellars of both houses were full of nightsoil to the depth of three feet, which had been permitted for years to accumulate from the overflow of the cesspools. . . . I would mention another case amongst many more in St Giles's Parish . . . Upon passing through the passage of the first house I found the yard covered in nightsoil, from the overflowing of the privy to the depth of nearly six inches and bricks were placed to enable the inmates to get across dryshod.

I found whole areas of the cellars of both houses were full of nightsoil to the depth of three feet

Henry Jephson, a member of the LCC who wrote an account of the development of London's drainage system, quotes a Medical Officer in Whitechapel as late as 1858 describing the effects of cesspools in his annual report:

> No cesspool ought to be allowed to exist in London, for wherever there is a cesspool, the ground in its vicinity is completely saturated with the foul and putrefying liquid contents, the stench from which is continually rising up and infecting the air which is breathed by the people, and in some instances poisoning the water which is drawn from the public pumps.[12]

On page 118 of his *Report* Chadwick remarked upon the difficulty of finding a market for the contents of the cesspools as agricultural manure. As London grew larger, farms became more remote and inaccessible and the transport and use of human waste as manure became less economical, though the records of the Grand Junction Canal company indicate that, as late as 1904, 45,669 tons of manure was being conveyed by barge from Paddington Basin to be applied to the Hertfordshire countryside.[13] Nightsoil men charged more for removing the waste a greater distance and poorer families, unable to afford the expense, allowed it to accumulate until it became a hazard. During the early 1840s the going rate for a load of human and animal waste sold by a nightsoil man to a farmer was 2*s* 6*d* but in 1847 guano (solidified bird droppings) from South America became available as a cheaper and more manageable fertiliser and the market for human waste collapsed. The alternative was to empty the waste into the street whence it would, with luck, make its way into the sewers and the river. This was not a new practice since Pepys recorded his neighbour doing this on 30 May 1660 but in the 1840s it became a commonplace necessity.

The going rate for a load of human and animal waste sold by a nightsoil man to a farmer was 2s 6d

The consequent pressures on the system, compounded by the lack of coordination and standardisation between neighbouring commissions, were illustrated by the surveyors Richard Kelsey and John Daw, giving evidence to the Select Committee on Metropolitan Sewage.[14]

> The sewers of the Holborn and Finsbury division having been greatly improved and enlarged, the City sewers became inadequate to carry off their contents, and a number of houses in the vicinity of the river were inundated after each fall of rain, the contents of their own drains . . . being actually forced back into their houses from the volume of water which occupied the main sewer.

Kelsey went on to describe the situation in Cheapside: 'The inhabitants of Cheapside, generally speaking, have got cesspools: they perforated the yellow clay or loam and got into the gravel, and whatever is thrown into the cesspool mixes with the water in the earth: that is for the benefit of the drinkers!'

Some areas were lacking even in properly constructed cesspools. In 1848 Hector Gavin, a doctor who lectured at Charing Cross Hospital, wrote an account of the sanitary conditions in Bethnal Green, which fell within the jurisdiction of the Tower Hamlets Sewers Commission. The book bore the strange title *Sanitary Ramblings* and was addressed to the Marquis of Normanby in his capacity as President of the Health of Towns Association of which

Gavin was himself a member. He described the situation in Bethnal Green in the following terms:

> House drainage is nearly entirely wanting in Bethnal Green . . . The inhabitants, therefore, are compelled to get rid of their fluid refuse by throwing it on the gardens, yards, or streets. Sometimes holes are dug in the gardens, or yards, to receive the refuse water. These holes are frequently closely adjacent to the wells whence the occupants derive their supply of water. [15]

Later in the same account Gavin described how the inhabitants dealt with the consequences of these methods of waste disposal. 'In numerous instances the inhabitants have piled, either in their yards, or in their houses or in the alleys fronting the houses, collections of dust and cinders, to conceal from the eye the soil which has oozed from the neighbouring privies or cesspools.'[16] As late as 1900 A.B. Hopkins wrote, 'To this day it is not unfrequently discovered, when a health officer is called in to investigate the case of an outbreak of illness in a house, that there is an old cesspool underneath.'[17]

The Coming of the Water-Closet

Further factors combined to precipitate the crisis that led to the creation of a unified Metropolitan Commission of Sewers in 1848. Of these the first was the growing popularity, from the late eighteenth century, of the water-closet. A water flushing device may be seen in the Minoan Palace at Knossos, dating from 1700 BC, but the technology was lost for over three thousand years before being rediscovered in the late sixteenth century by Sir John Harington, who described his invention in his book *The Metamorphosis of Ajax: a Cloacinean Satire* published in 1596. He installed one water-closet at his own home at Kelston, near Bath, and another at the palace of his godmother, Queen Elizabeth, at Richmond. For the next two centuries the invention was virtually ignored until, in 1775, a patent was taken out by a Bond Street watchmaker, Alexander Cumings, for an improved version of Harington's device. Further improvements were made to the valve mechanism by Joseph Bramah (1748–1814), a cabinet maker, who registered his patent in 1778.[18] By 1797 he had made over 6,000 closets and the company he founded continued to produce them until 1890.[19] In 1861 Thomas Crapper opened a competitive business in Chelsea with an improved flushing mechanism whose advantages were broadcast through the memorable advertising slogan 'a certain flush with every pull'. Crapper's business continued to trade from 120 Kings Road until 1966.

'A certain flush with every pull'

JOSEPH BRAMAH, 1748–1814

A prolific inventor who registered eighteen patents, Bramah was a Yorkshire farmer's son whose name was originally spelt Bramma. He was apprenticed to a carpenter and travelled to London to start his own business. In 1778 he was asked to install a water-closet in a private house and realised that he could improve the design. He patented the resulting mechanism (changing the spelling of his name in the process) and started to manufacture WCs in large numbers; their widespread adoption had devastating consequences for the antiquated sewers to which they were connected. He also invented an 'unpickable lock' and offered a prize of £200 to anyone who could pick it. The prize was eventually claimed long after Bramah's death by an American called Hobbs, who took up the challenge at the Great Exhibition of 1851. His other inventions included a hydraulic press, an ever-pointed pencil, a machine for numbering banknotes and an early screw mechanism for propelling ships.

In 1844 the London builder Thomas Cubitt, in evidence to the Royal Commission on the State of Large Towns and Populous Districts, estimated that in the previous twenty years the number of closets installed in London had increased tenfold.[20] A further stimulus was provided by the Great Exhibition of 1851 when 827,000 people used WCs installed for the occasion in Hyde Park by an enterprising manufacturer called George Jennings, many visitors no doubt experiencing the device for the first time. The effects of the adoption of water-closets by wealthier London households was described in the First Report of the Royal Commission on Metropolitan Sewage Discharge: 'About 1810 an invention was introduced which had a very important effect on the drainage system, namely the water-closet'.[21]

The report proceeds to describe how the greatly increased volume of water used by a WC as compared with an old-fashioned cesspool placed further strains on the drainage system, especially when WCs emptied into cesspools, causing them to overflow. The effect is illustrated by an article published in June 1859 which demonstrated how the volume of water used in London houses almost doubled in the six years from 1850 to 1856. The figures were:[22]

1850   270,581 houses used an average of 160 gallons each per day
1856   328,561 houses used an average of 244 gallons each per day

These figures, taken together, give a daily usage of 43.3 million gallons per day in 1850 and 80.8 million gallons per day six years later. A contemporary estimate of the pace at which water-closets were introduced to the capital was provided by three engineers who, in 1857, were asked to report on Bazalgette's main drainage proposals. In their report they wrote:

We believe that the introduction of water-closets in the metropolis, to any extent, may be dated from about the year 1810, from which time until 1830 their increase was only gradual; but since 1830 the increase has been very rapid and remarkable. The number of cesspools which have been discontinued in London, is stated to be not far short of two hundred thousand. [23]

The effects of the growing popularity of the water-closet were also noted by William Farr, the first statistician to the Registrar General of births, marriages and deaths, in his report on the cholera epidemic of 1866. On page 53 of the introduction to the report Farr wrote:

Almost coincidentally with the appearance of epidemic cholera [he is referring to the 1849 outbreak in London], and with the striking increase of diarrhoea in England, was the introduction into general use of the water-closet system, which had the advantage of carrying nightsoil out of the house but the incidental and not necessary disadvantage of discharging it into the rivers from which the [water] supply was drawn.

THOMAS CUBITT (1788–1855)

Thomas Cubitt's contribution to Victorian London above ground is comparable with Bazalgette's beneath. He was trained as a ship's carpenter and travelled in that capacity to India, saving enough money from his labours to set himself up as a builder upon his return. He was the first large-scale builder to employ a permanent (as distinct from jobbing) workforce of tradesmen embracing diverse crafts: carpenters, bricklayers, glaziers, etc. In order to maintain a steady flow of work for his employees he became engaged in speculative building and was thereby responsible for developing large areas of Highbury, Bloomsbury (including Gordon and Tavistock Squares), Belgravia (including Belgrave Square and Chesham Place), and some 250 acres of Clapham. At the request of Queen Victoria he modified and extended Osborne House on the Isle of Wight and built the familiar East Front (facing the Mall) of Buckingham Palace. At the request of Prince Albert he negotiated the purchase of the land on which the Kensington Museums were built with the profits of the Great Exhibition of 1851. He left over one million pounds in his will which, at 386 pages, was the longest on record.

Thomas Cubitt; builder of much of Victorian London, including the facade of Buckingham Palace and author of the longest will ever written. (By courtesy of the National Portrait Gallery, London)

George Cruickshank's view of the horrors surrounding the intake to the Southwark waterworks, about 1830.

Paradoxically, therefore, the improvements in the design of the WC and its more widespread adoption, while undoubtedly evidence of progress, were promoting epidemics because the infrastructure to which they were connected could not support the much greater volume of liquid waste that they generated. As a result some Victorian cities, including Manchester, discouraged the use of WCs among all classes 'because of the strain their outpourings imposed on the drainage and sewerage system'.[24] The Town Clerk of Manchester, as late as 1862, told a Parliamentary Select Committee that he would like to replace the troublesome devices with the old system of ashpits.

The increasing use of water for the WC and other purposes coincided with other social and regulatory changes which combined to bring about a sudden deterioration in the condition of the Thames. The social factor concerns the growth of London's population which increased as follows in the census years from 1801: [25]

Census Year	Population	Index
1801	959,000	100
1811	1,139,000	119
1821	1,378,000	144
1831	1,655,000	173
1841	1,945,000	203
1851	2,362,000	246
1861	2,807,000	293

Thus by the late 1840s a number of factors had combined to turn London's drainage system from a source of satisfaction to writers like Booth, Britton and Leigh to one of well-justified anxiety and criticism for its effects upon the health and comfort of the people. The population had more than doubled in forty years and, as usage of water-closets increased, the volume of waste increased disproportionately. The division of responsibility for the system among eight different commissions of sewers (with over one thousand commissioners),[26] set up in Tudor times to serve a much smaller community, created differences in workmanship and standards which meant that, when one part of the system was improved, it was liable to create insupportable pressures elsewhere, causing bursts of the kind described by Kelsey and Daw to the Select Committee on Metropolitan Sewage (see page 41 above). As the fields retreated before the growing urban population, the problems of disposing of the contents of the cesspools grew greater and, in the face of guano imports, the market effectively collapsed. As early as 1815, in an attempt to relieve pressure on the cesspools, the prohibition of earlier statutes on connecting house drains to the sewers was lifted as a result of lobbying by water companies who wanted to increase the number of households connected to their supplies.[27] Thomas Cubitt, commenting on the effects of this measure in his evidence to the Select Committee on the Health of Towns, observed that:

The problems of disposing of the contents of the cesspools grew greater

> Fifty years ago nearly all London had every house cleansed into a large cesspool . . . Now sewers having been very much improved, scarcely any person thinks of making a cesspool, but it is carried off at once into the river. It would be a great improvement if that could be carried off independently of the town, but the Thames is now made a great cesspool instead of each person having one of his own.[28]

If further incentives were needed to take seriously the need for improvements in the sanitary conditions of the metropolis it arrived with the threat of cholera. Its progress from India across Europe had been followed with great anxiety by the press before it finally reached England, via the port of Sunderland, in 1831. It was understood, though imperfectly, that cholera was associated with insanitary conditions. Following the Sunderland outbreak a Parliamentary Committee examined a scheme submitted by an artist called John Martin to improve London's sewerage. The scheme provided for the establishment of 'Grand Receptacles' on the Regent's Park and Grand Surrey canals, whence the sewage would be transported for sale to farmers. Stripped of these agricultural embellishments, Martin's scheme bore many of the characteristics of the one eventually devised by Bazalgette[29] and, though nothing came of the scheme (no body existed that could have carried it out), a number of Parliamentary initiatives then followed which led eventually to the establishment of the Metropolitan Board of Works for whom Bazalgette constructed the system.

Early Attempts at Reform through Legislation

In 1839 a Bill was drafted which included four features that are noteworthy in the light of later developments.[30] The Bill proposed to remedy the deficiencies of the Tudor legislation by giving greater powers to an overall authority, the Metropolitan Court of Sewers, to lay down standards and to require that buildings be connected to the sewers. The Court would operate through six new districts and would have full authority over the City of London whose jealously guarded independence would thus be removed by the unambiguous sentence 'This Act shall have operation in the City of London and the liberties thereof'. The six new districts were: The City; Western London; Finsbury; Poplar; Southern London; and Tower Hamlets. Members of Parliament for the respective districts would serve as commissioners and would also serve on the supervisory Court, where they would be joined by the Lord Mayor, the Presidents of the Royal Colleges of Physicians and Surgeons, and other figures of similar stature. This powerful body would have exercised more direct authority over the City than the Metropolitan Board later commanded and it was probably the opposition of the City fathers which caused the Bill to be lost since it disappears from the records shortly after being introduced by Henry Ward, MP for Sheffield, and Benjamin Hawes, MP for Lambeth,[31] on 23 April 1839.[32]. This early attempt at sanitary reform in London came to nothing but it was followed in 1843 by 'A Bill for the better regulating the Buildings of the Metropolitan Districts, and to provide for the drainage thereof', normally referred to as the Metropolitan Buildings Act, 1844. This required that no new building be constructed without being connected to the common sewer, provided this was within 30 feet of the building. A later amendment extended this distance to 100 feet. The same requirement applied to extensions to existing buildings and to buildings that were substantially reconstructed. Drains had to be at least 9 inches in diameter and 'must be built of brick, tile, stone or slate, set in mortar or cement'.[33] An 1847 amendment specified 'all cesspools and privies to be so constructed as to prevent escape save into drain or sewer'.[34] This Act ensured that new buildings would be connected to the sewers but had little impact on

'All cesspools and privies to be so constructed as to prevent escape save into drain or sewer'

existing buildings unless they were extended or rebuilt. The Nuisances Removal and Diseases Prevention Act, 1846, commonly known as the Cholera Bill,[35] remedied this shortcoming by providing a mechanism whereby existing buildings could be regulated, by enabling the Privy Council to issue 'any such new rules or regulations as to them may appear necessary or expedient' to prevent disease. These provisions were later used by the General Board of Health during the cholera epidemic of 1848–9, both to compel property owners to clean and whitewash their properties and to encourage them to make connections with the sewers.

The Metropolitan Commission of Sewers

In 1847 a Royal Commission was established to 'Inquire whether any, and what special means might be requisite for the health of the Metropolis, with regard more especially . . . to better house, street and land drainage'.[36] The Commission was chaired by Lord Morpeth (formerly George Howard, 1802–64), Commissioner of Woods and Forests. Morpeth, a close ally of Edwin Chadwick, was appointed to the Commission by the Prime Minister, Russell, along with many other of Chadwick's associates in the movement for sanitary reform. The Commission, strongly influenced by Chadwick, recommended that seven of the commissions of sewers which had been prescribed by Henry VIII's Bill of Sewers be amalgamated into one Metropolitan Commission of Sewers, the Commissioners to be appointed by Royal Warrant. The City Commission ensured its own survival as a separate unit by securing the passage of its own Sewers Bill. The recommendations of the Commission were accepted and the Metropolitan Sewers Act of 1848 gave jurisdiction over 'places or parts in the counties of Middlesex, Surrey, Essex or Kent, or any of them, not more than twelve miles distant in a straight line from St Paul's Cathedral, but not being within the City of London or the liberties thereof'.

> '*A Royal Commission was to inquire what special means might be requisite for the health of the Metropolis*'

Twenty-three commissioners were appointed to the First Metropolitan Sewers Commission, with Morpeth as the chairman. Other notable members included Chadwick himself, six MPs, three doctors (including the Queen's physician), Sir Henry de la Beche, (Director General of the Ordnance Survey), John Walter (proprietor of *The Times*) and four men who had served on the old commissions. The latter included John Leslie who, as a former member of the Westminster Sewers Commission, had played an active part in exposing corruption therein.[37] Leslie, 'a thoroughly unpleasant man, spiteful, offensive and ungenerous',[38] was to exercise a powerful destructive influence in the first two commissions, of which he was a member, and later in the Metropolitan Board of Works, to which he was also elected.

Thus twenty-three commissioners replaced the 1,065 commissioners who had nominally served on the former seven district commissions. The Act forbade the construction of houses without suitable drains and required them to be connected to public sewers provided there was one within 100 feet, thus echoing the provisions of the 1844 Metropolitan Buildings Act. In addition, all new houses had to have a WC or privy and ash-pit, on pain of a £20 fine. For the first time Commissioners were given the authority to order that existing properties be connected to the sewers. The Act enabled the Commissioners to insist upon the provision of WCs or privies and ash-pits in new or existing dwellings and, if property owners refused or failed to do so, the Commissioners could execute the work themselves and levy a charge. Further clauses enabled them to require the City authorities to carry out drainage works where they were considered necessary by the Metropolitan Commissioners. In 1849 these powers were further strengthened by an amendment which prescribed that, if a watercourse were considered by one of the commission's surveyors to be 'prejudicial to the health of the neighbourhood' then it might be 'abated without previous notice' and the owner required to pay. The 1848 Act thus created a body which wielded more power than its predecessors, including considerable influence over the City, though it did not have as much direct authority as the failed 1839 Bill would have conferred.

The Act enabled the Commissioners to insist upon the provision of WCs or privies and ash-pits in new or existing dwellings

Sir George Humphreys, who as Chief Engineer to the London County Council inherited Bazalgette's system, is rather dismissive of the achievements of the Metropolitan Commissions in his account of the development of London's main drainage: 'Numerous designs for improving the drainage system of London and for preventing the discharge into the River Thames were considered but no real advance made.'[39] This unflattering judgement does less than justice to the six short-lived and under-funded commissions which sat from 1848 to 1855. The First Commission began by asking the Ordnance Survey to prepare a survey of London's sewers to a scale of 5 feet to the mile, and a survey of house drains to a scale of 10 feet to the mile. The request immediately ran into a legal difficulty. On 18 May 1848 the minutes recorded that, in the opinion of the Attorney General and Solicitor General, a general Ordnance Survey could not be commissioned. It would be necessary for separate surveys to be ordered for each of the former districts. This problem having been overcome, the First Commission, in the words of the *First Report of the Royal Commission on Metropolitan Sewage Discharge* 'began zealously on the improvement of house drainage, the abolition of cesspools and the introduction of pipe-sewer communications between the houses and the main drains'.[40] Bazalgette himself described the process and its consequences in a paper delivered to the Institution of Civil Engineers:

> Within a period of about six years, thirty thousand cesspools were abolished, and all house and street refuse was turned into the river. . . . In times of heavy and long-continued rains, and more particularly when these occurred at the time of high water in the river, the closed sewers were unable to store the increased volume of sewage, which then rose through the house drains and flooded the basements of the houses.[41]

Moreover, since many of the sewer outlets into the river were tide-locked, discharge could take place only at low tide, the consequence of this being that the first movement of the sewage was upstream as the tide turned.[42] The need for the priority which the First Commission gave to promoting the connection of house drains to sewers is attested by Hector Gavin, who described the reluctance of builders and landlords to connect their properties to the public sewers.[43] He related how, in the period from 1838 to 1847, some 76,386 feet of sewer had been laid but only 750 connections made – less than one property for every 100 feet of sewer. He argued that 'this fact sufficiently proves that it is necessary to make it compulsory on owners of houses to form drains in connection with sewers'.

The Times, on 4 October 1849, quoted Chadwick, whose sanitary ideas dominated the Commission, as advocating: 'the complete drainage and purification of the dwelling house, next of the street and lastly of the river'. He successfully advocated a policy of flushing London's sewers into the Thames in an attempt to combat the cholera that had re-emerged after a respite in the winter of 1848/9. This policy was described by *The Times* as 'no filth in the sewers, all in the river'. Every two to three months the engineers reported to the Commissioners the volume of filth that had been flushed into the Thames in the previous months: 29,000 cubic yards in March–May 1848 and 80,000 cubic yards from September 1848 to February 1849.[44] The weakness of this approach, which was demonstrated in the cholera epidemics, was that by disposing of human waste in the river its most harmful elements returned in the capital's water supply, but at this time water was not recognised as a vehicle by which cholera was transmitted. Nevertheless the First Commission, though it drew up no plans for a system of intercepting sewers to protect the Thames, had taken the first steps towards cleaning the dwellings of the population as advocated by the sanitary reformers. It had also begun the Ordnance Survey which would be used by the

He successfully advocated a policy of flushing London's sewers into the Thames in an attempt to combat the cholera

future designers of the intercepting system. It was completed in 1858 at a cost of £23,630.

The Second Commission, which took office on 1 January 1849, was strengthened by the addition of new members who included three army engineers: Sir John Burgoyne, Captain Vetch (a member of the tidal harbour commission) and Captain Dawson of the Ordnance Survey. Other new members included Cuthbert Johnson, an authority on manure. His addition to the membership reflected Chadwick's interest in the use of sewage as manure (see Chapter Five). The new commission began experiments with different types and sizes of sewage pipe and addressed the question of an intercepting system. The commissioners asked their consulting engineer, Henry Austin, to prepare a design. Austin's proposal was for a 'converging system' in which sewage would be conducted to four reservoirs converging on a pumping station in Belgravia from which the sewage would be pumped for use in agricultural areas. Austin claimed that the system could be built:

> at a cost fully 30% below that of the most improved and economical arrangements under the present system' because 'the cost of engine power and of the suction and distributing pipes, together with the annual expense of working, would not be a charge upon the public, as it would be borne by the parties to whom the application of the refuse to agriculture would be entrusted.[45]

John Phillips, Chief Surveyor to the Metropolitan Commission, produced a rival plan for intercepting tunnel sewers running 19½ miles from Eel Pie Island at Twickenham to Plumstead marshes. It would cross the Thames eleven times and would be for sewage only: surface water could continue to run into the river via the old watercourses. The sewage would be made available for agricultural use along the route of the intercepting sewer and Phillips, like Austin, made some generous claims for the revenue that could be expected from this course. He estimated that the total cost of the sewer, with its associated machinery, would be £634,991 12s 10d.[46] A furious argument followed[47] as Austin and Phillips criticised each other's plans in terms which each, at different times, found insulting; Austin's faction was headed by Chadwick, Phillips' by the equally uncompromising John Leslie. The Commissioners could not agree on either plan so, on 20 August 1849 they issued a general invitation to engineers to submit their own schemes. At about this time, on 16 August 1849, they appointed Joseph Bazalgette to the post of Assistant Surveyor to the Commission at an annual salary of £250. They subsequently received 137 proposals in response to their

He estimated that the total cost of the sewer, with its associated machinery, would be £634,991 12s 10d

invitation but the Commission left office before evaluating them. Acrimony descended into farce when some members of the Commission attempted to organise meetings which excluded dissenters. The atmosphere had become so charged with distrust that Morpeth decided that a new Commission was essential and wrote to Chadwick on 29 September 1849, stating that 'neither of the prominent parties in the late disputes and differences should reappear in the new Commission' and adding that 'the government and public will require the sanction of the highest engineering authority that can be procured'.

'Neither of the prominent parties in the late disputes and differences should reappear in the new Commission'

The Engineers' Commission: a Plan Devised

Chadwick and Leslie were thus excluded from the new (Third) Commission which took office on 8 October 1849. It became known as 'the engineers' commission' because it included a number of eminent members of that profession. Robert Stephenson,[48] Member of Parliament for Whitby, agreed to join the Third Commission and he insisted on bringing with him, as fellow commissioners, a number of other prominent railway engineers. Frank Forster, who had also worked with Stephenson on railway construction, was appointed as Engineer to the Commission. A sub-committee was set up to examine the 137 plans submitted in response to the Second Commission's invitation for proposals and they delegated the work to Bazalgette and another Assistant Surveyor called Edward Cresy. Their report was read by Woolrych, Secretary to the Commission, at a special meeting held on 15 March 1850. The degree of public interest in the matter may be gauged from the fact that the commissioners' deliberations were described at length not only in professional publications like *The Builder* but also in *The Times* which devoted four columns to the subject on 16 March 1850.[49] Bazalgette and Cresy divided the schemes into seven categories:

1. Portable cesspool systems; using little water to reduce bulk and to avoid weakening properties of the sewage as agricultural fertiliser
2. Systems which discharged into the Thames
3. Intercepting tunnels or culverts adjacent to the Thames
4. Several tunnels or culverts at different levels
5. Cesspools from which sewage would be conveyed to rural areas
6. Converging reservoir systems, like Austin's earlier proposal
7. Systems described as 'almost exclusively confined to the consideration of processes and expedients for infiltrating, de-odorising and solidifying the sewage for the purposes of the market gardener'.

Of the 137 plans submitted, 116 were allocated to these categories while a further 21 were dismissed in the following terms: 'Numerous communications have come under our notice which may for the most part be described as vague, speculative, disquisitious or collateral . . . few of which can be said to possess any practical value.' One proposal, which was presented under the name 'Onalar', was described as 'a long, unconnected and unintelligible paper'. Several of the plans, including a proposal from the newsagent W.H. Smith (later a Member of Parliament), involved conveyance of sewage by rail while a variant of this was a proposal from J. Bethel for sewage pipes laid along railway lines. Another, submitted under the pseudonym 'Pontifex', proposed conveying solid manure by barge along the river and canal system while liquid would flow along a tunnel in the bed of the Thames.

'Pontifex' proposed conveying solid manure by barge along the river and canal system

After debating the matter the committee announced, on 8 March 1850, that none of the schemes submitted was entirely satisfactory. The commissioners decided to ask the Engineer to the Commission, Frank Forster, to design a new proposal. On 1 August 1850 he submitted plans for the south side drainage: it involved building a single intercepting sewer to be served by pumping stations at Ravensbourne Creek and Woolwich marshes before discharging into the Thames at Plumstead. On 31 January 1851 he submitted his plan for the north side which he had developed in conjunction with Colonel William Haywood, the City Engineer. This consisted of two sewers, each with branches leading to a pumping station at the River Lea. *The Builder*, commenting on the scheme, wrote that 16 square miles of Fulham and Hammersmith had been omitted from the system. This area was difficult to drain since it was low-lying and would require special arrangements in the scheme eventually devised by Bazalgette.

Some work for the system on the northern side had in fact already begun, in the form of the Victoria Street sewer which would run from Pimlico to Percy Wharf, Westminster (near Scotland Yard), via Parliament Square. The Victoria Street sewer was to be the source of great embarrassment to the Commission as a result of difficult terrain (quicksand), poor workmanship, changes in specifications, catastrophic collapses of work in progress and damage to nearby properties. The original estimate for the two construction contracts had been £12,300. The final cost of the sewers was £54,866. Difficulties over the Victoria Street sewer and over the final choice of an intercepting system provoked much criticism from metropolitan MPs, local vestries and *The Times*, and the critical climate was also manifested in Parliamentary debates.[50] In June 1852 the Third Commission (the engineers' commission) resigned because its revenue from the sewer rates was inadequate for the task it had to perform. It had lasted longer than either of its predecessors and had been responsible for devising schemes for intercepting sewers north and south of the Thames which bore many of the characteristics of the scheme later implemented by Bazalgette.

The Fourth Commission, which held office from July to October 1852, was divided over whether to support Forster's plan. During the Commission's brief term of office Forster died, the victim of 'harassing fatigues and anxieties of official duties'.[51] Some idea of the pressure on the Commissioners and their officers at this time is conveyed by Forster's obituary notice which commented that: 'A more general and hearty support from the Board he served, might have prolonged a valuable life, which as it was, became embittered and shortened, by the labours, thwartings and anxieties of a thankless office'.[52] Bazalgette, Forster's deputy at the Commission, was appointed as his successor.

The Fifth Commission: Financial Constraints

In late 1852 the Fourth Commission was succeeded by the Fifth which was, for a considerable time, distracted by a private Bill, promoted by John Morewood, for a private company called the Great London Drainage Company. This company, like many others that succeeded it,[53] proposed to make a profit from metropolitan sewage by applying it to agriculture. It proposed two tunnel sewers, one on each side of the Thames, and guaranteed the promoters 3 per cent per annum on an investment of one million pounds, to be paid out of the sewer rate. Any profits from the application of sewage to agriculture would be shared with the ratepayers. The prospectus for the scheme describes it as being designed: 'To Afford Means for Effectually Draining the Metropolis; To preserve the Thames from impurities at present passing into it and To collect all the produce of the sewers for application to agricultural purposes'.[54]

'To collect all the produce of the sewers for application to agricultural purposes'

Bazalgette was called to give evidence to the Select Committee considering the Bill, and the opinions he expressed are interesting in the light of his later work in constructing the intercepting sewers. He left the Committee in no doubt that, in his view, the priority should lie with constructing an additional thousand miles of street drains to draw off the waste from houses and streets rather than with cleaning up the river, thus reflecting the view expressed by Chadwick four years earlier (see page 50). Referring to suggestions that the smell from the Thames was offensive Bazalgette replied:

> The Commissioners of Sewers receive deputations, and memorials, and
> complaints of the want of sewers and drainage, at every court they hold,

and I do not remember one complaint (with one exception; I remember one complaint, and only one) of the offence of the sewers in the river . . . I think that evil has been very much exaggerated, and I think it is very much less than the benefit; not to be compared with the benefit which will be conferred on the public by the drainage into the Thames . . . I have not a word to say against the interception; I simply state, however · important it may be, or however desirable, I think it much more important to drain those localities that are now without drainage, where the people are really suffering from a want of it.[55]

The Bill was finally rejected after examination by a Select Committee in 1853. In the meantime Bazalgette, as Forster's successor as Engineer to the Commission, had worked with Haywood, engineer to the City of London, and prepared a modified version of Forster's plan which was approved by Robert Stephenson and William Cubitt, consulting engineers to the Commission, in 1854.

Lord Palmerston; could his weary expression reflect the fact that he has to receive another delegation from the Sewers Commission on the subject of London's sewage? (*Illustrated London News*)

The Fifth Commission also began a campaign to reform its finances. On 5 January 1853 the new chairman, Richard Jebb, wrote to the Home Secretary, Palmerston, reminding him that the Commission's income was limited to about £200,000 a year from the sewer rates whereas Forster's plan for the north side alone had been estimated to cost £1,080,000, excluding the purchase of land and houses for a pumping station and compensation for other landowners along the line of the sewer. On 13 October 1853 Jebb wrote again to Palmerston to inform him that the Commissioners would shortly be ready to enter into a contract for a portion of the high level sewer but that their attempts to raise the necessary capital sum on the money markets in the form of a loan against the sewer rates had been unsuccessful. Palmerston did not respond sympathetically to the Commission's financial difficulties and in the meantime a further difficulty had emerged in the form of an objection to the proposed scheme from the General Board of Health where Chadwick, excluded from the Sewers Commission because of his quarrels with John Leslie, was stirring up trouble for his former colleagues by insisting that they design separate systems for sewage and rainwater collection. Palmerston was receptive to these criticisms and this prompted the resignation of the Fifth Commission.

The Sixth Commission, which took office on 22 November 1854, differed from its predecessors in one significant detail. Evidence

taken by the Committee on John Morewood's Great London
Drainage Bill the previous year had convinced the MPs that the
membership of the Metropolitan Commissions should be altered. In
the words of John Thwaites, later to become Bazalgette's superior as
the first Chairman of the Metropolitan Board of Works:

> The information obtained during the examination of witnesses, had
> considerably enlightened Parliament, as well as the Metropolitan
> Constituencies on the subject, and so much opposition was evinced to
> intrusting (sic) the execution of works of such magnitude and cost, to a
> limited Crown appointed Commission, that Government, yielding to
> the expression of the general sentiment, infused a new element by the
> nomination to the New Board of one local representative for each of
> the Metropolitan Boroughs.[56]

The new commission recognised the urgency of the problems it had
inherited, particularly as they affected the southern bank of the
Thames, much of which lay below high water. On 23 January 1855
the Commission carried a motion to the effect that: 'This Court
therefore resolves that immediate steps be taken to carry into effect
the plans as set out by the late Mr F. Forster, with such alterations or
improvements, and extensions or curtailments of the branches, as
may be suggested to the Commission, as far as it relates to that part
of the Metropolis South of the Thames.'[57] The Commission then
discovered that it lacked the power to purchase land beyond its area
of jurisdiction which was essential if the sewer outfall was to be at
Plumstead marshes as Forster's modified plan required.

On 17 August 1855 the Metropolis Management Act received the
royal assent. Under its provisions the Metropolitan Board of Works
would take over all the responsibilities of the Metropolitan Sewers
Commissions with effect from 1 January 1856. Thwaites, who was to
become Chairman of the Metropolitan Board, therefore moved the
following resolution at the Commission's meeting on 21 August 1855:

*The Commission lacked
the power to purchase
land beyond its area of
jurisdiction which was
essential if the sewer
outfall was to be at
Plumstead marshes*

> That whereas the Metropolis Local Management Act will shortly come
> into operation, by which this Commission will be superseded, it is the
> duty of this Court immediately to provide plans, showing the existing
> sewers, for the use and guidance of the several District Boards to be
> formed under the said Act; that the proper officers of this Commission
> do with all diligence prepare such plans, that the same may be ready to
> be handed over to each of the said District Boards on or before the first
> day of January next.[58]

The motion was carried.

Six Commissions had, between them, held office for eight years. What had they achieved? They had brought into being the Ordnance Survey of the metropolitan area without which no comprehensive drainage plan could be devised. Their engineers, first Forster and later Bazalgette, had prepared a scheme which, for the first time, included two critical features of the plan which would eventually be adopted by the Metropolitan Board of Works: a unitary system combining sewage and surface water, and based upon the principle of interception, which would conduct the sewage to a tidal outfall beyond the limits of the metropolis. Finally, the principle that the body responsible for executing the works should include an element representative of the population of the metropolis rather than Crown appointees had been accepted in the constitution of the Sixth Commission. These developments foreshadowed both the constitution of the Metropolitan Board and the scheme it adopted, though only after many diversions into sewage manure, more distant outfalls and controversies over finance and methods of sewer construction. Nevertheless they were considerable achievements given the limited powers, duration and revenue of the Commissions and to that extent the dismissive judgement of Sir George Humphreys on the Commissions' achievements may be contested.[59]

CHAPTER THREE

A Government for London

There is no such place as London at all . . . {it is} rent into an infinity of
divisions, districts and areas . . . Within the Metropolitan limits the local
administration is carried on by no fewer than three hundred different bodies,
deriving powers from about two hundred and fifty local Acts.

(*The Times*, 1885)[1]

What is London?

Before an effective sanitary regime could be introduced to the
metropolis to deal with the problems described in the previous chapter,
it was first necessary to set in place an organisation with the wide-
ranging powers and the substantial financial resources required to
execute the work. The six sewers commissions which struggled with the
problem between 1848 and 1855 were wanting in both authority and
money. The creation of the Metropolitan Board of Works, which
eventually completed the project, was attended by fierce arguments
over the wisdom of creating a body that was seen by some
commentators as too powerful and by others as weak and ineffective.
The debate engaged some of the most influential polemicists of the
period including Edwin Chadwick, Benjamin Hall and a professional
campaigner called Toulmin Smith. They based their arguments upon
such concepts as economy, liberty and utilitarian philosophy. The issues
had to be resolved before London could be given the organisation it
needed to attend to its pressing need for better sanitation.

Some critics questioned what the word 'London' meant, if it meant
anything at all. Cobbett's 'Great Wen' had been described in
unflattering terms in the 1820s as if it were a recognised entity and in
1829 the establishment of the Metropolitan Police recognised the
existence of a 'metropolis', with defined boundaries (and excluding
the City) as a coherent unit for the purpose of policing. By 1830 the
word metropolis began to appear in map titles. Yet as the Metropolis

BENJAMIN HALL, 1802–67

Sir Benjamin Hall, whose removal from office in 1858 cleared the way for Bazalgette to begin work. (*Illustrated Times*)

An early campaigner for the Welsh language, the Welshman Benjamin Hall sat as MP first for Monmouth and later for Marylebone. In 1838 he became a baronet and in 1859 Baron Llanover. A vigorous Parliamentary campaigner, he directed his energies against the abuse of election expenses in Parliamentary elections and against sinecures in the Church of England. An opponent of Edwin Chadwick's authoritarian methods, he ousted Chadwick from the Board of Health in 1854 and effectively excluded him from further public office.

In 1855 he became Chief Commissioner of Works, in which capacity he was responsible for improvements to the royal parks and for the final stages of the rebuilding of the Houses of Parliament after the conflagration of 1834 (see page 73). Hall was a tall, imposing man, and 'Big Ben', the principal bell in the new Parliamentary clock in St Stephen's Tower, was named after him.

Local Management Bill made its way through Parliament *The Times* could comment, in the words that open this chapter: 'there is no such place as London at all. [it is] rent into an infinity of divisions, districts and areas . . . Within the Metropolitan limits the local administration is carried on by no fewer than three hundred different bodies, deriving powers from about two hundred and fifty local Acts'.[2]

Sir Benjamin Hall described the situation to Parliament in 1855 when he introduced the Metropolis Local Management Act. Outside the boundaries of the City itself, about two million people were governed by the vestries of more than ninety parishes, precincts and liberties, ranging in size from the Liberty of the Old Artillery Ground, Bishopsgate, with fifteen hundred inhabitants, to the parish of St George's, Hanover Square, with sixty thousand. Some of these vestries were 'open' and elected by ratepayers, while others were 'close' or 'select' vestries. In these the vestrymen were put forward by thirty or more 'principal inhabitants' whose forebears had been nominated for this purpose in the Act of Parliament which set up the vestry.

St George's, Hanover Square, and St Marylebone, two of the largest parishes, were select vestries. One of the largest and most chaotic areas, St Pancras, had reconstituted its vestry from an open to a close form by a local Act of 1819. Of the 122 vestrymen created, seven were noblemen, two-thirds were parishioners with parish property valued at £150 or more and the remainder were parishioners with parish property valued at £56 or more.[3] Overlaying this fragmented apparatus was a system of about three hundred different boards responsible for paving, lighting, drainage and other amenities which had been established by over two hundred and fifty Acts of Parliament, creating some ten thousand commissioners for the purpose. The rector of Christchurch, Regent's Park, wrote to the General Board of Health to enquire what steps he could take to improve sanitation in his parish and had been told:

> In the parish of St Pancras, where you reside, there are no fewer than sixteen separate paving boards, acting under twenty-nine Acts of Parliament, all of which would require to be consulted before an opinion could be pronounced as to what might be practicable to do for the effectual cleansing of your parish as a whole.[4]

Sir Benjamin Hall claimed, in his speech to Parliament when he introduced the Metropolis Local Management Bill, that St Pancras had nineteen separate boards. In the Strand alone, nine different paving boards served three-quarters of a mile of road.[5] *The Times*, commenting upon the need for the reform of London's government in the period leading up to the introduction of the Bill, observed that London had 'a greater number and variety of governments than even Aristotle might have studied with advantage' and commented that, within St Pancras, the seventeen paving districts 'have no more to do with each other than the pavement of our St Paul's with that of St Peter at Rome'.[6] It is significant that the General Board of Health, Sir Benjamin Hall and *The Times* could not even agree how many paving boards served the beleaguered inhabitants of St Pancras. Some commentators wished to preserve such distinctions and privileges, basing their arguments on such well-defended grounds as civil liberties, the rights of property and the need for rigid economy in public expenditure. Others opposed them, citing public health, the philosophical principles of Bentham and J.S. Mill and, again, the need for economy in public expenditure.

Evidence that state intervention would be necessary before any reforms could occur became available from a survey carried out by the Health of Towns Association in 1848. Towns were sent a questionnaire which asked 'Have the authorities of the town given any indication of their knowledge of the kind and degree of influence which the condition of suburban districts exercises over the health of the town?' The reply from Canterbury was:

> A few of the town council are quite aware of the influence which defective drainage has upon the public health but a large number will

State intervention would be necessary before any reforms could occur

not acknowledge it and the greater number are so much opposed to public expenditure for any purpose that there is no hope of effectual means being resorted to by them for the public good.[7]

A question to Oxford about its plans for obtaining a clean and economical supply of water drew the answer 'never, and not likely to until compelled by Parliamentary interposition'. Dr John Snow, who hypothesised that cholera epidemics were water-borne, drew attention to the problems which arose from such attitudes while addressing the Social Science Congress in Bristol in 1849. He stated that 'our present machinery must be greatly enlarged, radically altered and endowed with new powers', above all with the power of 'doing away with that form of liberty to which some communities cling, the sacred power to poison to death not only themselves but their neighbours'.[8]

Chadwick and many other advocates of strong central administration (and accompanying public expenditure) based their arguments on economic grounds: the effects of poor sanitation upon the Poor Rates. His views on the relative importance of the various elements that could promote or obstruct the cause of better sanitation are expressed in a letter that he wrote in 1842:

'The sacred power to poison to death not only themselves but their neighbours'

> The chief remedies consist in applications of the science of engineering, of which the medical men know nothing; and to gain powers for their applications, and to deal with local rights which stand in the way of practical improvements, some jurisprudence is necessary, of which the engineers know nothing.[9]

Local rights, in Chadwick's opinion, were something to 'deal with'.

Vested Interests

Such a comprehensive prescription was certain to bring Chadwick and his supporters into conflict with every kind of vested interest: commissioners of sewers, vestries, local paving boards, private water companies, each with its own agenda and means of influence. The contrary beliefs that such measures would be ineffective, or would require burdensome taxes, or would require an unacceptable degree of interference with personal liberty, found many eloquent advocates. In 1848, *The Economist* criticised attempts to improve public sanitation in the following terms:

> Suffering and evil are nature's admonitions; they cannot be got rid of; and the impatient attempts of benevolence to banish them from the world by legislation, before benevolence has learned their object and their end, have always been more productive of evil than good.[10]

Other commentators viewed the processes of sanitary reform as an interference with personal freedom and, particularly, with property. Following a public meeting in 1850, presided over by Charles Blomfield, Bishop of London, the bishop, Lord Ashley and others went as a deputation to the Prime Minister, Lord John Russell, to press for reform. Russell told them that 'In this city there is very naturally and properly great jealousy of any interference either with local rights or individual will and freedom from control'. Russell may have been complacent but he was not unrepresentative. He probably knew that he was reflecting the views of voters like the one who signed himself 'A. Ratepayer' in a letter to the *Morning Chronicle* about the 'centralising' tendencies of the Public Health Act: 'Even in Constantinople or Grand Cairo where plague and cholera are decimating the population, it is doubtful whether such a Bill would be desirable'.[11]

The most ardent critic of centralisation, for sanitary reform or for any other purpose, was a barrister of Lincoln's Inn, J. Toulmin Smith, who wrote a series of pamphlets criticising all legislative measures which he regarded as directed to that purpose. In 1849, in a turgid document of 380 pages entitled 'Government by Commissions Illegal and Pernicious' he invoked Magna Carta, Sir Edward Coke and the Common Law in attacking the centralising tendencies of commissions, referring to the Metropolitan Commission as 'one of the best illustrations of the vices of the system'.[12] He founded a journal, *The Eclectic Review*, to publicise his 'Anti-Centralisation Union' which called on Anglo-Saxon traditions ' to take its stand on our historical constitution, not on any novel theories' and which declared itself opposed to 'that sweeping experimental legislation to which there is now so great a disposition'.[13] At a meeting of the Institution of Civil Engineers in 1852 he argued that nature should be left to carry away rainfall, sewers being an unnecessary expense for this purpose, and he attacked both the engineering profession and the General Board of Health for suggesting otherwise.[14]

The Creation of the Metropolitan Board of Works

In 1853 the Royal Commission on the Corporation of the City of London considered the matter of London's government. The Royal Commission, in its final report, gave twenty-seven recommendations concerning the internal organisation of the City, followed by two recommendations suggesting a government for London outside the City based on the seven Parliamentary Boroughs of Tower Hamlets, Westminster, Finsbury, Lambeth, Southwark, Marylebone and Greenwich. Each of these, except Greenwich, contained more inhabitants than the City itself. A further recommendation was:

'Even in Constantinople or Grand Cairo where plague and cholera are decimating the population, it is doubtful whether such a Bill would be desirable'

'We further suggest the creation of a Metropolitan Board of Works composed of members deputed to it from the Council of each metropolitan municipal body including the Common Council of the City. The public works in which all have a common interest should be conducted by this body'.[15]

When Sir Benjamin Hall introduced the Metropolis Local Management Bill to Parliament on 16 March 1855 he briefly considered the Royal Commission's proposals to base London's administration on the seven Parliamentary Boroughs but dismissed the idea on the grounds that they were too large and, conversely, that he did not wish to burden them with the expenses of mayors and their retinues. He turned instead to his own proposal which was that the metropolis be divided into administrative areas based upon existing parish boundaries, without creating corporations. The Bill, as presented to Parliament, represents an attempt to balance the need for a powerful metropolis-wide body with enough authority to execute the drainage and other works of common interest with the competing claims of vestry interests. Some of the resulting tensions were expressed in the course of the Parliamentary discussion of the measure.

His own proposal was that the metropolis be divided into administrative areas based upon existing parish boundaries

The Bill is a long one, running to 112 pages, but the critical provisions as they affected the drainage works may be briefly summarised. For the purposes of the Act the metropolis would be defined as the area covered by the Registrar-General's thirty-six metropolitan registration districts, as used in the 1851 census so that 'London as a governmental unit began as a statistical area'.[16] Within this area the local government of London would continue to be based upon vestries, as in the past, but henceforward all vestries would be 'open': that is, elected by all ratepayers whose properties were rated at £40 or more in most areas, though a lower figure of £25 was substituted in certain poorer areas. Vestries would then elect members of a central Metropolitan Board of Works according to a formula which allocated more members to vestries with larger populations, giving a total of forty-six members, of whom one-third would retire annually. The chairman of the Board would be elected by the other members and would receive a salary of between £1500 and £2000. No other member would receive payment for his services.

Vestries and District Boards would be responsible for the construction and repair of local sewers, subject to the approval of their plans by the Metropolitan Board which was given the power to raise rates for the construction of the intercepting sewers, for which it alone was responsible. Its rating power extended to the City despite protestations on the matter from that quarter. Clause 135, concerned with the powers and duties of the Board, instructed that: 'The Metropolitan Board of Works shall make such sewers and works as they may think necessary for preventing all and any part of the sewage of the Metropolis from flowing into the River Thames in or near the Metropolis.' But it was the following clause, 136, that was to dominate the first three years of the Board's existence and prevent it from taking any active steps to carry out this instruction:

> Before the Metropolitan Board of Works commence any sewers and works for preventing the sewage from passing into the Thames as aforesaid, the plan of the intended sewers and works . . . shall be submitted by such Board to the Commissioners of Her Majesty's Works and Public Buildings; and *no such plan shall be carried into effect until the same has been approved by such Commissioners.* [Author's italics]

It seems that, having created a body in which local vestry interests would be strongly represented, Parliament was still unwilling to confer upon the Board the powers necessary to design and execute the system of intercepting sewers. A power of veto was retained. Further constraints upon the Board were inserted in Clause 144, which stated that expenditure upon improvement works of over £50,000 had to be approved in advance by the Commissioners of Works and Public Buildings while expenditure in excess of £100,000 had to be approved by Parliament. Further clauses allowed ratepayers to appeal to the Quarter Sessions if they felt that the amount the Board spent on works in their area was inadequate in relation to the rates they were paying. This additional constraint on the Board's powers was to cause endless litigation and delay until it was repealed.

Ratepayers could appeal to the Quarter Sessions if they felt that the amount the Board spent on works in their area was inadequate

The debates on the Bill were poorly attended. Only five members spoke in the debate on the first reading, one of them being Lord Ebrington who reflected the anxieties of MPs that 'there was a danger that the proposed local Parliament . . . would discuss politics instead of sewerage questions, and threaten to overshadow the authority of the Speaker and that of the Imperial Parliament'.[17] Outside Parliament the debate was conducted with more vigour. On 14 August, following the passage of the Act, *The Times* published a leader welcoming the new body and, commenting on its powers over the City, wrote that 'a very large handful of feathers has been plucked from the civic bird'. Prominent among the opposition to the measure was the redoubtable Toulmin Smith who in 1857 published a clause-by-clause commentary on the Act in which he placed it in a long and dishonourable line of authoritarian measures that 'sought to extend the system of Functionarism and to destroy the traces of every principle which characterises English institutions and responsible government'.

John Thwaites: Chairman of the Metropolitan Board of Works

Hall's careful judgement in creating a body over whose plans he had, in effect, a power of veto in his capacity as Chief Commissioner of Works, was put to the test as the Board began what the Hackney Medical Officer in 1860 characterised as 'a war of the community against individuals for the public good',[18] a phrase which effectively summarises the debates between centralisers and de-centralisers which had preceded the creation of the Board. The Board took office on 1 January 1856. Instead of forty-six members it had forty-five since John Thwaites, soon to be elected chairman, had been returned as representative for two vestries, Southwark and Greenwich. Born at Meaburn, Westmorland, in 1815 and educated at a school in Reagill, in the same county, Thwaites left Westmorland for London in 1832, and became a partner in a draper's business in Southwark after first serving an apprenticeship. Thwaites was knighted on 18 May 1865 for his work as chairman of the Board and died at Meaburn House, Upper Richmond Road, Putney, on 8 August, 1870.[19] An account of him which appeared in the *Illustrated London News* in July 1858 revealed that his experience of local administration included the role of Poor Law Guardian in the parish of St Paul, Deptford, where he resided. He had also been chairman of a gas consumers' committee which had been instrumental in exerting control over gas prices in the area. He had represented Southwark on the former Metropolitan Sewers Commission. *The Elector*[20] described him in flattering terms:

'A war of the community against individuals for the public good'

> Mr. Thwaites is a type of the time we live in. He is the natural product of London matter-of-factism . . . In the celebrated Guildhall of the most important city on earth you may see, enthroned in the highest Metropolitan authority a man who, a short time ago, was the vendor of broadcloth.

Referring to his role as chairman of a Board whose discussions were often acrimonious *The Elector* wrote:

> The frequent use of his hammer proves how active his mind must be in balancing the merits of every statement, and the amount of disorder he has to check . . . He bears with great calmness the odium of actions he has done all he could to prevent, and the charge of inaction he has made every effort to avoid.

Other members of the Metropolitan Board were of similar character. Poor Law guardians, magistrates, mayors, lawyers, MPs, lecturers and businessmen were all well represented in its membership.

A False Start

The Board, from its earliest days, was in doubt about its priorities. Although it had responsibility for streets and many other activities besides sewers, it moved swiftly to the problem of drainage. The members elected Thwaites as chairman on 22 December 1855, and on 1 January 1856 asked Bazalgette to continue to act as Chief Engineer,[21] thus extending his former responsibilities as Chief Engineer to the Metropolitan Sewers Commission. The Board swiftly passed the resolution on 18 February 1856 'that this Board, impressed with the necessity of at once proceeding with the works necessary for the complete interception of the sewage of this Metropolis, request the Chief Engineer to report to the Board at the earliest possible period as to the plans necessary for the accomplishment of such object'.[22]

Bazalgette was appointed as Chief Engineer to the Board on 25 January 1856, in competition with eight other candidates, his application for the post being supported by testimonials from numerous eminent engineers including I.K. Brunel, Robert Stephenson and William Cubitt. Some contemporary commentators forecast that Thwaites and Bazalgette would soon be at odds with each other and *The Observer* went so far as to suggest that Bazalgette's appointment had been backed by City interests in order to control Thwaites because 'they calculate that it will place Mr Thwaites in an unpleasant position if the Chief Officer holds views diametrically opposed to the chairman'.[23] There is no evidence that this was so, but the story arose from an incident some years earlier which did Bazalgette no credit. Edwin Chadwick, through one of the numerous public bodies on which he served, had attempted to force the Fifth Metropolitan Sewers Commission to make their sewers from earthenware pipes, rather than from bricks.[24] The Sewers Commissioners did not like being given instructions by Chadwick and had asked their engineer, Bazalgette, to produce a report on the relative merits of the two systems by checking their effectiveness in the metropolis and five other towns. Bazalgette had come down strongly in favour of brick. Subsequent enquiries suggested that Bazalgette's inspections had been hurried, biased and sometimes surreptitious, at least one of them being conducted at

Isambard Kingdom Brunel, who in 1856 provided a flattering testimonial in support of Bazalgette's successful application to become Chief Engineer to the Metropolitan Board of Works. (By courtesy of the National Portrait Gallery, London)

night without the knowledge of the local engineer. Thwaites, in a contemporary account of the affair, criticised Bazalgette's methods and implied that his task had been to assemble evidence to support the prejudices of his masters rather than to carry out an objective appraisal. The controversy also brought Bazalgette into conflict with another engineer, John Grant, who was so critical of Bazalgette over the matter that Bazalgette threatened to sue him. The episode was an embarrassment to Bazalgette but it says much for his personal qualities that he worked effectively with Thwaites in often difficult circumstances and appointed John Grant as his deputy.

Bazalgette was as familiar as anyone with the numerous proposals that had been advanced for metropolitan drainage since 1849, when he had been appointed Assistant Surveyor to the Second Commission of Sewers. He had been responsible for examining and evaluating the 137 plans submitted to the Third Commission in 1850 and had worked on the Commission's own scheme with Frank Forster, whom Bazalgette succeeded as Chief Engineer upon the death of Forster in 1852. Bazalgette was therefore well acquainted with the multitude of solutions to London's drainage problems that had been proposed over the previous seven years. Following the instruction issued by the Board on 18 February 1856 Bazalgette was able to submit plans for the southern drainage on 4 April and for the northern drainage on 23 May.[25] He presented the plans with a modesty that was to become his hallmark:

Almost every suggestion which can be made upon the subject has been so often repeated in some shape or other that it would be difficult to detect which were the first authors of the various schemes propounded. Having had the advantage of access to all, I cannot pretend to much originality; my endeavour has been practically to apply suggestions, originating in a large measure with others, to the peculiar wants and features of different districts, with which my position has made me familiar.[26]

Sir George Humphreys, who as Chief Engineer of the London County Council assumed responsibility for Bazalgette's system in the twentieth century, took a more flattering view of his predecessor's work in his account of the development of London's drainage system. Commenting in 1930 on Bazalgette's modest claims he wrote that:

This fair and frank statement, disclaiming credit which he considered was not due to him, must not be allowed to deprive Sir Joseph Bazalgette . . . of the great credit to which he is entitled as the engineer who not only evolved a practical scheme out of these various proposals but also carried it out in so efficient a manner that to-day, with trifling exceptions, the whole work is still carrying out the function for which it was created.[27]

'With trifling exceptions, the whole work is still carrying out the function for which it was created'

The area north of the river was to be served by three sewers and that
south of the river by two, with some sewers also having branches. At
Abbey Mills, West Ham, in the north the low level sewer's contents
would be pumped up to a level with the middle and high levels;
thence the combined flow would proceed via the three outfall sewers
to Barking where it would be discharged into the Thames just west
of the River Roding (Barking Creek) which formed the metropolitan
boundary. At Deptford, on the south side, the contents of the high
level sewers would discharge to an outfall and the Low Level sewer's
contents would be lifted to the outfall which would run to Crossness,
on Plumstead marshes.

On 3 June 1856 Bazalgette's plan was sent to the First
Commissioner, Sir Benjamin Hall, for his approval, as the Act
required. There followed a protracted, frustrating and sometimes
acrimonious debate between Hall and the Board concerning the
interpretation of the Act, particularly as it affected the positions of
the outfalls into the Thames. From the beginning of the project Hall
showed a keen awareness of his responsibilities for supervising the
Board's affairs though this appears to have been prompted by
diligence rather than by distrust of the Board. Hall submitted the
Board's plans to an independent consultant, Captain Burstall, who
reported on them in little more than three weeks, on 30 June 1856.[28]
On 2 July Hall sent the plans back to the Board accompanied by a
letter which made plain his own reservations about them:

> By the Metropolis Act of 1855 it is provided that the Metropolitan Board
> of Works shall make sewers and works for preventing *all or any part of the*
> *sewage of the Metropolis from flowing or passing into the Thames in or near the*
> *Metropolis.* [Author's italics] But the scheme submitted for the approval of
> the First Commissioner actually provides that the sewage shall flow into
> the Thames at a point within the Metropolis. The First Commissioner
> feels that he cannot undertake to do this and, considering that the scheme
> is entirely at variance with the intentions of the legislature as set forth in
> the Act which passed last August he considers it to be his duty to return
> the plans which were submitted for his approval.[29]

It is hard not to feel sympathy for Benjamin Hall in the disputes that
occupied the next two years. On the one hand he had the Metropolitan
Board, Bazalgette and the vestries who did not want the project to be
more costly or complicated than was absolutely necessary. On the other
hand he must have known that, if the sewage was not discharged at a
safe distance from the metropolis, and particularly from the Houses of
Parliament, his career would end in acrimony and ridicule.

In the weeks that followed, numerous alternative plans were
devised by Bazalgette and debated by the Board, the most radical of

*If the sewage was not
discharged at a safe
distance from the
metropolis, and
particularly from the
Houses of Parliament,
his career would end in
acrimony and ridicule*

which required Bazalgette to prepare a plan for carrying the southern sewage across the river via a tunnel starting near Greenwich marshes and then proceeding by one channel to an outfall at Mucking Creek just short of Canvey Island, Essex, 20 miles beyond the metropolitan boundary. The numerous resolutions and heated debates which characterised these few weeks are no doubt a reflection of the pressure felt by the Board, on the one hand to conform with the Act and on the other to do so at a cost that would be acceptable to the Vestries and Districts whose rates would have to pay for it. As it wrestled with this dilemma the Board was the object of some severe criticism, such as that which came from the *Illustrated London News*:

> In sullen, Pistol-like compliance with Sir Benjamin Hall's desire they have, a fraction at a time, amended their plan for Thames purification; though in this respect their latest effort is still a half-measure. It will, however, ensure the destruction of the riverborne fish trade, ruin the waterside towns and waste upon the unthankful flood the fertilising matter.[30]

On 5 November Thwaites and Bazalgette visited Hall to submit a modified plan, together with an offer to site the outfalls further downstream at the government's expense. The plan did not really suit anyone and, in the words of *The Builder*, 'it would appear that the deputation was considerably snubbed'.[31]

'It would appear that the deputation was considerably snubbed'

The Referees' Plan

On 31 December 1856 Hall referred the Board's modified plan to a committee of three referees: Captain Douglas Galton of the Royal Engineers; James Simpson, engineer to two London water companies; and Thomas Blackwood, engineer to the Kennet and Avon Canal.[32] Their terms of reference were broader than those of Burstall since they were allowed to put forward their own proposals and were especially enjoined to consider the possibility of using the sewage for agricultural purposes: a matter which was to influence, and often confuse, the deliberations of the Board over the following years. Seven months passed before the referees submitted their 500-page report to Hall on 31 July 1857.[33] They recommended that, on the north side, the outfall be situated near Mucking lighthouse in Sea Reach and on the south side at Higham Creek – 20 miles beyond the metropolitan boundary on the north side and 16½ miles on the south side – since 'these are the only places in the river, either above or below, which appear to us entirely to fulfil the conditions essential to the objective in view'. The proposed outfalls would be open channels (in effect canals of liquid waste) and were designed to run to an outfall some 15 miles beyond the lowest points at which the Board considered it necessary to discharge. Moreover the additional drop in the level of the outfalls at the point of discharge, caused by the additional 15-mile incline, was such that the outflow could take place only at low tide, thereby ensuring that the initial movement of the sewage would be upstream towards the population centres. Finally, the referees added that the construction of the system should not be dependent upon the development of proposals for sewage utilisation though it was hoped that some of the sewage would be siphoned off from the channels in order to fertilise the barren Essex marshes through which it would pass on its long journey to the outfalls.[34]

The construction of the system should not be dependent upon the development of proposals for sewage utilisation

In the meantime, during the summer of 1857, Hall was starting to come under pressure to bring about some improvements in the condition of the river flowing past the Palace of Westminster itself. The Lord Chamberlain wrote to Hall complaining that 'the pestilential state of the atmosphere at times in and about the New Houses of Parliament has on several occasions compelled me to leave the terrace and I am frequently obliged to close the door of my office'.[35] Similar pressure in the following summer, that of 1858, proved to be more decisive.

The referees' report was submitted to the Board in October 1857 and was greeted with a predictable lack of enthusiasm. The referees estimated that it would cost £5,437,265, a sum that compared unfavourably with the estimates for Bazalgette's plans, which ranged from £2,135,196 to £2,413,376.[36] On 5 November a meeting was held attended by Sir Benjamin Hall, two of the referees (Galton and Simpson), Thwaites and Bazalgette. In response to a question from Thwaites and Bazalgette concerning the additional cost of carrying the outfalls so much further downstream Hall 'stated that in his opinion Parliament will refuse to make any contribution to the works in question'.[37] This news prompted such an adverse reaction from the Vestry and District Boards that on 16 November the Metropolitan Board passed a resolution to the effect that it would be contrary to the provisions of the Metropolis Local Management Act to charge metropolitan ratepayers with the cost of the extension. The argument continued with mounting bitterness during the hot, dry summer of 1858 in a correspondence which the 1884 *Report of the Commissioners Appointed for the Purpose of Enquiring into the Effect of the Discharge of the Sewage of the Metropolis into the River Thames* characterised as having 'taken a somewhat acrimonious and personal tone'. In the meantime events had occurred which had the effect of relegating the engineering disputes to the margin.

The Great Stink

In February 1858 Palmerston's government fell and was replaced by a Conservative administration led by Lord Derby who appointed Lord John Manners as First Commissioner of Works in place of Hall. In the months that followed the hot, dry summer reduced the Thames to a condition which the press named the 'Great Stink'. It raised to irresistible levels the pressure to resolve the disputes over London's drainage in circumstances which were described in a leading article in *The Times* on 18 June:

> What a pity . . . that the thermometer fell ten degrees yesterday. Parliament was all but compelled to legislate upon the great London nuisance by the force of sheer stench. The intense heat had driven our legislators from those portions of their buildings which overlook the river. A few members, bent upon investigating the matter to its very depth, ventured into the library, but they were instantaneously driven to retreat, each man with a handkerchief to his nose. We are heartily glad of it.

Eleven days earlier Hansard recorded a claim by one honourable member that 'It was a notorious fact that Hon. Gentlemen sitting in the Committee Rooms and in the Library were utterly unable to remain there in consequence of the stench which arose from the river'.[38] *The Times* writer went on to predict that the discomfort suffered by the Parliamentarians would finally lead to a remedy and on the same day the House of Commons debated the state of the river in response to a question by a member, R.D. Mangles, MP for Guildford, who 'rose to ask the Chief Commissioner of Works what steps he has taken, or proposes to take, to preserve the health of the members of the two Houses of Parliament from being destroyed by the present pestilential condition of the River Thames'. Mangles proceeded to make several unflattering references to the Metropolitan Board of Works who, he had heard, proposed to take a voyage in a steamboat for the purpose of inspecting the river:

The Hon. Gentlemen were utterly unable to remain there in consequence of the stench which arose from the river

> If they were to go on that voyage of inspection, he hoped that they would take a good supply of brandy and other condiments with them for the purpose of obtaining relief from the sickening sensations they must experience. . . . he believed that the House has committed a great mistake in handing over a matter of that importance to any municipal body. The question was really one of an imperial character and ought to have been so treated by the legislature.[39]

The debate that followed attracted much press comment, led by the *City Press* which wrote on 19 June that 'Gentility of speech is at an

Father Thames introducing his offspring to the city of London; *Punch*'s view of the condition of the Thames in July 1858, as the Great Stink reached its climax. (*Punch*)

end – it stinks; and whoso once inhales the stink can never forget it and can count himself lucky if he live to remember it'. *The Observer* reported in similar terms two days later while a later commentator has written that 'The Thames, which had become more and more heavily used as a sewer, finally made its point by stinking out the Commons Committee'.[40]

On 2 June 1858 the Metropolitan Board passed a resolution on the drainage to the effect that they would 'defer all consideration of it until the middle of October next, leaving the whole summer to pass without any care for the state of the river'.[41] In his contribution to the Parliamentary debate Sir Benjamin Hall, now out of office, hinted that the Metropolitan Board was taking advantage of the discomfort caused by the stench of the adjacent river to exert pressure upon the Members to resolve the engineering and financial arguments in its favour. Hall went on to ask whether 'the Government should consider whether it would not be better to take the whole of this great work into their own hands . . . works of such magnitude that it was impossible that they could be paid for wholly out of local rates'.[42]

A week later, on 25 June, the House debated the matter again when Owen Stanley, a Welsh MP, quoted a letter addressed to the Speaker by Mr Goldsworthy Gurney, who was responsible for lighting and ventilation of the House. Gurney had written that he 'can no longer be responsible for the health of the house' and Stanley went on to describe interruptions to the business of the Court of

Queen's Bench where the surgeon Dr John Bredall had testified that 'it would be dangerous to the lives of the jurymen, counsel and witnesses to remain. It would produce malaria and perhaps typhus fever.'[43] It should be remembered that at this time most MPs would have believed in the 'miasmatic' explanation of disease propagation and would have been easily persuaded that the stench was potentially fatal as well as very unpleasant.

Against this background the movement for reform proceeded. On 15 July Disraeli, as leader of the House, introduced the Metropolis Local Management Amendment Act: 'An Act to alter and amend the Metropolis Local Management Act (1855) and to extend the powers of the Metropolitan Board of Works for the purification of the Thames and the Main Drainage of the Metropolis'. The first clause amended the original Act in a subtle but significant way by instructing the Board as follows:

> The Metropolitan Board shall cause to be commenced as soon as may be after the passing of the Act and to be carried on and completed with

SIR GOLDSWORTHY GURNEY, 1793–1885

A Cornishman, Goldsworthy Gurney practised as a surgeon in Wadebridge while remaining an enthusiastic student of engineering and chemistry. In 1820 he moved to London and delivered a series of lectures on chemistry which greatly impressed the young Michael Faraday, then at the beginning of his career. Gurney developed the process for producing limelight, the very bright light used in theatres; and a steam jet which was adopted by the Stephensons to power *The Rocket*. Gurney also patented a steam-carriage in which he travelled from London to Bath and back in 1829 at an average speed of 15mph. He installed a heating and lighting system in the House of Commons. In 1834 the building was burned down as a result of a well-intentioned but misguided attempt to fuel the boilers with medieval exchequer tally sticks (receipts for taxes paid) whose rotting wood proved excessively combustible. Gurney then installed a new heating, lighting and ventilation system in the rebuilt House – hence his anxieties and responsibilities during the Great Stink.

Goldsworthy Gurney. Inventor of limelight and the steam jet, he had the misfortune to be responsible for ventilating the Houses of Parliament at the time of the Great Stink. (By courtesy of the National Portrait Gallery, London)

all convenient speed according to such plan as to them may seem proper the necessary Sewers and Works for the Improvement of the Main Drainage of the Metropolis, and for preventing *as far as may be practicable* [author's italics], the sewage of the Metropolis from passing into the River Thames within the Metropolis.

The italicised phrase effectively resolved, in the Board's favour, the arguments over the positioning of the outfalls which had involved Bazalgette, Burstall and Sir Benjamin Hall's three referees for the previous two years, since it effectively repealed Clause 135 of the original Act with its unambiguous prohibition on 'all or any part of the sewage of the Metropolis . . . passing into the Thames in or near the Metropolis'. This had prompted Hall to reject the Board's original plans in July 1856. Clauses 4 and 6 enabled the Board to raise £3,000,000 by bonds or debentures and allowed the Treasury to underwrite these instruments, thus enabling the Board to obtain the money at low rates of interest, often from insurance companies. Clause 25 repealed clauses 136 and 144 of the original Act – the two clauses which had, in effect, enabled Parliament in the form of the First Commissioner to veto plans for the main drainage and any expenditure on any project in excess of £50,000. Further clauses removed the rights of ratepayers to appeal to the Quarter Sessions against the rates they were paying.

The introduction of the Bill was preceded by debates on the state of the Thames and was itself debated on 22, 23 and 24 July 1858. On the day before the debate started, *The Times*, in a long article, expressed its frustrations in the most trenchant terms:

> The truth is, that this is a case where the fool's argument that 'something must be done' is applicable . . . the sewage of a mighty city lies in a broad stream under our very noses. The actions of the [Metropolitan] Board were crippled in two most important respects. It had no money and it had no power; it had no authority to raise the means required, and its engineers were liable to be confronted with engineers appointed by government and armed with a veto . . . if we wait for a concurrence of opinions on this subject, we shall never stick a spade in the ground or construct either a drain or a tunnel, or get, in fact, a single inch beyond the recent expedient of correcting Thames water with tons of lime. . . . The stench of June was only the last ounce of our burden. That hot fortnight did for the sanitary administration of the Metropolis what the Bengal mutinies did for the administration of India.[44]

This is a case where the fool's argument that 'something must be done' is applicable

At the same time the *Journal of Public Health and Sanitary Review*, in an article called 'Is the Thames Pernicious?', reported 'stories flying of men struck down with the stench, and of all kinds of fatal diseases, upspringing on the river's banks'.[45]

Several members including Robert Stephenson, Lord John Manners and Disraeli referred to the need to deodorise the waste before it was discharged and the Prime Minister, Derby himself, during the debate in the Lords on 27 July, made a more specific reference to this question.

> It is generally understood, although there is no express provision in the Bill to that effect, that the modus operandi is to be by intercepting sewers, whereby the sewage of the Metropolis will not be allowed to be poured into the river until it shall have undergone, at such place or places as shall be determined on, the process of de-odorisation.[46]

The implication of Derby's 'general understanding' and of the thrust of the debate on the matter, was that, if sewage were to be allowed to drift with the tide to within the boundaries of the metropolis, then deodorisation would have removed its most offensive properties. Such deodorisation was normally accomplished by the addition of lime but the only reference to the subject in the Amendment Act itself was Clause 23 which prescribed that the sewage would be deodorised 'in the meantime and until the works required by the Act for the purification of the River Thames are completed'. This ambiguity became significant in a later dispute about the outfalls.

Benjamin Disraeli. His Bill in 1858 gave the Metropolitan Board and Bazalgette the authority and money they needed to construct the main drainage. (By courtesy of the National Portrait Gallery, London)

On 2 August 1858 the Metropolis Local Management Amendment Act became law, just eighteen days after Disraeli had introduced it. It gave the Board all it needed to carry out the main drainage. The Parliamentary veto was removed and the Board was empowered to borrow £3,000,000, guaranteed by the Treasury, to be repaid by the proceeds of a threepenny rate levied over forty years. In 1863 the Board was authorised to raise a further £1,200,000 on the same terms. The Act also gave the Board discretion over the siting of the outfalls. It did not mark the end of criticism of the Board. In 1861, with the drainage works well advanced, *The Times* compared the municipal government of London with that of Paris, to the detriment of London, and it advocated a directly elected body to govern the whole metropolis, including the City, arguing that such a body 'would have strength enough to double the work of Hercules and to cleanse not only the filthy stables but the river which runs through them'.

In a late contribution to the debates on the Amendment Act Viscount Ebrington, who had experienced some of the problems of the earlier Sewers Commissions, was close to the truth when he 'remarked that this Bill had been forced upon the government by a panic rather than with dignity'.[47] A later commentator observed, more succinctly, 'the "'Great Stink" concentrated minds wonderfully'.[48] Whatever the reasons, the 'centralisers' had won. Parliament had given the Board more authority than any of its predecessors had enjoyed to construct a new system of drainage for London according to its own judgement, with little danger of interference either from Parliament or from the vestries. Thwaites and his colleagues had gained a degree of autonomy which Chadwick had sought in vain.

Bazalgette could at last begin to build.

The 'Great Stink' concentrated minds wonderfully

CHAPTER FOUR

'The most extensive and wonderful work of modern times'

In various parts of the metropolis, small wooden sheds, surmounted by tarpaulins {sic} may be seen . . . in these spots has been commenced, within the last week, one of the heaviest operations London has witnessed in recent times . . . For good or for evil, the metropolis has entered upon a work of no common magnitude.

(*The Builder*, 1859)[1]

This chapter will consider the construction of the intercepting system, the problems that arose during that long process, extending over almost twenty years, the ways in which the numerous contracts were managed, and the changes that were made as the construction progressed. It will also examine the public reaction to the project, as reflected in the comments by politicians, newspaper writers and other parties. The volume of such comments and the prominent places in which they were found, including leading articles in major newspapers, clearly demonstrate the high degree of public interest that the project aroused, but also reflect the skilful way in which the Metropolitan Board of Works maintained public support and interest by cultivating influential politicians, vestrymen and writers. The chapter will also consider the extent to which the system responded to early demands on its capacity and the changes that were finally forced upon a reluctant Board and Engineer.

Bazalgette's plan, which was modified in some details as construction progressed, proposed a network of main sewers, running parallel to the river, which would intercept both surface water and waste, conducting them to the outfalls at Barking on the northern side of the Thames and Crossness, near Plumstead, on the southern side.

Bazalgette as Chief Engineer to the Metropolitan Board of Works, about 1865. (Thames Water plc)

A particular difficulty arose from the fact that much of London, especially the area around Lambeth and Pimlico, lies below the high water mark, thus making it necessary to lift the sewage from these areas to a level at which it could flow by gravity into the rest of the system. The broad outline is as follows,[2] as illustrated in the map overleaf.

Bazalgette's Plan: the Northern Drainage

The northern drainage called for the construction of three main intercepting sewers, the high level, middle level and low level sewers, the last two having a number of branches. The high level sewer ran from Hampstead Heath to Old Ford, Stratford, on the River Lea, a distance of almost 9 miles, intercepting the sewage and surface water from the northern part of the metropolis. It lay at a depth of between 20 and 26 feet below the surface and its fall was rapid, at least 4 feet per mile. For this reason it was lined with specially made bricks called Staffordshire Blues,[3] which were baked to an exceptionally high temperature to allow them to withstand the scouring motion arising from the rapid fall. Among the hazards the sewer encountered were the New River, the Great Northern Railway and the Grand Union Canal, each of these being traversed by means of tunnels. At Old Ford the sewer formed a junction with the middle level sewer which drained the central area. At the junction was a chamber from which the contents of both sewers could be discharged into the northern outfall. The middle level sewer ran at a depth of up to 36 feet from Kensal Green to its junction with the high level sewer at Old Ford, with a branch from Piccadilly and another parallel with Gray's Inn Road, giving a combined length of about 12 miles. Much of the sewer was formed by tunnelling, including a section beneath the Regent's Canal, but the greatest engineering problem was presented by the need to cross the Metropolitan Railway without stopping the traffic. This was done by constructing an aqueduct 5 feet above the intended level and then lowering it into position a few inches above the engine chimneys. The northern low level sewer was a much more complex enterprise since it lay for much of its length along the northern (Victoria) Embankment which, besides the intercepting sewers themselves, was also to house a subway, the Metropolitan underground railway, gas pipes and other services. The work involved in constructing the embankments is examined in Chapter Seven.

The greatest engineering problem was presented by the need to cross the Metropolitan Railway without stopping the traffic

The low level sewer began in Pimlico and followed the line of the river from the vicinity of Vauxhall Bridge. From Westminster Bridge to Blackfriars it was one of the many structures contained in the Victoria Embankment but from Blackfriars it headed north beneath

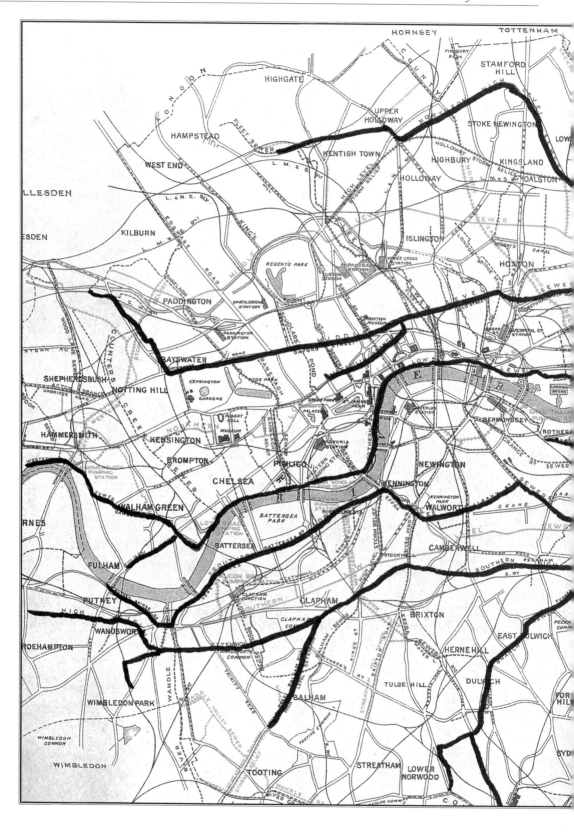

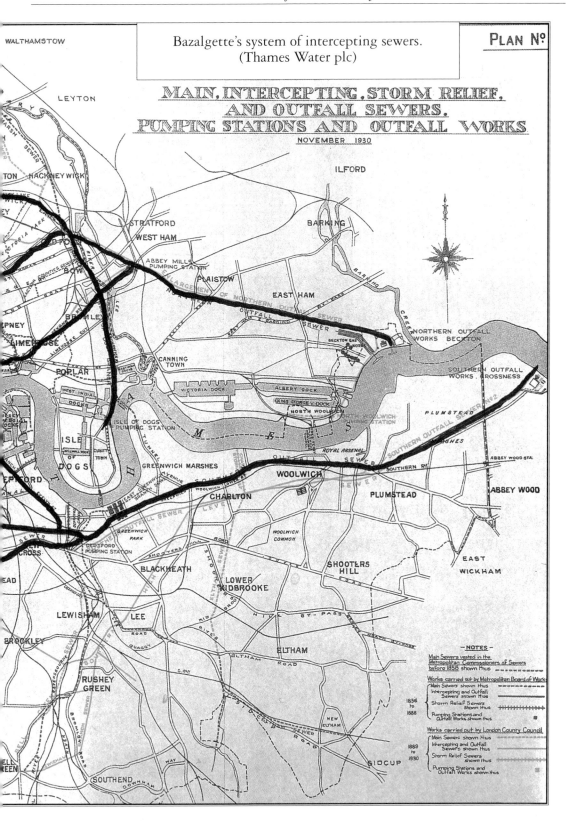

Bazalgette's system of intercepting sewers.
(Thames Water plc)

Queen Victoria Street and on to Tower Hill, Cable Street and Bow. It passed beneath the River Lea in a tunnel. Two branches extended to Homerton and the Isle of Dogs, giving a combined length of about 12 miles. At Abbey Mills a pumping station of exotic oriental design was constructed, with eight beam engines which lifted the low level sewage 36 feet into the outfall sewer. There it joined the contents of the high and middle level sewers and flowed, with them, a distance of 5 miles to the outfall reservoirs at Barking and thence into the Thames. The northern outfall sewer was a particularly complicated project since it required the construction of massive embankments to carry the outfalls across low-lying marshy land and it also had to negotiate a dense network of roads, rivers and railway lines. It was the most costly contract of the whole system, requiring the construction of a temporary cement works to produce the large quantities of material the project required and a temporary railway to convey the cement to the points at which it was used. The Barking and North Woolwich railway lines had to be lowered to enable the outfall to be carried over it without an excessive fall in the sewer. Similarly, five roads had to be raised by between 6 and 16 feet to enable the outfall to pass beneath them. It cost £669,762 and took the contractor, Furness, five years to complete. Furness also constructed the northern outfall reservoir at Barking, where the sewage was stored until it could be released at high tide.

Raising the Money

Bazalgette estimated that the cost of constructing the intercepting system would be £2,836,601.[4] The Metropolis Local Management Amendment Act of 1858 had authorised the Board to borrow £3,000,000, underwritten by the Treasury, to be repaid from the proceeds of a threepenny rate over forty years, but as the work progressed it soon became clear that additional funding would be required. Bazalgette presented evidence of increases in the prices of materials and labour to meetings of the Board, referring to the 'remarkable rise in the value of materials and labour', much of the increase in cost being caused by the demands of the main drainage itself. Bricklayers had seen their wages rise from 5s a day to 6s or more.

Bricklayers had seen their wages rise from 5s a day to 6s or more

In May the Board reviewed its financial position and estimated that the continuing growth of the Metropolis was such that the increase in the rateable value of properties within the metropolis was averaging £164,000 a year. This would enable the Board to support an additional loan of £1,200,000, to cover the additional costs of the works as estimated by Bazalgette.[5] On 13 June 1863 Thwaites wrote to the Chancellor, Gladstone, requesting authority to borrow this sum against the security of the additional rates. In July 1863 Parliament granted the Board the power to borrow the sum required.[6]

The Western Drainage

This left the low-lying western area around Fulham, Pimlico and Hammersmith which could not discharge by gravity into the rest of the system. Bazalgette's original plan proposed that the sewage from this area of about 21 square miles should be conducted to a reservoir at Fulham Fields where it would be deodorised by the addition of perchloride of iron and discharged into the Thames to the north of Chelsea Bridge.[7] The population of this area at this time was relatively small and it was estimated that about one-and-a-half million cubic feet per day of liquid would need to be discharged in this way whereas the system as a whole was designed to cope with sixty-three million cubic feet a day.[8] The Board presumably hoped that this modest discharge would pass unnoticed but in 1862 it came to the notice of Dr Burge, the Fulham Medical Officer. Burge called a special meeting of the Society of Medical Officers of Health which passed a resolution condemning the proposal as: 'ineffective in its operation, pernicious in its influence on the river, and entirely subversive of the principle on which the intercepting scheme was originally based'.[9]

In January 1863 the Society sent a deputation to the Board to protest about the proposed arrangements. The Board immediately altered its decision and announced that it would build a pumping station in Chelsea which would lift the western area sewage 19 feet into the northern low level sewer at an additional cost of £180,000.

A resolution condemned the proposal as: 'ineffective in its operation, pernicious in its influence on the river, and entirely subversive of the principle on which the intercepting scheme was originally based'

The Southern Drainage

The southern drainage was similar in conception to the northern though the area covered was smaller and the population little more than a third of the numbers living north of the river. The southern high level sewer ran from Clapham High Street 9½ miles to Deptford Creek where it was linked to Dulwich via the old Effra sewer. It flowed into the northern outfall at Deptford. The southern low level sewer ran from Putney High Street to Deptford, with a branch to Bermondsey, and the two sewers drained an area much of which was below the high water mark and previously subject to frequent flooding by the contents of the old sewers. The combined length of the sewer and branch was a little over 12 miles. The sewer was carried in tunnels beneath the Greenwich railway and Deptford

Creek. At Deptford the Board built a pumping station which opened in 1864 with four beam engines lifting the sewage 20 feet to the southern outfall sewer which ran from Deptford to Crossness. Of the 7½ miles, almost a mile of the outfall sewer was built in a tunnel beneath Woolwich. At high tide the sewage was discharged directly into the river but at other times it was lifted 21 feet into a reservoir to await high tide, this being accomplished by four huge beam engines, built by James Watt and Co. These were the largest ever built and they remained in use until 1953, surviving the attentions of scrap merchants because they were deemed too large to be removed. They are now being restored by the Crossness Engines Trust.

Bazalgette conveyed the scale of the work and the engineering problems involved in his paper to the Institution of Civil Engineers in 1865, by which time much of the system was in operation.[10] The intercepting sewers were in total 82 miles in length, laid to a minimum fall of 2 feet per mile, and consumed 318,000,000 bricks and 880,000 cubic yards of concrete, requiring the excavation of 3,500,000 cubic yards of earth. The system itself placed strains upon the suppliers of materials. In the second year of the work Bazalgette commented in his annual report on the shortage of bricks: 'the supply became quite unequal to the demand created by the extensive character of your works, and thus the price of bricks was enhanced from forty to fifty per cent'.[11]

Managing Contractors

The late eighteenth and early nineteenth centuries witnessed the emergence of the concepts of contract management which were necessary before large-scale engineering works such as railways and sewers could be undertaken. Large-scale contracting had developed in response to government contracts for the construction of barracks during the Napoleonic wars, a contractor called Alexander Copland earning over £1,300,000 for such contracts between 1796 and 1806. Thomas Cubitt (1788–1855), whose early career had been that of a ship's carpenter, is an early example of the large-scale general contractor with a permanent workforce of craftsmen which at times numbered more than two thousand. This made possible the development of open competitive tendering for large projects and replaced the earlier arrangement whereby the client made arrangements with each master craftsman.

Cubitt built the London Institution by these methods in 1855 and in the 1840s the new Houses of Parliament were built largely by such general contractors, much of the work being supervised by the

(Opposite)
Constructing the Northern outfall at Barking, 1861. This picture from the *Illustrated London News* shows the scale of the project; a concrete mill was constructed to produce the huge quantities required and a temporary railway was laid down to convey the materials to the site. (*Illustrated London News*)

SUPPLEMENT, Nov. 30, 1861.] THE ILLUSTRATED LONDON NEWS 551

L O N D O N M A I N D R A I N A G E.

FORTY years ago good salmon were taken in the upper reaches of the Thames, and good fish of various kinds caught between Vauxhall and London Bridges; indeed, a thriving community of fishermen resided there in those picturesque old streets about the Archbishop's Palace who prosecuted their calling in the immediate neighbourhood. The walks along the shores of the Thames were pleasant places in those days, where the Londoners wandered on summer evenings to enjoy fresh air. The river was a comparatively clear stream, bearing on its surface hundreds of pleasure-boats; and the houses which had back gardens or lawns extending down to the river were highly prized as dwellings by the wealthiest citizens. How changed now is both the river and its banks! The former has become a filthy sewer, the fish have been destroyed, and those who travel on it do so only as a matter of business; on the latter the dwellings are abandoned and property immensely deteriorated in value, unless occupied by wharfingers and others whose necessities compel them to locate there. And what has brought all this great change about? Simply the fact that there is poured into the River Thames every day about sixty millions of gallons of sewage, the filthy washings, scourings, and cleanings of the three millions of people who inhabit the mighty city that has grown up on its banks.

It is with not a little pleasure, then, that we have taken up for illustration and description the main drainage works now being carried out, because, according to the report of the engineer who superintends them, we may hope, in the course of two years or thereabouts to see the Thames assume its original character. We cannot make sure of catching salmon at London-bridge so soon as that, but we may certainly expect at the expiration of the time stated to see the Thames a clear, wholesome stream, attractive for its natural beauties and adding to the healthiness of the metropolis generally.

The object sought to be carried out by the works called the London Main Drainage is to intercept the sewage in its progress towards the river, and divert it by covered channels to Barking Creek, on the north side, and Erith Marshes on the south. These points are about fourteen miles below London-bridge, and it is intended that the entire mass of sewage shall be cast into the bottom of the river here during the first two hours of the ebb tide only. The period of discharge is restricted to these hours because then the sewage would be deodorised and diluted by a volume of water twenty times greater than that which now dilutes it at London, and because each ebb tide would, in returning to the sea, convey it to points twelve miles below the outfalls, or twenty-six miles below London-bridge, through a constantly-enlarging flood.

When once this system is got into working order there will be no reason why the Thames may not ebb and flow through London a perfectly clean stream, as the whole of the sewage launched at the first of the ebb will have got so far down before low water that (Continued on page 555.)

THE CONCRETE MILLS AT PLAISTOW.

CONCRETE FOUNDATION FOR THE NORTHERN OUTFALL TUNNELS.

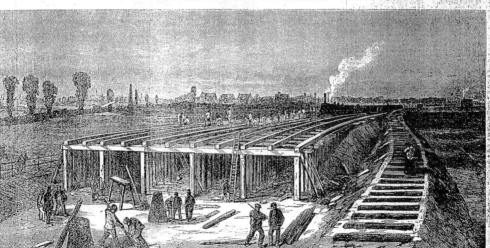

THOMAS BRASSEY, 1805–70

Son of a prosperous Cheshire farmer, Thomas Brassey became one of the greatest railway contractors in the heroic age of railway construction, as well as carrying out major works for Bazalgette. Articled to a land surveyor, in 1834 he caught the eye of George Stephenson who awarded Brassey his first railway contract, for the Penkridge viaduct in Staffordshire. Brassey then built much of the London to Southampton railway and executed railway contracts in Italy, France, Canada, the Crimea, Australia, Argentina, India and Austria. At one time he employed six thousand men on the Great Northern Railway contract alone. In a brutal age Brassey was noted for his humane treatment of labourers of all races. He appears to have had many friends and admirers, and no enemies. His son, also Thomas (later Earl) Brassey, was a minister under Gladstone, who used to take summer cruises in his luxury yacht, *Sunbeam*.

Chief Commissioner of Works, Sir Benjamin Hall. In the period between 1844 and 1862 a series of legislative measures governing joint stock and limited liability companies made it much easier for large enterprises like Cubitt's to be established. Bazalgette and the Board of Works depended upon large civil engineering firms, notably those of Thomas Brassey, William Webster and George Furness, to execute much of the work on the main drainage.

By the time the main drainage work was being undertaken there had emerged three types of contract. The first was the measure and value contract in which a full specification was given for all items to be completed and the materials to be used. The contractor specified the cost of each item and the total cost of the contract. The second type of contract was the cost plus profit method and the third was the lump sum and contractor's risk in which the contractor quoted a fixed sum which included his profit and made no allowance for contingencies. Bazalgette used the measure and value contract in most of the main drainage works, and it is possible to gain some insight into the means by which contracts were awarded and managed by examining the contracts themselves and by reading Bazalgette's monthly progress reports.[12]

For each contract a set of drawings was produced in plan and section showing the depth and line of the sewer, dimensions at each point, the method of construction and the materials to be used. The plans were superimposed on the Ordnance Survey map, thus clearly showing the position of the sewers in relation to the streets above them. The contract drawings for the northern middle level sewer may be taken as an example.[13] They comprise the main sewer itself from Kensal Green to Old Ford and two branches, one running beneath Piccadilly and the other East of Gray's Inn Road: about 12 miles of sewer altogether. At Kensal Green the dimensions of the sewer were specified as 4 feet 6 inches by 3 feet, increasing to 9 feet 6 inches by 12 feet at the junction with the high level sewer at Old Ford. The main line was to be by the 'cut and cover' method, with the exception of the 4-mile section from Saffron Hill to Notting Hill via Oxford Street, where the contours of the land prompted Bazalgette to specify tunnelling. About two thousand feet of the two branches were also made by tunnelling. The materials to be employed were specified, taking as an example the following clause covering the largest part of the main sewer:

> Construct in Open Cutting, 4,430 feet run, of brick sewer, 9' 6' in height by 12' wide, of the form and dimensions shown in Section, Drawing no. 4; the upper arch in mortar, the rest in cement, from a junction with the Northern high level Sewer . . .[14]

Having completed the drawings and specification of materials, Bazalgette passed them to a quantity surveyor who calculated the quantities of work required to complete each contract. A number of these Bills of Quantities have survived, including one for the southern low level sewer prepared by a surveyor called D.W. Young, John Grant being named as the resident engineer.[15] For this sewer Young's calculations included: 400,317 cubic yards of excavation; 250,287 cubic yards of infill; 57,410 cubic yards of concrete; and

Constructing the Southern sewers at New Cross, 1861. (*Illustrated Times*)

Bricks and other materials
being delivered by sailing
barge to Barking, to build the
Northern outfall, 1865.
(Thames Water plc)

3,505 rods of brickwork. The estimated quantities were then issued
to tenderers together with details of payment methods. Accounts
were to be submitted monthly, within a week of the month's end.
Initially 90 per cent of the estimated value would be paid; a further
5 per cent after three months; 2½ per cent after six months; and the
balance after a year. The work was to be completed by 24 December
1863, a penalty of £50 a day being imposed for late completion.

In evidence to the *Royal Commission Appointed to Inquire into Certain
Matters Connected with the Metropolitan Board of Works*, Bazalgette
described the procedures he followed when contracts were put out to
tender.[16] Having secured the agreement of the Board to his proposed
works he would advertise for tenders in publications such as *The
Builder*. The documents were printed and issued for a fee of £5 to
every tenderer and the tenders, when received, were opened at the
Board meeting immediately following their receipt.

The contractors then submitted bids based on the quantities
calculated by the surveyor and these were incorporated in the
contract in the form of a Schedule of Prices. The schedule submitted
by Thomas Brassey for the northern middle level sewer contract
included the following:[17]

Digging, shoring and fencing:	2s 6d per cubic yard
Tunnelling:	6s 6d per cubic yard
Lime cement:	6s 6d per cubic yard
Portland cement:	13s per cubic yard
Brickwork:	£14 per rod
Stockbricks:	35s per thousand
Staffordshire Blue bricks:	84s per thousand

Day labour rates per ten hour day:

Labourer:	3s 6d
Miner (for tunnelling):	5s 6d
Bricklayer:	6s[18]

An examination of Bazalgette's sectional drawings shows that he used the tunnelling method where the sewers were 30 feet or more beneath street level, preferring the 'Cut and cover' method for most of the system. In this choice he was no doubt influenced by the greater costs of tunnelling, as reflected in the figures given above both for tunnelling and for the higher wages paid to 'miners'. Tunnelling could also be dangerous, a number of fatalities being incurred in the 5,000 foot tunnel beneath Woolwich.

The Board did not always accept the lowest tender since, as Bazalgette explained:

> if there is a contractor whom they well know, and whose tender is not materially above the lower one, they will naturally prefer it. It is a very great mistake to employ a contractor who has not the means of carrying out his contract thoroughly. It always leads to constant wrangling, difficulty, stoppage and very often eventual failure.[19]

It always leads to constant wrangling, difficulty, stoppage and very often eventual failure

In this judgement Bazalgette was no doubt influenced by the early failure of Rowe, the original contractor for the northern middle level sewer who gained the contract on 24 February 1860 and failed shortly after beginning, having executed only £12,451 of work. The contract was eventually completed by Thomas Brassey for £349,869. When a dispute arose between a contractor and the Board over sums owed for work completed, Bazalgette effectively acted as arbitrator, having considered the claims of the contractor and the estimates of the quantity surveyors who supervised the work on behalf of the Board. No bill was paid unless it was authorised by Bazalgette. The stress involved in constantly drawing up plans, supervising numerous simultaneous contracts, working and arbitrating in disputes eventually affected Bazalgette. A year before his death, in an interview with Cassell's *Saturday Journal* he described how he often worked until one o'clock in the morning.[20] On 29 October 1869, with all but the western drainage in operation, the Board declared that the engineer 'be authorised and requested to absent himself from all his duties for a period of three months, with a view to the restoration of his health' and a week later John Grant was appointed to deputise for Bazalgette during the latter's absence. Bazalgette returned to his duties after a little more than a month.[21]

In his evidence to the Royal Commission Bazalgette claimed that his advice to the Board on the choice of contractors was confined to informing them whether the tenderer had previously worked for the Board, whereas checking credit worthiness was undertaken by the Board's solicitor, though this view – that Bazalgette exerted little influence on the selection of contractors – was challenged in the 'Odessa contract'.

Bazalgette was 'authorised and requested to absent himself from all his duties for a period of three months, with a view to the restoration of his health'

The Odessa Contract

An embarrassing episode for Bazalgette concerned the 'Odessa contract'. On 11 November 1863 the *Clerkenwell News* published a letter from 'A. Ratepayer' who was very well informed about the tenders for the northern outfall reservoir and the main contract for the Northern Embankment, both of which had been awarded to a contractor called George Furness whom the Board often employed. The writer claimed, correctly, that a contractor called Ridley, one of thirteen who had tendered for the contract,[22] had bid £495,000 for the Embankment against Furness's winning tender of £520,000. The writer questioned 'how far Mr Bazalgette is fitted to be retained in his present office of Chief Engineer to the Board of Works' since it seemed that 'acceptance goes by favour and not by merit'.[23] The following week J.A. Nicholay, Board member for Marylebone, replied to 'A. Ratepayer' in terms that were very critical of Bazalgette. Nicholay stated that Ridley would have won the tender:

but for the circumstances of our engineer emphatically stating he should place more reliance on Mr Furness whose knowledge, experience and capabilities were far superior. I have every reason to believe that such result would not have been obtained had the members known at the time that our engineer was about to receive from twelve thousand pounds and upwards as commission from Mr Furness for work to be carried out by him at Odessa.[24]

In the previous year Sir John Rennie had consulted Bazalgette on the suitability of Furness to execute a contract for draining and paving the city of Odessa, in the Ukraine. Bazalgette had recommended Furness, who agreed to pay 5 per cent of the contract price to

Rennie, of which 1¾ per cent was to be paid to Bazalgette. In fact Bazalgette had made extensive enquiries into Ridley's background and had established that, although he had considerable experience as a sub-contractor on railway works in Canada,[25] he had no experience of tidal or harbour works and none of executing works on the scale of the Embankment contract, the second largest that the Board ever awarded. In Bazalgette's words:

> I believe him to be an active and industrious man, capable of successfully completing a straightforward job; but I do not think he is competent, either from past experience, or from his judgement and engineering knowledge, to cope with . . . the great risks which must arise in the execution of that very important work.

In addition, Bazalgette had received confidential information from Waring Brothers, former employers of Ridley, to the effect that Ridley had appropriated a sum of £100 which should have been used to pay his workmen.[26] The Board set up a Committee of Enquiry into the affair and in his final evidence to it Bazalgette stated: 'it is most important that the contractor should be a person of skill and experience and *possessed of great resources*. [author's italics] I was bound to advise the Board to this effect and Mr Ridley's tender was rejected'.[27]

Ridley had appropriated a sum of £100 which should have been used to pay his workmen

Bazalgette reminded the committee that he had originally recommended that the contract be awarded to a firm called Baker and Son but that this firm had wanted to impose an arbitration clause that the Board found unacceptable. Bazalgette had then recommended that the contract be re-advertised but this advice had been rejected and it was awarded to Furness. The committee declared that: 'there has been nothing reflecting in any way on Mr Bazalgette's personal or professional honour and that he has throughout discharged his duties, both to the Board and their contractors, with ability, impartiality and integrity'.[28] The Committee nevertheless indicated their disapproval of the arrangement into which Bazalgette had entered and noted that he had agreed to forgo his commission.

Public Interest: a '*most extensive and wonderful work*'

The construction of the system was closely followed in the press and in Parliament, receiving a degree of attention and comment which reflected both its significance in the life of the metropolis and the importance attached by the Board to gaining and keeping support for the project among opinion formers. The first such comment appeared in the *Illustrated London News* on 19 February 1859 with an illustration of the commencement of the works on the high level sewer in Victoria Park, Hackney, together with an expression of gratitude to:

> Old Father Thames [for] having last summer so loudly remonstrated against our tardiness in cleansing his bosom, and having threatened us with some sore disease if we continued to pollute him, for the fact of the spade, the shovel and the pick having at last taken the place of pens, ink and debate.[29]

Within two years a note of wonder was evident in the pages of the previously critical *Observer*. In April 1861 the newspaper commented:

> It is two years since the most extensive and wonderful work of modern times was commenced, and yet the inhabitants of this metropolis, who are so deeply interested, seem to take little interest in the undertaking . . . It is hardly possible that such an undertaking could be finished in three years, or at a cost of only three millions of money.[30]

Crossness under construction, 1865. The storage reservoirs have yet to be roofed over, and the pumping station is under construction in the background. (Thames Water plc)

The concrete mill at Crossness, 1865. The Southern outfall sewer may be glimpsed in the distance. (Thames Water plc)

The three years and the three millions were both significantly exceeded but such unqualified appreciation of works executed at the public expense is an interesting and unfamiliar reflection of the importance that was attributed to the project. Such praise for a public project is certainly hard to imagine in the late twentieth century. Similar views were reflected in the *City Press* five months later. In a leading article entitled 'The Main Drainage' the writer commented:

> Looking at the results attained so far, we must do the Board the justice of uttering our opinion that it has accomplished wonders and if we were to contemplate the transference of its powers to the hands of government we should at the same time entertain grave doubts if the future progress of these immense undertakings would be prosecuted with one-tenth the speed or with anything like the same efficiency. As to the cost, vast as it is, no one can charge the Board with waste; in the proper mission for which it was created it has practised rigid economy and stern prudence, and let it have the praise it as well deserves.[31]

Even the astringent *Marylebone Mercury* was won round. In March 1861 an article entitled 'The Uselessness of the Board of Works' took the members to task for wasting their time in naming streets and dealing with vestry grievances, but in October it was generous with its praise for the engineer and his works, stating that 'To Mr Bazalgette no tribute of praise can be undeserved' and wondering at

The railway built to transport workmen to and from Crossness; it was pressed into service in July 1864 to convey home inebriated vestrymen who had missed the returning steamer. (*Illustrated Times*)

the fact that, in tunnelling beneath Woolwich, 'So accurate were the designs that, when the different bodies of men met, there was not a deviation of a quarter inch in their projection'.[32] These flattering comments followed a visit of inspection on which the newspaper's editor had been a guest the previous week and which appears to have created the favourable impression the Board desired.

Such visits became a regular feature of the Board's public relations and were evidently effective in maintaining support for the enterprise. On 6 July 1862 *The Observer* contained a favourable account of a visit by 150 members of the Lords and Commons to inspect the northern and southern outfall works and declared that 'every penny spent is sunk in a good cause'[33] while two years later the *Marylebone Mercury* carried a long, humorous and good-natured account of a visit to the outfalls by members of Vestry and District Boards, five steamers being chartered by the Metropolitan Board for the visit which took place on 27 July 1864. The account was headed 'The Main Drainage Works' and the opening sentence stated 'That has at last been accomplished, which not long ago would have been regarded as an engineering castle in the air'. Having described the works and the visit of inspection the *Mercury* described the lively lunch that followed and the toasts and cheers that accompanied the attempts of Thwaites, Bazalgette and others to address the gathering.

However, the writer then lamented that a 'most indecorous scene marred what had hitherto been a merry gathering':

> Mr Marley, a gentleman well-known and respected as a member of the Saint Pancras Vestry, rose at the conclusion of the regular programme of addresses, and endeavoured to say a few words, but he had hardly risen, before he was assailed from several quarters by large pieces of bread that remained from the luncheon.[34]

Mr Marley abandoned his attempts at speechmaking and the company, evidently fortified by their luncheon, proceeded to exercise themselves on the shoreline by organising barefoot races among themselves. Some of the more inebriated members of the company missed the returning steamers and had to be conveyed home via the temporary railway that had been laid to convey workmen and materials to the site. The indulgent tone of the account suggests that this was a particularly successful piece of news management by the Board.

The City, some of whose privileges had been weakened by the authority of the Board, remained a critical onlooker, particularly with regard to the Board's finances, and in May 1865 the Court of Common Council became exercised by a reported plan to reward Bazalgette and his team of engineers with a special bounty. This proposal had originated with a member of the Board called Miller, a Member of Parliament, who on 28 April 1865 had proposed to the Board that: 'in consequence of the near completion of the Main Drainage works, it be referred to the Main Drainage Committee to consider the propriety of granting a special remuneration to the Engineer and Assistant Engineers'.[35]

A fortnight later the Committee supported the proposal:

Crossness nears completion, April 1865. (*Illustrated London News*)

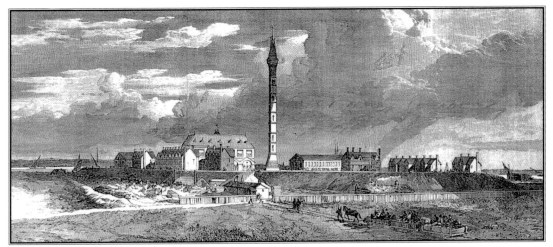

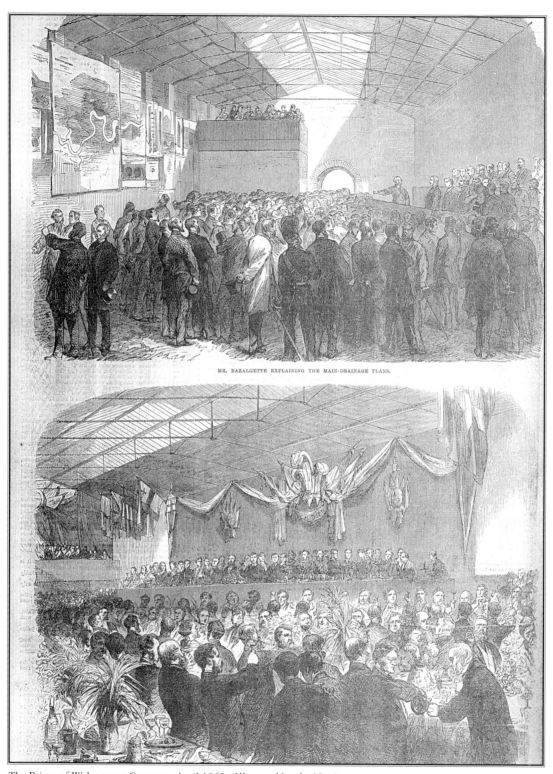

MR. BAZALGETTE EXPLAINING THE MAIN-DRAINAGE PLANS.

The Prince of Wales opens Crossness, April 1865. (*Illustrated London News*)

It appears to your Committee that a very general feeling exists that
there should be some recognition of the valuable and eminent services
of the Engineer and his Assistants, in the successful carrying out of the
scheme of the Main Drainage of the Metropolis, which is universally
pronounced to be one of the greatest works of this or any other age.

The committee proposed a payment of £6,000 to Bazalgette (a huge
sum, three times his annual salary) with a further £4,000 to be
divided between the three assistant engineers. Following protests
from some of the vestries the Board dropped the idea though the
City, despite its critical comments on the Board's management of its
finances, 'was not prepared to say that Mr Bazalgette was not entitled
to some recognition of the great talent he had displayed in carrying
out the main drainage work'.[36] The fact that the Board was prepared
to contemplate paying such a large bounty to Bazalgette and his
assistants at a time when parsimony was the dominant characteristic
of public expenditure is a firm indication of the depth of public
interest and approval that appears to have characterised the work.

The official opening took place on 4 April 1865 and the
importance attributed to the occasion may be judged by the fact that

The Prince of Wales starts the
engines at Crossness, one of
them named after himself,
April 1865. (*Illustrated London
News*)

Crossness, with its magnificent Victorian ironwork, pictured following the opening, April 1865. (*Illustrated London News*)

the Prince of Wales was accompanied by other royalty, Members of Parliament, the Archbishops of Canterbury and York, the Lord Mayors of London and Dublin and numerous other dignitaries, among them Edwin Chadwick. After inspecting the works in progress at Abbey Mills, the party crossed to the southern bank where Bazalgette explained the workings to His Royal Highness who switched on the four great beam engines, named Victoria, Prince Consort, Albert Edward and Alexandra, thus marking the official inauguration of the system. Construction work continued for many more years. Crossness was not completed until 1867 and Abbey Mills was opened in 1868. The western area was completed in 1875. Nevertheless, the official opening on 4 April 1865 was a significant date in the project and was recognised as such, being extensively reported in influential metropolitan publications such as *The Times*, the *Marylebone Mercury* and *The Builder*, which was particularly generous in its praise: 'That the Board has been admirably served by Mr. Bazalgette and all the engineering staff, we need not say; that fact is shown by structural work that is the admiration of all who have seen it'.[37]

The Board appears to have planned an opening for Abbey Mills almost as grand as that for Crossness but these plans were scaled down when the Duke of Edinburgh was unable to perform the ceremony and the Board learned that the Parliamentary recess would mean that prominent politicians would also be unavailable.[38] Instead, the Board issued three tickets for the ceremony to each member and also invited members of Vestry and District Boards as well as representatives of the press.[39] The opening took place on 30 July 1868 but once again the Board took advantage of the occasion to draw attention to its continuing activity. In the second week of August 1868, VIPs visited the new pumping station from Monday to Thursday and on the Friday the workmen who had built it, with their wives and families, inspected the installation as the guests of the Board and sat down to a meal.[40] Such was the enthusiasm for the new system that it was even allocated a place in the defence of the realm. Some critics had suggested that the outfalls were vulnerable to attack by an invading force sailing up the Thames (the French being the chief suspects at this time) but on 29 January 1870 *The Builder* asserted that, on the contrary: 'The sewage of London, North and South, suddenly discharged upon an advancing fleet, would inevitably produce a panic and retreat, or death by poison'.

The engine house, Crossness, 1865 (now being restored). (*The Builder*)

Besides building the intercepting sewers the Board was also responsible for maintaining the network of main sewers previously constructed by the Commissioners of Sewers and their predecessors. Thus in its annual report for the year 1863/4 the Board reported that, with most of the contracts for the main drainage under way, it had been turning its attention to repairing and enlarging the older sewers, on which it had spent £800,000 during that year.[41] The Board eventually reconstructed 165 miles of old main sewers (twice the length of the intercepting system itself), together with storm relief sewers, while 1,100 miles of new local sewers were constructed by Vestries under the supervision of the Board, all the plans being inspected and approved by Bazalgette.[42]

Testing the System – Rain

In preparing his plans Bazalgette had to make assumptions about the likely future population of the area over which his responsibilities

Abbey Mills pumping station, 1868. The ornate chimneys were demolished during the Second World War because it was believed that the Luftwaffe was using them as a navigation aid. (*Illustrated London News*)

extended and the quantities of sewage that each would generate. He allowed for a population of 3,450,000, of which two-thirds would be north of the river and one-third south. This was about 25 per cent more than the population at the time he designed the system.[43] Bazalgette also estimated that the water supply to the population would increase from the figure then prevailing, of 20 to 25 gallons per day, to a more generous 30 gallons per day. Subsequently both estimates were greatly exceeded. By the time of Bazalgette's death in 1891, the population had already reached 4,225,000, more than 20 per cent above Bazalgette's estimate, and greater increases followed in the twentieth century, while *per capita* consumption of water grew to 90 gallons per day. In Bazalgette's lifetime the system proved adequate to cope with the greater volumes of sewage and, when further growth of the metropolis began to put strains upon the capacity of the system, further sewers were added.

However, Bazalgette also had to accommodate rainfall whose volume over short periods was far less predictable. He designed the system to cope with ¼ inch of rain falling during the six daytime hours of maximum sewage flow, a larger volume being accommodated when there was less sewage flowing (for example at

Interior of Abbey Mills
following the opening
ceremony, 1868. (*Illustrated
London News*)

night). However, as Bazalgette also observed in his 1865 paper to the
Institution of Civil Engineers, violent rainstorms can occur in which
as much as 2 inches of rain can fall in an hour. It would have been
impractical to build sewers with the capacity to handle these
exceptional flows which, he estimated, would occur on a maximum
of twelve days a year. He therefore constructed:

> overflow weirs, to act as safety valves in times of storms . . . on such
> occasions the surplus waters will be largely diluted, and, after the
> intercepting sewers are filled, will flow over the weirs, and through
> their original channels into the Thames.[44]

The system was subjected to its first severe test in the early hours of
26 July 1867. Between midnight and 9 a.m. 3¼ inches of rain fell,
more than had ever previously been recorded in such an interval, and
amounting to about one-eighth of the average annual rainfall. *The
Builder* reported that the intercepting system had coped.[45]
Bazalgette, in his report to the Board on 'The Extraordinary Rainfall
on Friday, 26th July 1867',[46] observed that: 'the pumps were that
day lifting a volume of water equal to nearly half an inch of rain over
the whole of the low level area, nearly double the quantity they were

intended to lift'. He commented that serious flooding had been confined to an area in Battersea in which houses had been built since the main drainage plans had been published; yet they had been built with basements in some cases 12 feet below high water mark – a level at which they could not be effectively drained by the intercepting system.

Testing the System: Problems at the Outfalls

One of the consequences of the pollution of the river in the 1840s had been the disappearance of fish from the Thames, so in its annual reports the Board made careful note of the favourable effects of the main drainage on the condition of the river. In the report for 1865–6, following the official opening at Crossness, the Board referred to 'the return of fish in large quantities to those parts of the river which, previous to the execution of the works, were in the most polluted condition'[47] and in the following years such comments became a regular feature of the Board's reports. Nevertheless, even before Abbey Mills was opened in July 1868, doubts were being expressed about whether the problems of pollution had been solved or simply moved downstream. In May 1868 the vicar and 123 other inhabitants of Barking presented a petition to the Home Secretary concerning the condition of the river near the outfalls, claiming that the local water supply was being polluted.[48] An enquiry established that pollution was caused by poor sewers in Barking itself and by chemical pollution of the River Roding which entered the Thames close to the outfalls.[49]

'The return of fish in large quantities to those parts of the river which, previous to the execution of the works, were in the most polluted condition'

On 29 July 1874 the Thames Conservators informed the Board of the existence of banks of deposits in Halfway Reach, a little way downstream from the outfalls, implying that the outfalls were responsible. On Bazalgette's advice the Board responded to the Conservators' complaint by asserting that it had been taking soundings in the vicinity of the outfalls since 1867 and that, far from creating banks, the outfalls produced a 'positive scour and improvement in the depth of the river referred to, to the extent of three hundred thousand cubic yards, or in other words that part of the river is actually ten inches deeper than in 1867'.[50] In June 1877 the Conservators raised the matter again, suggesting that the Board was responsible for the banks and that it should remove them by dredging at its expense. To support their case they appointed Captain Calver RN, who produced a report on 15 October 1877 which asserted that:

offensive accretions had recently formed within the channel of the
Thames; that a material portion of these were within the

neighbourhood of the sewage outfalls . . . that the constituents of these accretions were the same as those of the sewage, and that the latter was discharged in sufficient quality to account for them, the tidal streams in the neighbourhood of the outfalls being the effective cause.[51]

Calver's conclusions were discussed in *The Times*[52] and brought a swift reply from Bazalgette who argued that 'were Captain Calver's theory correct, the Thames and all other tidal rivers of the universe would long ago have ceased to exist'. Calver had claimed, in his report, that Bazalgette had advised that the sewage of Glasgow should be purified before release into the Clyde, while condoning the release of untreated sewage into the Thames. Bazalgette explained that his recommendations that Glasgow's sewage be purified before discharge into the Clyde had been influenced by the fact that the banks of the Clyde were suitable for residential development 'whereas the neighbourhood of the metropolitan outfalls is surrounded by bone boilers and glue and artificial manure works and they can bear no comparison'. Bazalgette added that, in 1858, the Thames had become so offensive that 'It was suggested that Parliament would have to abandon its sittings at Westminster whereas now I have the evidence before me of flounders being frequently caught in the neighbourhood of Westminster'.[53]

'The neighbourhood of the metropolitan outfalls is surrounded by bone boilers and glue and artificial manure works'

The Princess Alice

On 3 September 1878 there occurred an accident which sharpened the dispute but did little to resolve it. The pleasure steamer *Princess Alice* collided with the freighter *Bywell Castle* causing the *Princess Alice* to sink, with the loss of many lives.[54] The collision occurred close to the outfalls at the time of discharge and it was suggested in some quarters that many fatalities had resulted from poisoning rather than drowning.[55] Woolwich Board of Health commissioned a chemist called Wigner to produce a 'Report on the State of the Thames with special reference to the question as to whether the water was so contaminated by sewage discharge on 3rd September 1878 as to cause the death of any of the passengers on the *Princess Alice*'. He reported that such deaths could have been caused by 'uncontrolled vomiting' and his conclusions were reported in *The Times*.[56]

Further correspondence between the Board and the Conservators failed to resolve the question of who was responsible for the banks. On 4 November 1879, therefore, three arbitrators were appointed by the Board of Trade. Twenty-five sittings were held between 4 November 1879 and 24 March 1880 and the findings of the arbitrators were unanimous. They concluded that river navigation had actually improved since the outfalls were constructed; that the banks complained of resulted from the Conservators' own dredging operations, which had altered the flow of water; and that 'we are therefore of opinion that the Metropolitan Board of Works should not be called on to remove or contribute any portion of the expense of removing the three banks or any of them'.[57] Bazalgette added his own riposte in his evidence to the Commissioners, repeated in his annual report, declaring that 'Captain Calver's imaginary sewage zone in the lower reaches of the river can have no existence'.[58]

Another Great Stink?

On 7 March 1882 a group of merchants, traders, shipowners and the representatives of dock and shipping interests on the Thames held a meeting and drafted a memorial to Gladstone asking that a Commission be appointed to enquire into the condition of the river. Sixteen MPs from the metropolitan area were included in the 159 signatories who announced that they had formed themselves into the 'General Committee for the Protection of the Lower Thames from Sewage'. The memorial was supported by the secretary to the Local Government Board in a letter dated 15 May. On 22 June a Royal Commission was appointed, chaired by Baron Bramwell, a retired judge, and including two civil engineers, a professor of chemistry from University College, a doctor and an army surgeon. The Metropolitan Board argued unsuccessfully that the Commission should be postponed until October 'and not made in the hot summer months when decomposition is more rapid'. It is hard to resist the conclusion that this was a further defensive move by the Board to protect its own narrow interests.

A further defensive move by the Board to protect its own narrow interests

The Commissioners produced two reports. The first, published on 31 January 1884, stated that 'the discharge of the sewage, in its crude state, during the whole year, without any attempt to render it less offensive, is at variance with the original intentions and with the understanding in Parliament when the 1858 Act was passed',[59] this being a reference to Derby's speech on the Act when he had stated:

> It is generally understood, although there is no express provision in the Bill to that effect, that . . . the sewage of the Metropolis will not be allowed to be poured into the river until it shall have undergone, at such place or places as shall be determined on, the process of deodorisation.[60]

The Home Secretary, Harcourt, supported the Commissioners and wrote to the Board on 29 July 1884 to the effect that 'The Secretary of State thinks it greatly to be regretted that, instead of disputing the existence of the evil when it was first urged upon their attention in the early part of the year 1882 by the Secretary of State, on the representation of the Corporation of London and other persons, the Metropolitan Board did not at once take measures to remedy so serious a mischief'. The Board had in fact resolved to increase the reservoir capacity by 50 per cent three years earlier in order to be able to hold all the sewage pending the arrival of the ebb tide but had later resolved to postpone the work pending the outcome of the Royal Commission.[61]

The Second and Final Report of the Commission was unequivocal and, having considered the possibility of sewage utilisation as a full and permanent solution, its fourteen recommendations included the declaration that 'it is neither necessary nor justifiable to discharge the sewage of the Metropolis in its crude state into any part of the Thames' and suggested that, having separated the solids for sale as manure, the remaining liquid should be conveyed to Hole Haven, near Canvey Island, for discharge into the Thames estuary.[62]

The Board was alarmed at the expense of these proposals, involving further massive engineering works to convey the sewage, from both the northern and southern banks, the 20 miles to Canvey Island. For these reasons Bazalgette carried out a series of experiments as a result of which he reported that the sewage could be disposed of by extracting the solid elements through the addition of lime and sulphate of iron. The solids could then be burnt, given to farmers or dumped at sea while the much larger volume of liquid, rendered harmless by the process, could be discharged to the river.

By the autumn of 1885 *The Times* was publishing material which was alarmingly similar to that which had appeared in its pages during 'The Great Stink' twenty-seven years earlier, writing: 'Anybody who has frequented the Thames would, though he has been years away and returned blind, recognise its stream by the dull brooding atmosphere of odours the Metropolitan Board of Works brews from its London sewage.'[63] In January 1886 the *Pall Mall Gazette* took the Board to task, asserting that 'The Royal Commission on the Sewage Discharge returned a verdict of guilty on the Board on January 31st 1884' [the date of the first report of the Commissioners] and asking why the Board did not order Bazalgette to take the necessary steps. The writer added:

> There are not wanting those who say that Sir Joseph is master of the Board and will not give them definite advice on the difficulty. They argue that it is his own scheme that he is called upon to correct, and that the natural man in him puts off the evil day of having to admit

'Sir Joseph is master of the Board and will not give them definite advice'

failure. Canvey Island may claim whatever credit belongs to the fact that it is as clearly designed for the treatment of London sewage as the belt of chalk under the English Channel was created by Providence for the construction of the channel tunnel – which latter fact the world has on the unquestioned authority of a railway chairman.[64]

The reference to Canvey Island concerned a proposal made by two promoters called Colonel A.S. Jones and J. Bailey Denton who, anticipating that the Board would convey the sewage to Hole Haven, proposed that the Board should pay them £110,000 per annum to dispose of the sewage. Denton and Jones, who had purchased an interest in Canvey Island, had proposed the scheme to Gladstone and continued to lobby the Board and its advisers for the next two years, long after other proposals had been adopted.[65]

The Works and General Purposes Committee of the Board reported on this and other proposals on 26 March 1886. Bazalgette had calculated that the annual cost of conveying the sewage to Hole Haven, including the cost of capital, would amount to £215,000 whereas the precipitation and disposal process would cost £118,000. This would generate 850 tons of pressed sludge a day. Tests had shown that burning it produced offensive smells and limited results had been achieved by giving it to farmers, so it would be dumped at sea.[66] Unsurprisingly, the Committee recommended the adoption of this process. In January 1887 the Board engaged a contractor to construct thirteen precipitating channels at Barking, at a cost of £406,000 and this was followed in May 1888 by a similar contract for channels at Crossness at a cost of £259,816.[67] Six sludge vessels were ordered, the first one, the *Bazalgette*, arriving from the Naval Construction and Armaments Company, Barrow, in June 1887 at a cost of £16,353.[68]

Burning sludge produced offensive smells and limited results had been achieved by giving it to farmers, so it would be dumped at sea

The Board had slowly, with great reluctance and with a strong rearguard action, come to accept that it could no longer discharge raw sewage into the Thames. A solution which had been greeted with enthusiasm in the 1860s was no longer acceptable in the 1880s, in which period London had grown in population by almost 50 per cent and the previously sparsely inhabited communities of Barking and Plumstead had become substantial metropolitan suburbs instead of the 'bone boilers and glue works' described by Bazalgette in 1877.[69] A much later historian agreed with the contemporary judgement, quoted above, of the *Pall Mall Gazette*. Bazalgette, 'an old and tired man . . . had been with the Board for so long that he had, perhaps, gained an excessive influence over its decisions', and consequently they were reluctant to make significant changes to the system which he had devised thirty years earlier and for which he had

Thames Water's sludge-boat, the SS *Bazalgette* was finally replaced in December 1998 by an incinerator. (Thames Water plc)

been widely praised.[70] His system was nevertheless easily adapted to the process of precipitation and disposal at sea and this practice continued successfully until 1998.[71]

Post Script

In 1995 Thames Water 'exported' 4.3 megawatts of electricity to the National Grid from their CoGas (Combined Gas and Steam) power plant at Barking, generated by igniting the methane gas which is naturally present in sewage. In 1998 the company began to operate much more advanced incineration plants at Bazalgette's treatment works at Barking and Crossness, thereby enabling them to conform with European directives which required that marine disposal of waste should cease by the end of 1998.[72] The new plant compresses the sludge recovered from the settlement tanks at the treatment works and incinerates it through a sand bed at a temperature of 850 degrees centigrade. The heat generated is recovered and used to drive a steam turbine which provides electricity to run the treatment works while leaving a substantial surplus for 'export' to the National Grid. The remaining liquid is treated by an aerobic process which promotes bacterial activity to remove remaining impurities before the treated liquid is released to the Thames, having been raised to a level of cleanliness greater than that of the water in the river itself. It is intended that the small quantity of ash which remains after the incineration process will be marketed as breeze blocks.

CHAPTER FIVE

Where there's Muck there's Brass?

Not to know the particulars of the last movements on the sewage question is to be quite unfit for the drawing-room where scientific and social subjects are freely mingled in the elements of elegant conversation.

(*City Press*, 1864)

It is hard for us to imagine today that proposals for the utilisation of sewage as manure would regularly engage the attention of leader writers in popular newspapers yet such was the case in the late 1860s as politicians, sanitary reformers, engineers and entrepreneurs debated the merits of one scheme after another. An examination of the pages of the leading trade publication, *The Builder*, in the year 1868 reveals that scarcely a week passed without correspondence or editorial commentary on the subject. Daily and weekly newspapers like *The Times* and *City Press* regularly joined the debate. This chapter will consider the origins of this interest in the concept of sewage utilisation; the many attempts in London and elsewhere to introduce successful schemes; the difficulties which these schemes caused both for their promoters and for the Metropolitan Board as it constructed the intercepting sewers; and the progressive acceptance of the view that, instead of being exploited as a source of income, opportunities for the utilisation of sewage should be regarded as an aid to overcoming the problem of disposal. This latter view is reflected in twentieth-century schemes found in areas as diverse as the Thames Valley in England and the Australian capital Canberra.

Economics: Early Experiments

As observed in Chapter One, it had been the practice since the Middle Ages to convey the contents of cesspools to the fields which surrounded towns and to sell the sewage to farmers as fertiliser for their crops. From the early nineteenth century large quantities of sewage had been conveyed up the Grand Union Canal to Hertfordshire for this purpose and the traffic continued into the twentieth century. Nevertheless, as early as 1842 Edwin Chadwick had commented on the increasing difficulty of finding a market for the contents of London's cesspools as the metropolis grew larger and the fields, in consequence, more remote.[1] The problem was compounded by the fact that, from about 1820, other forms of fertiliser were becoming available which were more easily handled and cheaper. The development of agricultural chemistry by the German chemist Justus von Liebig and the consequent availability of mineral fertilisers like sulphate of ammonia, together with the importation of guano from South America from about 1847, made sewage relatively more expensive and less necessary. However, not everyone was satisfied with this arrangement. The price of guano increased from £10 to £12 a ton between the late 1840s and the early 1860s and at the same time developments in agricultural chemistry had made it possible to compare the fertilising ingredients of sewage and guano and thereby to estimate the theoretical value of sewage.[2] In November 1859, as Bazalgette began the work of construction on the intercepting sewers, *The Times* published one of many letters on the subject from J.J. Mechi, a London alderman who was a regular contributor to correspondence on the subject of sewage utilisation. Mechi, of Tiptree Hall, Kelvedon, in Essex, quoted Liebig in support of his argument that failure to utilise sewage would lead to the exhaustion of the land. He wrote critically of:

> the gradual but sure exhaustion of the soil of Great Britain by our new sanitary arrangements, which permit the excrements (really the food) of fifteen million people, who inhabit our towns and cities, to flow wastefully into our rivers. The continuance of this suicidal practice must ultimately result in great calamities to our nation.[3]

According to Alderman Mechi, Liebig had estimated that Britain was importing half a million tons of guano annually.

Three years later *The Builder* reviewed Liebig's book *Agricultural Chemistry* and quoted extensively from its introduction which criticised the harmful effects of English sanitary practices:

> The introduction of water-closets into most parts of England results in the loss annually of the materials capable of producing food for three and a half million people; the greater part of the enormous quantity of manure imported into England being regularly conveyed to the sea by the rivers . . . like a vampire it hangs upon the breast of Europe, and even the world; sucking its life-blood.[4]

'The continuance of this suicidal practice must ultimately result in great calamities to our nation'

JUSTUS VON LIEBIG, 1803–73

Justus von Liebig was described by a contemporary English writer as 'the Isaac Newton of agricultural science' and he certainly has a strong claim to be the father of modern agricultural methods, in particular the use of chemical fertilisers. His early training was as an apprentice in a pharmacy but it was his work as a professor of chemistry at Giessen (whose university is now named after him) which earned him his reputation. He identified the importance of minerals like potassium and phosphates in plant nutrition though he underestimated the importance of nitrogen. He was very critical of England for disposing of its sewage at sea while importing guano (solidified bird droppings) from South America, making this the basis of an extravagant claim that England 'like a vampire hangs upon the breast of Europe and even the world, sucking its life blood'. His wildly optimistic assessments of the agricultural value of London's sewage set Bazalgette upon the evaluation of many futile schemes for its utilisation. While visiting a scientific friend called Muspratt, in Liverpool, he devised a meat extract for Muspratt's sick daughter, aiding the child's recovery. His name is remembered in the company that exploited this technique: Brooke Bond Liebig, makers of the Oxo cube.

Many of those who advocated the use of sewage as manure did so on clear economic grounds, a view plainly expressed in *The Builder* in 1875 in a few words: 'The round of nature is ever a perfect circle. Food makes the muck-heap and the muck-heap makes food.'[5] This view was attractive to utilitarians like Chadwick and to others who believed that the money to be made from sewage utilisation would pay much of the cost of drainage systems.

While the debate on the general economics of sewage utilisation schemes proceeded, a series of proposals was put to the authorities charged with managing the sewage of the metropolis. As early as 1843 a man called Richard Rowed proposed the construction of cast-iron sewers on either bank of the Thames which would conduct sewage to Kent and Essex where it would be discharged into receptacles similar to gas holders. Filters and quicklime would be used to separate liquids from solids and the latter would be 'formed into blocks of any shape or size best fitted for conveying to any part of the empire'. Street refuse would be swept into the sewers every twenty-four hours and Rowed quoted George Stephenson in support of his contention that 'the soil of England, if properly treated, will produce four times the amount of food that it yields under the present system'. Like many later advocates of similar schemes he made generous claims for the financial viability of his scheme, assuring the readers that 'it would form a legitimate source of revenue of upwards of one million sterling annually'.[6]

As early as 1848 William Shaw, editor of the *Mark Lane Express* and an early member of the Royal Agricultural Society of England, made a generous estimate of the value of sewage to the London Farmers' Club, claiming: 'I believe that we are wholly in the dark as to the mine of wealth which may be worked in connection with sewage manure – wealth which is unjustifiably, day by day, suffered to run to waste, whilst we are expending large sums in the purchase of foreign manure to enable us to produce the food of the people'.[7]

Contemporary entrepreneurs like Thomas Plum, of Camberwell, took up the challenge with a proposal that, in London:

> tight cesspools be formed, at certain intervals under the public roadways . . . the emptying process is to be accomplished by means of the airtight nightsoil cart recently invented . . . the pecuniary value of the contents for agricultural purposes, upon the most moderate estimation, would produce sufficient to repay the original cost in a short time.

A critic of this scheme observed that it would require 3,000 horses and carts worked by 4,500 men every twenty-four hours if it were to work successfully.[8]

In December 1851 interest in such schemes was promoted by the General Board of Health which published a 167-page document entitled 'Minutes of Information on the Application of Sewer Water and other Town Manures to Agricultural Production' which was distributed to local Boards of Health. The document made the extravagant claim that, as a result of the application of sewage to land: 'the value of land is quadrupled, the produce is largely increased, and no other manure is equal to it. Land manured with it will support half as much more stock as highly cultivated land on which solid manure is used.'[9]

'The value of land is quadrupled, the produce is largely increased, and no other manure is equal to it'

The document was inspired and probably largely written by Edwin Chadwick who remained a strong believer in the potential profitability of sewage utilisation schemes in the face of mounting contrary evidence. As late as 1870, after many schemes had foundered in the face of engineering and financial difficulties, Chadwick led a delegation to Breton's Farm, Hornchurch, Essex, which had been purchased by the Romford Board of Health to dispose of its sewage and he declared that 'this movement would lead to an enormous increase of the productive power of the soil'.[10] In 1877, at a discussion at the Institution of Civil Engineers on the application of town sewage to agricultural use, Chadwick defended another of his pet projects, tubular earthenware sewers, on the curious grounds that they delivered faeces to watercourses more quickly than brick sewers which, he believed, would become clogged, giving the faeces time to become putrescent. He argued that fresh faeces would produce fat, healthy fish and be good for agriculture whereas decomposed faeces from brick sewers would be harmful!

During the 1850s numerous schemes were proposed to sell sewage at a profit to farmers, the extravagance of their claims being matched by the enthusiasm with which they were welcomed in official circles. In 1853 a chemist called William Higgs told a Parliamentary Committee that, using a process which he had patented, 125,000 tons of dry manure could be recovered each year from the sewage of the metropolis, to be sold at an annual profit of £190,000. In support of his claim he cited a scheme using his process operated by prisoners at Cardiff Gaol which, the governor confirmed, yielded 3 tons of manure a year for local farmers.[11] When pressed, he conceded that the release on to the market of 125,000 tons of metropolitan sewage might depress the price he had achieved by making 3 tons at Cardiff: a view which was endorsed by the Parliamentary Committee. During the 1850s numerous other schemes were advanced, including one, promoted in the columns of *The Builder*, which proposed to construct railways within the sewers which would collect, compress and convey the manure to the point of sale 'while the expense of the necessary works would be partially, if not wholly, covered by the sale of the same'. Such enterprises were no doubt encouraged by the enthusiastic advocacy of such commentators as Liebig's collaborator Alderman Mechi, mentioned above, who in 1860 told the *Farmer's Magazine*: 'If the money value of our sewers could be shown to the British farmer in bright and glittering heaps of sovereigns he would gasp at the enormous wealth, and make great efforts to obtain the treasure.'[12]

In 1857 a Royal Commission was established 'to Inquire into the Best Mode of Distributing the Sewage of Towns and Applying it to Beneficial and Profitable Uses'. The Commissioners visited eight towns in Britain and one in Italy, Milan, where sewage was being applied to land and concluded that, in most circumstances, large quantities of sewage could not be economically applied to the land because of the huge quantities of nutrition-less water which had to be expensively removed before the sewage had any value as manure. However, the advocates of sewage utilisation did not give up easily. Five years later, in 1862, they secured the appointment of a Parliamentary Select Committee to reconsider the matter and produced some formidable witnesses to support their case. The redoubtable Alderman Mechi assured the committee that his land in Tiptree had increased in value by £3 an acre as a result of the process; Sir Joseph Paxton, MP, designer of the Crystal Palace, recommended rye grass and mustard and cress as suitable crops; and a chemist called Augustus Hofmann calculated that the annual value of metropolitan sewage was £1,385,540, one of many similarly optimistic assessments which were to be a feature of the next two decades. Contrary evidence came from the town clerk of Manchester,

'If the money value of our sewers could be shown to the British farmer in bright and glittering heaps of sovereigns he would gasp at the enormous wealth'

SIR JOSEPH PAXTON, 1801–65

Sir Joseph Paxton, designer of the Crystal Palace and advocate of the use of sewage as fertiliser. (*Illustrated London News*)

Son of a farmer, apprenticed to a gardener, Paxton so impressed the Duke of Devonshire with his enthusiasm and ingenuity that the duke appointed Paxton head gardener at Chatsworth and took him on a tour of Europe to gather ideas. Paxton created the famous Chatsworth fountain, 267 feet high, and a 300-foot glass conservatory which he based on the structure of a lily brought home from South America by a botanist. The success of the conservatory inspired him to design, on similar principles, the 23 acre Crystal Palace (the name sneeringly coined by Punch in a critical article) for the Great Exhibition of 1851 after 233 other designs had been rejected by the organising committee. He completed the design, based on pre-fabricated, interchangeable panels, in nine days. It held 14,000 exhibits, was visited by six million visitors and generated enough profit to build the Kensington museums. The structure was dismantled and re-erected at Sydenham, South London, by a group of navvies whose work so impressed the authorities that they used them as a model for the 'Works Corps' employed in the Crimean War. They later developed into the Pioneer Corps. The Crystal Palace was destroyed by fire in 1936.

Joshua Heron, who reported a very different experience since in that town: 'All attempts to catch and utilise the sewage waters have been utterly unsuccessful. Great expense has been incurred, and no return obtained, the product having been found valueless; so much so, that for agricultural purposes it has not proved to be worth the expense even of the cartage.'[13]

The Select Committee, like the earlier Royal Commission, concluded that, in most circumstances 'the evidence leads to the conclusion that a solid manure cannot be manufactured from town sewage with profitable results'.[14]

The Metropolitan Board of Works

Members of the Metropolitan Board had, from its earliest days, shown awareness of the need to consider the question of sewage utilisation. In April 1856, the fourth month of the Board's existence, the following motion was proposed by one of the members, a solicitor called Charles Few:

That it is expedient to invite persons to send in to this Board, Essays on the practicability of applying the sewage of London to agricultural

purposes, and that a committee be appointed to consider and report
the best course to be pursued in order to obtain such Essays . . . and
especially as to the amount of premiums to be given to the authors of
those adjudged most excellent.[15]

The Observer applauded Few's initiative and drew attention to the fact
that imported guano was sold very profitably at £8 to £10 a ton. The
paper criticised Bazalgette's plan for intercepting sewers on the
grounds that it 'proposes to leave this question unprovided for, and
to throw into the Thames that which ought almost to defray the
original cost of his intended works'.[16] After discussion the motion
was withdrawn. At the same meeting, the Board discussed a proposal
from a Lambeth civil engineer called William Morris who proposed
to construct an intercepting sewer on each bank of the Thames from
which he would draw off the contents and manufacture manure.
A condition of Morris's offer was that he should replace Bazalgette as
the Board's Chief Engineer. The Board declined. Over the next few
months the Board considered a series of 'memorials' from numerous
parties who expressed interest in utilising the sewage of the
metropolis and on 22 October 1856 John Leslie proposed a motion
that the Board 'not embarrass itself with Deodorizing or Sewage
Manure schemes', a motion voted down by 17 votes to 15.[17]
Nevertheless no further steps were taken in 1857 or 1858 beyond
referring a number of unsolicited proposals to the Main Drainage
Committee. At this time the Board was, of course, pre-occupied with
the problems of the Great Stink and with pressurising Parliament to
accept the main drainage scheme and, in particular the position of
the outfalls.[18]

On 27 May 1859 the Board, which by now had a backlog of
schemes submitted by hopeful entrepreneurs, returned to the subject,
resolving 'That Dr Hofmann and Dr Frankland be requested to
undertake the duty of advising the Board as to the various schemes of
deodorisation, and the several systems of dealing with sewage matter,
which have been submitted to the Board', voting a fee of up to £100
to be paid to each.[19] The thirty-eight schemes submitted were
evaluated by these two chemists, both Fellows of the Royal Society,
in a report which was presented to the Board in August 1859 and
printed in full in *The Builder*. The two authors wearily commented
that 'not the least arduous part of our labours consisted in the careful
examination of the numerous, and in many cases ponderous,
documents addressed to the Board on this subject'.[20] The proposals
included one for distributing sewage by rail, another which involved
the use of electricity, 'a process for the precipitation of sewage in
reservoirs, of which no further description was obtained' and another

*'Not the least arduous
part of our labours
consisted in the careful
examination of the
numerous, and in many
cases ponderous,
documents addressed to
the Board on this
subject'*

Bazalgette in middle life. (Thames Water plc)

Commander Joseph William Bazalgette RN. He was wounded shortly before the battle of Trafalgar in 1805. See page 9. (Derek Bazalgette)

The inventor of the water-closet, Sir John Harington, attributed to Hieronimo Custodis, fl. 1589. See page 42. (By courtesy of the National Portrait Gallery, London)

Knights' bridge, crossing the Westbourne river which still flows, hidden beneath the streets of Knightsbridge, surfacing only in the Serpentine in Hyde Park. See page 27. (By courtesy of the Guildhall Library, Corporation of London)

The New River Head, with part of the town of Ware. See page 21. (By courtesy of the Guildhall Library, Corporation of London)

Hampstead Pond, source of the Fleet river. See page 27. (By courtesy of the Guildhall Library, Corporation of London)

The royal barge of King William and Queen Adelaide returning to Somerset House on the Thames after the opening of London Bridge and before the building of the Victoria Embankment by Bazalgette. See also page 2. (By courtesy of the Guildhall Library, Corporation of London)

The building in Leicester Square designed to contain Mr Wylde's 'Great model of the Earth'. See page 170. (By courtesy of the Guildhall Library, Corporation of London)

The British department of the Great Exhibition of 1851. See page 43. (By courtesy of the Guildhall Library, Corporation of London)

The Fleet Sewer, *c.* 1830. Following Bazalgette's great works, the Fleet became a river again and still runs beneath London's streets. See page 28. (By courtesy of the Guildhall Library, Corporation of London)

Artists' impressions of the Victoria Embankment commissioned by Sir Joseph Bazalgette.

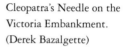

Cleopatra's Needle on the Victoria Embankment. (Derek Bazalgette)

The landing stairs, roads and ornamental gardens on the embankment between Hungerford and Waterloo bridges. (Derek Bazalgette)

York Gate on the Thames embankment. York Gate was later moved to Embankment Gardens. (Derek Bazalgette)

Aerial photograph of Crossness sewage treatment works, with Beckton in
the background. The largest treatment works in Europe, it is now operated
by Thames Water plc. (Thames Water plc)

Abbey Mills pumping station. Built in 1869, it is still in use today. (Thames
Water plc)

Elaborate Victorian ironwork at
Crossness. The roundels contain the
initials of the Metropolitan Board of
Works. (Author's collection)

Bazalgette's low level sewer which runs to the north of the Thames. Built in the 1860s it remains in use, protecting the Thames from pollution. (Thames Water plc)

which was described as 'not chemical, and is communicable only by personal interview'. The chemists concluded that the deodorisation of sewage would best be effected by the addition of quantities of perchloride of iron before discharging it to the river.[21] In the summer of 1859 the Board spent £17,733 on chemicals for this purpose.[22] The chemists' report made no recommendations on sewage utilisation so, the following January, the Board resolved to advertise for 'tenders from parties who may be willing to treat with the Board for taking the sewage of London' and six months later, on 6 July 1860, the four communications submitted were opened and read. A note of scepticism may be detected in the Board's account of the response which it had received to its advertisements, a response which did not appear to reflect the amount of attention the matter had received in Parliament and elsewhere:

> It has been very generally supposed that a large class of persons are so persuaded of the vast value of the sewage of the Metropolis, that they only await an opportunity of putting their schemes into practical operation; this has not, however, been borne out by the experience of this Board. They advertised extensively, inviting tenders for the Metropolitan sewage; and in answer to these advertisements they received only four proposals.[23]

In January 1862 the Board considered the Committee's report on the schemes, including two schemes which had been received after the deadline for the tender. One of these was from Mr Thomas Ellis, an Irish solicitor, who proposed to pump the sewage to the top of Hampstead Heath on the north side (close to the beginning of the northern high level intercepting sewer) and Shooters Hill on the south, allowing it to flow thence on to half a million acres of farmland. The other was from the Hon. William Napier and Lieutenant-Colonel William Hope, VC, the latter being described as General Manager of the International Financial Society, Director of the Lands Improvement Company and of reclamation and irrigation works in Spain and Majorca.[24] This scheme proposed to convey the northern sewage by a 44-mile culvert to Rawreth in Essex and thence via two branches to Dengie Flats and Maplin Sands where it would be used to reclaim an area of about 20,000 acres from the sea on either side of the estuary of the River Crouch. The Committee explained the priorities which it had set itself in evaluating the various schemes:

> Two very material points were to be secured; the first, the absolute necessity for guarding the Board against the consequences which would arise in the event of a nuisance being created by the application of the sewage; and the second, the desirability of adopting, if possible,

The chemists concluded that the deodorisation of sewage would best be effected by the addition of quantities of perchloride of iron a scheme which should hold out a prospect of some benefit, in a financial point of view, ultimately accruing to the ratepayers of the Metropolis. These objects are, in the opinion of your committee, more likely to be effectually attained by the scheme propounded by the Hon. William Napier and Mr Hope than by either [sic] of the others which have been submitted to your Hon. Board.[25]

Bazalgette, in his report to the Main Drainage Committee, also observed that this was the only scheme which was furnished with plans that were adequate for presentation to Parliament for its approval.[26]

Further delays now ensued as the Metropolitan Board waited upon the deliberations of yet another Select Committee which was set up in 1864 'to Enquire into any Plans for Dealing with the Sewage of the Metropolis and other Large Towns, with a view to its Utilisation for Agricultural Purposes'.[27] The Committee was particularly impressed by the evidence of Professor Way who informed them that the annual value of the metropolitan sewage was equivalent to 10s 6d per person. Since income and property taxes, he calculated, averaged 10s 3d per person he concluded that, if applied nationally, 'the sewage would be equal to the local taxation of England, Ireland and Scotland'.[28] Other authorities, using data gathered from such diverse quarters as the bodyguard of the Grand Duke of Hesse, estimated that the agricultural value of human waste was as high as 16s per person and that, appropriately used, it would pay half the interest on the national debt. Such reasoning was as attractive to Members of Parliament in 1864 as it would have been a hundred years later and, for this reason, they were very critical of Thwaites and Bazalgette for the measures the Board had taken in insisting that 'All tenders must contain a full description of the works proposed' and that they should also include the names of sureties who would indemnify the Board in the event of the failure of a contractor. Thwaites explained that, besides being normal practice, these measures were a prudent means of protecting the Board against highly speculative schemes and in defence of his position he drew attention to some of the stranger schemes which had been submitted. The Committee felt that the Board was thereby discouraging enterprise and concluded that:

'The sewage would be equal to the local taxation of England, Ireland and Scotland'

Your Committee has come to the conclusion, that it is not only possible to utilise the sewage of towns, by conveying it, in a liquid state, through main [sewers] and pipes to the country, but that such an undertaking may be made to result in pecuniary benefit to the ratepayers of the towns whose sewage is thus utilised. Your committee, having examined the chairman and engineer of the Metropolitan Board of Works, are of the opinion that more might have been done by that Board towards the profitable use of the sewage of London; and that the completion of the outfall sewerage of the Metropolis ought, at the earliest possible moment, to be followed by the adoption of a system which may convert that sewage from a nuisance into a permanent and increasing source of agricultural fertility.[29]

The Hope-Napier Scheme

On 15 November 1864 the Board voted to accept the Hope-Napier scheme, despite a late and well-orchestrated protest by the City of London. The Court of Common Council had concluded that the scheme was wasteful, having calculated that the annual value of metropolitan sewage was £2,899,972. In support of this contention they produced a letter from Professor Liebig dated 4 October 1864 in which the eminent German agriculturist, writing from Munich, was dismissive of the Hope-Napier scheme:

It is in vain to think of transforming the Maplin Sands into a fertile soil . . . The project of Messrs Napier and Hope is one of the most curious . . . It appears to me like a soap bubble, glistening with bright colours, but inside hollow and empty. There is not the slightest doubt that every penny expended in that frivolous undertaking would be irretrievably lost. The carrying out of this scheme would not only be a squandering of an enormous amount of money, but before long would be looked on as a national calamity.[30]

Liebig claimed that Maplin had the wrong kind of soil to benefit from sewage irrigation and this encouraged the City men in their belief that the Metropolitan Board was making inappropriate use of such a valuable commodity by allowing it to be applied merely to 'redeeming twelve thousand acres of quicksand on the shores of the German Ocean'.[31] In correspondence with the Lord Mayor, Liebig had made the most optimistic assessment yet achieved of the value of London's sewage, proposing that it could be worth £4,081,430.[32] The committee of the Common Council accordingly insisted that: 'The scheme of Messrs Hope and Napier, if it could be carried out, would be a glaring violation of the laws of agricultural science, from which the least possible increase to our home supplies of food would be obtained.'[33] *The Times* sided with the Board, writing that: 'The Corporation, instead of rejoicing as it would have done three years ago, over the bargain which the Board had made for them, now cry out with extraordinary indignation on this wasteful anticipation of Metropolitan resources.'[34]

In its decision the Board had been influenced by the fact that, for much of its 44-mile length, the culvert conveying the sewage would run through agricultural land which would itself be suitable for

Maplin had the wrong kind of soil to benefit from sewage irrigation

irrigation and that, if these adjacent areas did not want the sewage, it could be discharged upon the barren and uninhabited Maplin Sands,[35] well beyond the metropolis itself. The capital cost of the scheme was estimated as £2,100,000 and the cost of pumping as £10,000 to £13,000 a year. William Hope, the promoter, estimated that total operating expenses would amount to £35,000 a year, giving profit before interest of £365,000, which would be shared with the ratepayers of the metropolis.[36] Hope expected to be able to let the reclaimed land to dairy farmers at a rent of up to £40 an acre.[37] Thomas Ellis, proponent of the rival scheme to pump the sewage to the top of Hampstead Heath, had modified his scheme to spare Hampstead in favour of pumping the sewage to Brentwood instead, well outside the metropolis, but this failed to persuade the Board.

Despite the reservations of the City the scheme was greeted with lyrical enthusiasm by the *City Press* which pronounced that 'there can be no doubt that the Maplin Sands can be made to smile with golden harvests by means of the fertilising slush that has so long been devoted to the poisoning of the Thames'.[38] The company was formed under the name of 'The Metropolitan Sewage and Essex Reclamation Company'. In the meantime the Board had drawn up Articles of Agreement with the company. These conceded the northern sewage to the company for fifty years, provided for division of the profits between the Board and the company according to a formula which enabled the company to pay interest on its capital on a sliding scale and prudently included a requirement for a deposit of £25,000, to be repaid by the Board when the construction work was completed. Five years was stipulated as the maximum time for this to be accomplished.[39] The work began towards the end of 1865, the company entering into a contract with Webster, a very experienced builder who executed many contracts for the main drainage itself. At this time the Board itself seems to have been reasonably confident about the prospects of the scheme since in its *Report* for the year ending 25 March 1866 it wrote: 'There appears to be no reason whatever to doubt the ultimate success of the undertaking to be carried out by the company on the Maplin Sands.' In 1866 the company purchased a tract of land at Lodge Farm, at Barking in Essex, which was used as an experimental sewage farm, the experiments yielding satisfactory crops of strawberries, celery and wheat.[40] A further experiment was carried out at Breton's Farm, Romford.[41] However, construction work soon ended, difficulty being experienced in raising the necessary capital at a time when there was a financial crisis in the City precipitated by the collapse of the Overend Gurney bank. In its *Report* for 1867–8 the Board reported that 'the construction of these works has been in abeyance for some

'The Maplin Sands can be made to smile with golden harvests by means of the fertilising slush that has so long been devoted to the poisoning of the Thames'

time'.[42] William Hope, still struggling to revive the scheme, changed tack and argued that sewage farms had restorative properties so that: 'London beauties might come out to recruit their wasted energies at the close of the season, and, attired in a *costume de circonstance*, with coquettish jack-boots, would perhaps at times listen to a lecture on agriculture from the farmer himself, while drinking his cream and luxuriating in the health-restoring breeze'.[43]

'London beauties, with coquettish jack-boots, luxuriating in the health-restoring breeze'

After 1871 there is no further reference to the Hope-Napier scheme in the Board's reports and the plan was dropped. The Board retained the £25,000 bond.[44] In the Board's own words 'This, it may be mentioned, is the only money the ratepayers of London have ever received in respect of their sewage, which was once considered to be of so much pecuniary value.'[45] But the failed scheme was not the last one that the Board had to consider. In April 1865 it invited tenders for utilisation of the southern sewage and received five tenders, one of which bore the familiar name of the ever hopeful Thomas Ellis. Nothing came of the scheme beyond brief references in the Board's *Minutes* and in its 1868–9 *Report* to the effect that no progress had been made.[46]

On 23 December 1869 the Board received a communication from the Native Guano Company seeking a concession of the southern sewage for conversion to manure by its 'ABC process' which involved the addition of alum, blood and clay and certain other chemicals. At the invitation of the company the Board visited its works at Leamington where it saw the process operating on a small scale and, despite the inconclusive nature of its observations, the Board resolved in January 1871 that: 'the Native Guano Company be permitted to erect, at their own expense, and for a period not exceeding twelve months, works at Crossness for the purpose of treating by their ABC process about a half a million gallons of sewage daily'.[47]

In January 1873 the company's activities were checked by Bazalgette and the Board's chemist, Keates, who reported on the experiment, concluding that: 'The quantity of manure resulting from the operations was about 142 tons . . . and the total expenditure was £895 3s 3d, which made the cost of manufacture £6 6s 4d per ton . . . On the other hand, with the exception of a few shillings, the company's books showed no returns in the shape of sales of manure.'[48] The most generous estimate that Keates could place on the value was £1 a ton. Moreover an analysis by Augustus Voelcker of the 'native guano' thereby produced concluded that the product was almost worthless for agricultural purposes.[49] The scheme was pronounced a failure and the Native Guano Company's works at Crossness were removed. Further schemes were similarly unproductive.

Sewage Utilisation in Retreat

More prosaic assessments were now beginning to prevail. On 16 May 1871 a paper was read at the Institution of Civil Engineers 'On the treatment of Town Sewage', in which the author, Arthur Jacob, emphasised that successful sewage irrigation depended upon the proximity of land of suitable size and composition. Six years later the Institution heard a more comprehensive paper on the subject, based on a study of eleven towns, read by Norman Bazalgette, himself a civil engineer and son of Sir Joseph. He concluded: 'that where land can be reasonably acquired, irrigation is the best and most satisfactory known system for the disposal of sewage. That no profit must be expected from the cultivation of crops by the sanitary authority and only a moderate one by the farmer.'[50] He also argued that towns on coasts or tidal rivers would find that disposal to the coastal waters would offer the most economic and efficient solution. Discussion of the paper extended over five evenings and in its summary of the discussions *The Builder* commented:

> There is a very strong, and we believe a spreading, conviction, that the advance of the sanitary question has been more hampered and throttled by the idea that sewage is to be utilised than by anything else. The idea is certainly becoming more general that what is wanted is not utilisation but destruction.[51]

'What is wanted is not utilisation but destruction'

In 1872 one of the first acts of the newly established Local Government Board was to denounce sewage irrigation schemes as uneconomic and to turn down a plan submitted to them by the West Ham local board on these grounds, paying particular heed to its chief engineer Robert Rawlinson (who had installed sewers in the area twelve years previously), whose report contained 'a distinct denial of the commercial success of irrigation, which should only be adopted under the pressure of absolute necessity'.[52] Three years later, in June 1875, the Local Government Board directed Rawlinson to investigate the matter. A committee of the Board, including Rawlinson, visited thirty-eight British towns as well as Leyden, Amsterdam, Berlin, Brussels and Paris, and their report, published in 1876, concluded that:

> so far as our examinations extend, none of the manufactured manures made by manipulating town refuse, with or without chemicals, pay the contingent costs of such treatment. . . . the chemical value of sewage is greatly reduced to the farmer by the fact that it must be disposed of day by day throughout the entire year, and that its volume is generally greatest when it is of the least service to the land.[53]

The Metropolitan, commenting favourably upon the practical view taken by Rawlinson's report, reminded its readers that 'since the year 1856 there have been no fewer than 417 patents obtained for dealing more or less with sewage and manures' and that the protagonists of the schemes had believed that: 'all there was to do was to extract [the chemicals], pack them up, and offer them for sale, when a grateful host of farmers would rush to give well-filled bags of gold for the wonderful stuff'.[54]

In 1875 Bazalgette, who had more experience than most of evaluating schemes of widely varying merits, commented on the wisdom of incorporating sewage utilisation provisions in a drainage scheme to cover the Beckenham area of Kent. He wrote:

> The purification of the sewage of towns by chemical or mechanical agents has been fairly tested during the last quarter of a century in this country and, as a practical means of dealing with the sewage it has, in every case I am aware of, failed. The disposal of sewage by irrigating lands has, to a considerable extent, been successful; but it is not a system which can be applied, without objection, to a suburb of London, thickly studded with the ornamental residences of those who are daily engaged in business in the metropolis.[55]

'Since the year 1856 there have been no fewer than 417 patents obtained for dealing more or less with sewage and manures'

Postscript

Despite the final verdict of the Board on the prospects of making a profit from the utilisation of sewage, others have not been deterred from similar enterprises, albeit on a more modest scale than Hope and Napier. In the 1950s a writer called J.C. Wylie calculated that 200,000 tons of nitrogen was lost annually in the process of sewage disposal, an amount that approximated to the quantity purchased in the form of chemical fertilizers[56] and at about the same time a processing plant was built near Bazalgette's outfall works at Barking where a proportion of the solid matter was dried, bagged and sold direct to the public as 'Dagfert' ('Dagenham fertiliser') to be used as garden manure. The experiment was discontinued in the 1970s in the face of competition from chemical fertilisers which, like the South American guano of the 1860s, could be produced more economically than could treated sewage.

Advances in techniques for processing sewage, together with more favourable public attitudes towards 'green' or recycled products encouraged Thames Water, the ultimate successors to the Metropolitan Board of Works, to undertake further experiments in the 1980s. In 1987 Thames Water established a pilot plant at its Little Marlow sewage treatment plant in Buckinghamshire which processes the sewage for a population of about ninety thousand in the vicinity of High Wycombe. The use of the waste is governed by a Department of the Environment Code of Practice which reflects the fact that, as processing techniques have advanced, so have the problems which they have to overcome, not least because of the increasingly complex industrial chemicals which can find their way into sewage treatment works.[58] The plant trades under the name Terra Eco Systems. The waste is held in conventional settlement tanks after which the liquid is run off for further treatment before being returned to watercourses while the sewage sludge is offered for sale in four forms. The most basic product is Terra Organic Fertiliser which is sold to farmers (some of them in the locality of the treatment works but many in East Anglia) by the tanker load as a general fertiliser to be spread on fields. Further processing, including the addition of lime, produces Terra Lime Plus, a bulk solid which is used to balance lime-deficient soils and Terra Soil Builder which is used for landfilling and for landscaping. The highest added-value product is Terra Multi-Purpose Compost which is produced by mixing sewage sludge with straw and leaving it to be broken down by bacteriological activity before being sold under that name through garden centres. In the summer of 1996 this was incorporated into a Grow-Bag for sale through the same channels. In 1998 the products were featured in a prize-winning garden at the Chelsea flower show and in a drought-resistant garden at London Zoo. The process is seen as an alternative to other methods of disposing of waste in appropriate topographical areas. The enterprise is being extended to other areas where the additional cost of processing and marketing the waste is more than compensated by the sale value. These schemes are thus perceived to be making a useful financial contribution to the continuing problem of disposing of sewage in a way which is ecologically acceptable, rather than as a money-making device *per se*, as conceived by Victorians like Chadwick.

The products were featured in a prize-winning garden at the Chelsea flower show and in a drought-resistant garden at London Zoo

As the Victorian promoters discovered, one of the greatest difficulties associated with making money from sewage utilisation arises from the fact that a comparatively small proportion of nutritional material is conveyed in huge volumes of water. This makes it difficult to move to the point of consumption and also requires expensive processing to extract the small volume of saleable matter. However, in areas where water itself is a scarce commodity this characteristic is being exploited as a water conservation measure and this particularly applies in Australia, the world's driest inhabited continent. Within the Australian Capital Territory, Canberra, research is being undertaken into means of recycling 'grey water' – the waste from baths and domestic appliances – with a view to using it for toilet-flushing and irrigation and thereby conserving fresh water for drinking and food preparation.[59] Small-scale treatment technology is being developed which can be installed to recycle the waste water for small neighbourhoods. Research is also being undertaken into the use of 'composting toilets' for urban use, a device which would enable individual households to recycle their own waste products for use in their own gardens and which would, in effect, mark a sophisticated reversion to the medieval practice of using human waste from cesspools to fertilize neighbouring fields. The concept of 'water mining' is also being explored whereby effluent is extracted from sewers and separated into liquid and 'sludge'. The water is diverted to irrigation, thereby conserving fresh supplies, while the small volume of sludge is returned to the sewer, freed of most of its liquid content, and conveyed to the treatment works. An experiment of this kind has been conducted at Townsville, Queensland.

Each of the Victorian schemes had to be considered, researched and reported upon by Bazalgette and his team at a time when they were heavily engaged in designing and constructing the main drainage. Some of them may now appear to have been a foolish distraction and they must often have seemed so at the time to those whose working hours were spent evaluating them. Yet the numerous attempts to devise successful schemes and the extravagant claims that were made for them are evidence of the attractions they held for people like Edwin Chadwick and Justus von Liebig who believed not only in the restorative qualities of the sewage when applied to the soil but also in its powers to reduce or eliminate the need for local taxation. In the twentieth century the development of more sophisticated processing techniques and the heightened awareness of the environmental consequences of dumping untreated sewage have led to a revival of interest in schemes which Bazalgette and his contemporaries would no doubt have recognised as being descended from those upon which they had to pass judgement, though their twentieth-century promoters are prompted more by ecological and less by financial motives than were their Victorian predecessors.

CHAPTER SIX

Cholera

Although great differences of opinion existed, and continue to exist, as to the causes of the disease, yet an inspection of the houses in which deaths occurred was sufficient to show that, however occult might be the connection between death and defective drainage, the places formerly most favourable to the spread of disease became quite free from it, when afterwards properly drained.

(Joseph Bazalgette, 1864)[1]

In the mid-nineteenth century London suffered four major outbreaks of cholera, the deaths in the capital being recorded as follows:[2]

1831–2:	6,536
1848–9:	14,137
1853–4:	10,738
1866:	5,596.

In the first three outbreaks death rates exceeding 50 per 10,000 were found in the East and West Ends of London and both north and south of the river. In the fourth outbreak, high death rates were confined to the East End between Aldgate and Bow.

The 1866 epidemic was confined to that part of the metropolis which was not fully protected by Bazalgette's intercepting system. The completion of the system in the 1870s rid London for ever of water-borne diseases though continental cities continued to be ravaged by epidemics, with a particularly virulent attack on Hamburg in the 1890s. Fear of cholera, which affected all classes of society, killing by nightfall citizens who had breakfasted in good health, was one of the major impulses towards the reform of London government which was necessary before Bazalgette and the Metropolitan Board of Works could gain the authority they needed to transform the sanitary condition of the capital. What is more surprising is that, despite compelling evidence, the connection between good sanitation, clean drinking water and good health was long overlooked or denied by many of the most prominent reformers of the Victorian era.

CHOLERA

A disease attributable to the *Vibrio cholerae* first identified by the German bacteriologist Robert Koch in India in 1883. Commonly known as the *comma bacillus* because of its characteristic shape, it causes acute diarrhoea, draining the body of nutrients and fluids, leading to dehydration, kidney failure and death, often within a few hours of the onset of the disease. The disease is almost always transmitted when drinking water is contaminated by the faeces of sufferers. In the nineteenth century four pandemics, starting in India, made their way across the Middle East and Europe, causing tens of thousands of deaths and prompting numerous riots. The disease spread rapidly because drinking water supplies were contaminated by inadequate sewers in towns and cities. Modern sanitation, based on engineering works like Bazalgette's, eliminated the epidemics. Cases in the developed world are now extremely rare though it remains a major health problem in third world countries and epidemics are a familiar horror in refugee camps where sanitation is poor.

The Miasmic Orthodoxy

From the late 1820s the spread of cholera from India across Asia, via the Caspian Sea and continental Europe, was the cause of much anxious comment and speculation as to its causes, both in medical journals like *The Lancet* and in newspapers like *The Times*. Each epidemic was the cause of intense public debate concerning the nature of the disease and the means by which it was propagated. The anxiety that attended its arrival in Britain in 1831 (where it first came ashore in Sunderland) was unprecedented since the seventeenth-century plagues, thirty riots being caused by concern about the disease in 1832. Each subsequent outbreak prompted further theorising, over 700 works on the subject being published in London alone between 1845 and 1856. In 1883 the German bacteriologist Robert Koch isolated the cholera bacillus and confirmed that cholera is usually spread by water which has been contaminated by the faeces of someone infected with the disease.[3] In the absence of this knowledge the epidemics that afflicted Britain between 1831 and 1866, and their possible remedies, were the subject of conjecture which was sometimes informed by despair.

In November 1831, early in the first cholera outbreak that struck Great Britain, *The Lancet* reported from Vienna that a community of Jews in Wiesnitz had escaped its effects by rubbing their bodies with a liniment containing wine, vinegar, camphor powder, mustard, pepper, garlic and ground beetles.[4] In 1853, as the third great cholera outbreak was observed making its way across Europe towards Great Britain, *The Lancet* speculated on the nature of the disease:

> What is cholera? Is it a fungus, an insect, a miasma, an electrical disturbance, a deficiency of ozone, a morbid off-scouring of the

ROBERT KOCH, 1843–1910

Robert Koch, the German scientist who isolated the cholera bacillus in infected water in 1883. (*Illustrated London News*)

This German bacteriologist identified the organisms that cause anthrax (1876) and tuberculosis (1882). He visited India and Africa to identify the sources of epidemics and in 1883 he both identified the cholera bacillus in India and established that it was conveyed in polluted water – as John Snow had suggested thirty-five years earlier. Koch's reputation underwent a temporary setback in 1890 when he announced that he had found a cure for tuberculosis. Within days some 1,500 doctors had converged on Berlin only to learn that he was mistaken.

Nevertheless, for his pioneering work in the field of bacteriology Koch was applauded in both political and scientific circles. and for twenty-five years he was a powerful influence in the Imperial Health Office in Berlin. The draconian powers granted to him by Kaiser Wilhelm II to deal with the outbreak of cholera in Hamburg in 1892 were resented by the Burgomeister but were eventually successful in ending the epidemic. In 1905 he was awarded the Nobel prize for medicine.

intestinal canal? We know nothing; we are at sea in a whirlpool of conjecture . . . Every analogy leads to the conclusion that the essential cause of cholera consists in a morbid poison, which under certain congenial conditions becomes developed into activity, and ferments in the blood'.[5]

In 1853 *The Lancet* was no better informed than *The Times* had been four years earlier when, over three days at the height of the second cholera epidemic, the newspaper had published a series of articles in which the possible causes of the disease, and its remedies, were debated.[6] On 13 September the writer listed the current theories, starting with the 'Telluric theory [which] supposes the poison of cholera to be an emanation from the earth'. He then considered the 'Electric theory' which attributed the disease to atmospheric electricity and the 'Ozonic theory' which laid the blame on a shortage of ozone. He briefly considered the idea that the epidemic was caused by 'emanations from sewers and graveyards . . . for such an hypothesis we can find no solid foundation'. More space was devoted to the 'Zymotic theory' which was particularly associated with the German professor of organic chemistry at the University of Giessen, Justus von Liebig, a friend of Michael Faraday (see above, page 110). Liebig believed that some compounds were inherently unstable and that, under the influence of temperature, electricity or friction, they could be prompted into a condition of fermentation, similar to that associated with yeast. He suggested that the putrefaction of bodies which had suffered from the disease could produce ammonia, thereby creating a 'miasma' in the atmosphere which would spread the infection.

The idea that illness was spread by an infected atmosphere had a long history. Hippocrates had noted that certain fevers were associated with warm weather and with wet, poorly drained places where the air was dank and foul. Among Bazalgette's contemporaries, Florence Nightingale was a strong advocate of this 'miasmic' theory and in her classic text *Notes on Nursing* she criticised the practice of laying drains beneath houses, suggesting that odours would escape from them, penetrate the dwellings and cause epidemics of scarlet fever, measles and smallpox,[7] while some nineteenth-century prison reformers even maintained that moral, as well as physical, degeneracy could be spread through infected air. Professor Booth, in his letter to *The Builder* in 1844 (see Chapter One, page 17), had advocated a policy of watering the streets so that the consequent evaporation: 'will carry up with it into the atmosphere, and above the reach of mischief, the various decomposing and decomposed organic matters floating about, and which otherwise allowed to remain would be productive of contagious miasms'.[8]

Florence Nightingale: a severe miasmatist who believed that foul smells rather than foul water were the cause of epidemics. (*The Hornet*)

Edwin Chadwick: 'all smell is disease'

In this, as in so many other matters, Edwin Chadwick was an ardent if sometimes misguided campaigner and went to his grave firmly believing the 'miasmic' or 'atmospheric' theory of disease causation. In 1846, in evidence to a Parliamentary Committee which was considering the problem of metropolitan sewage, he pronounced confidently: 'All smell is, if it be intense, immediate acute disease; and eventually we may say that, by depressing the system and rendering it susceptible to the action of other causes, all smell is disease'.[9]

From this shaky premise Chadwick drew the conclusion that it was more important to remove smells from dwellings than to free the Thames of sewage since, according to him, the smells were the causes of disease. He further argued that small earthenware pipes were better than large brick-built drains since pipes had smaller surface areas from which noxious fluids could evaporate and he proceeded to claim that this reasoning had prompted Frederick Doulton,[10] at Chadwick's request, to produce the first glazed earthenware pipes at his Lambeth pipeworks. Chadwick never altered his belief in the miasmic theory despite the fact that, during his lifetime, the work of Pasteur, Koch and others clearly demonstrated the existence of water-borne organisms. In the year of his death, 1890, Chadwick attended a discussion at the Royal Society of Arts on the disposal of sewage and, in the words of *The Builder* which reported the occasion: 'Sir Edwin concluded his somewhat prolix communication by advocating the bringing down of fresh air from a height, by means of such structures as the Eiffel Tower, and distributing it, warmed and fresh, in our buildings.'[11]

Other respected contemporaries, some of them close associates of Chadwick, were equally emphatic. Dr Neil Arnott, whose earlier work for the Poor Law Commissioners had led to the preparation of Chadwick's 1842 *Report on the Sanitary Condition of the Labouring Population of Great Britain*, informed a Parliamentary committee in 1844 that:

> The immediate and chief cause of many of the diseases which impair the bodily and mental health of the people, and bring a considerable proportion prematurely to the grave is the *poison of atmospheric impurity* [Arnott's italics] arising from the accumulation in and around their dwellings of the decomposing remnants of the substances used for their food and in their arts, and from the impurities given out by their own bodies.[12]

Dr W.H. Duncan, who in 1847 became the first medical officer appointed in any English city, Liverpool, had calculated the medical effects of breathing within the city: 'By the mere action of the lungs of the inhabitants of Liverpool, for instance, a stratum of air sufficient to cover the entire surface of the town, to a depth of three feet, is daily rendered unfit for the purposes of respiration.'

In other quarters the theory took even more eccentric forms. Sir Francis Head, a former colonial governor, reviewed Chadwick's *Report*

SIR FRANCIS BOND HEAD, 1793–1875

Head was descended from a Portuguese Jew called Ferdinando Mendez who came to England in 1662 as physician to Catherine of Braganza, wife of Charles II. The family name was changed to Head in the following century. Francis Head became a lieutenant in the British Army in 1811 and fought at Waterloo. In 1824 he was appointed manager of the River Plate Mining Association and was despatched to Argentina at the head of a potential workforce of Cornish and German miners. After a 1,000-mile march they learned that the mining concession had also been sold by the local authorities to a rival concern who had arrived first. A further 1,200 miles of marching in search of other workable seams proved equally fruitless. In 1835 Head was appointed Lieutenant-Governor of Upper Canada where he quelled a revolt by pro-American sympathisers, setting their boat, *The Caroline*, on fire and despatching it over Niagara Falls. He was made a baronet in 1836 and afterwards returned to England (taking a circuitous route to avoid a rumoured assassination attempt by his earlier victims). He devoted the remainder of his life to writing alarming pamphlets and articles with titles like 'The Defenceless State of Great Britain', prompted by his alarm at the supposed threat from Napoleon III, emperor of the French.

in the pages of the influential journal *Quarterly Review*. He applauded Chadwick's criticism of poor drainage and ventilation and, in supporting the miasmic theory, argued that some of the new settlements in America had been rendered dangerous by the practice of ploughing virgin soil, thereby releasing miasms from decaying vegetable matter which had previously been safely buried.

In the absence of any clearly defined germ theory of the propagation of disease it must have been very tempting to conclude that epidemics were spread exclusively by the foul-smelling air which was so evident rather than by water which looked clean, unless examined under a powerful microscope. The widespread belief that cholera, and other fatal diseases, were caused by foul smells also helps to account for the panic that afflicted the Houses of Parliament as the 'Great Stink' was borne in through the windows of the Palace of Westminster in the summer of 1858. It also explains why the legislators were so uncharacteristically prompt in taking action to clean up the river.

John Snow on Cholera

In the meantime the most significant contribution to an understanding of the true causes of cholera epidemics was being made nearby. Dr John Snow (1813–58), a pioneer anaesthetist, began to practise medicine from premises at 54 Frith Street, Soho, in 1843. In 1849 he published a

THE SILENT HIGHWAYMAN
'Your money or your life'.

'The Silent Highwayman' – *Punch*'s view of cholera on the Thames at the height of the Great Stink, July 1858. (*Punch*)

DR JOHN SNOW, 1813–58

Born in York, and apprenticed to a Newcastle surgeon, John Snow became a vegetarian and total abstainer from alcohol during his days as a student: a most unusual phenomenon. An early anaesthetist, he was one of the first to use ether and chloroform for this purpose, administering chloroform to Queen Victoria for the birth of Prince Leopold in 1853. He is best remembered for his seminal paper *On Cholera* whose significance was appreciated by very few at the time. The site of his surgery in Broad Street (now Broadwick Street, off Carnaby Street) is now occupied by a pub called the John Snow and the site of the pump whose cholera-infected water was the subject of his paper is marked by a granite stone.

---

paper *On the Mode of Communication of Cholera* in which he suggested that water polluted by sewage might be the vehicle by which cholera was transmitted. He further argued that the practice of flushing sewers into the river made the 1849 epidemic worse[13] and developed this thesis in a series of articles in the *Medical Times and Gazette*.[14] He drew attention to the role of water-closets in helping to spread the disease: 'If the general use of water-closets is to continue and to increase, it will be desirable to have two supplies of water in large towns, one for the water-closets and another, of soft spring or well water from a distance, to be used by meter like the gas.'[15]

During the 1854 epidemic Snow observed that a high incidence of cholera was occurring among persons drawing water from a well in Broad Street, Soho, near Golden Square, close to his medical practice. Further investigation revealed that a sewer passed close to the well. These observations supported the arguments of his papers of 1849. Snow persuaded the parish council to remove the handle which operated the pump. While some medical authorities were prepared to acknowledge that polluted water had some role in the propagation of disease, acting with other environmental factors such as filth and moral depravity to weaken the system and make it vulnerable to attack by disease, few were prepared to acknowledge it as the specific cause, despite the evidence of Snow's observations and the lucidity of his arguments:

> Rivers always receive the refuse of those living on the banks, and they nearly always supply, at the same time, drinking water of the community so situated . . . the water serves as a medium to propagate the disease amongst those living at each spot and thus prevents it from dying out through not reaching fresh victims.[16]

Few were convinced by his hypothesis so, in 1857, the year before his early death, Snow published a study of mortality rates in two South

Opposite.
'Death's dispensary' – a water pump shown dispensing disease in this picture from the inaptly named *Fun*, 1860. (*Fun*)

DEATH'S DISPENSARY.
Open to the Poor, Gratis, by Permission of the Parish.

Chelsea waterworks about
1830; the intake worryingly
close to the Ranelagh sewer to
the right of the picture.
(Thames Water plc)

London parishes. He compared the incidence of mortality in
Lambeth, whose water was supplied mostly by the Lambeth water
company, with that in Southwark, which was supplied by the
Southwark and Vauxhall company. In the 1849 outbreak the
mortality rates in the two parishes had been similar, with Lambeth
being slightly higher. In the 1853–4 outbreak the position was
reversed, the incidence in Southwark being almost six times greater
than that of Lambeth. In the intervening five years James Simpson,
engineer to the Lambeth company, supplying the healthier parish,
had moved its water intake to Seething Wells, Thames Ditton, above
Teddington Lock, as required by the Metropolis Water Act of 1852,
where it was untainted by sewage borne upstream by the tide. The
Southwark and Vauxhall company, however, continued to draw its
water from the tidal stretch near Vauxhall. Snow offered this as
further evidence that the cholera was water-borne.[17] The marked
difference in the incidence of disease between the customers of the
two companies, living in the same streets and breathing the same air,
cast further doubt on the 'miasmatic' explanation. Snow advocated
the use of filters by water companies and advised that water be boiled
before use during cholera outbreaks.

John Simon and the City of London

The first Metropolitan Sewers Commission took office in 1848 and
was immediately beset by the second great cholera epidemic. As the
Commissioners struggled to improve the sewerage of the remainder

of the metropolis the City defended its territory against intruders. On 12 April 1847 the City Sewers Commission had declared that 'the City of London, for health, cleanliness, effective drainage and supply of water to its inhabitants cannot be surpassed'. To this comment the Lord Mayor added: 'there could be no improvement in the sanitary condition of the City – it was perfect'.[18] This view was not universally shared even before it was disastrously refuted by the ravages of cholera in the 1848–9 epidemic. In 1848 the Health of Towns Association published an insulting pamphlet on 'The Sanitary Condition of the City of London' and the Prime Minister, Russell, who was the MP for the City, announced that the City would fall under the jurisdiction of the Metropolitan Sewers Commission. The Lord Mayor warned Russell that in such an eventuality the Prime Minister would have to find another constituency so a compromise was agreed. A separate City Sewers Act maintained the City's independence but in return the City appointed its own Medical Officer, John Simon.

'There could be no improvement in the sanitary condition of the City – it was perfect'

Simon, like Bazalgette, was of French extraction (the name is pronounced *Simone*) and was one of the most influential medical practitioners of his time. He was an early practitioner of disinfection processes in surgery and later lecturer in pathology at St Thomas's Hospital Medical School. He was also, like Chadwick, a strong supporter of the 'miasmatic' theory of disease propagation. Simon made some early proposals to secure regular returns of disease and mortality in his 'General Suggestions on Preliminary Arrangements in the Sanitary Affairs of the City'.[19] The City Commission refused to pay the cost but Simon achieved his aims by making enterprising use of the Nuisances Removal and Diseases Prevention Act, 1846 (the 'Cholera Bill', see Chapter Two, page 48) after the onset of cholera in 1848. Using the same methods he also encouraged Harvey, the City Police Commissioner, to inspect and suppress insanitary practices in the dwellings of the City. Harvey reported the results of his inspections in October 1849 and *The Times* carried a full account of them:[20]

15,010	houses were inspected
2,524	had 'offensive smells from bad drainage or other causes'
720	had 'filth or rubbish in the cellar'
446	were 'in an offensive or unhealthy state from bad or deficient drainage'
1120	had 'privities [sic] and water-closets in a very offensive state'
223	had 'cesspools full of soil'
30	'cesspools had burst or overflowed'
21	had 'cellars used as cesspools'

Thus, 5,084 houses, over one-third of the total, were revealed as suffering from serious drainage problems and Simon used the experience of the 1849 epidemic to press for reforms. On 6 November 1849 he presented his first annual report in which he observed that 'animals will scarcely thrive in an atmosphere of their own decomposing excrement; yet such, strictly and literally speaking, is the air which a very large proportion of the inhabitants of the City are condemned to breathe'.[21]

The report advocated six measures: better house drainage; improved water supply; control of 'offensive trades'; cessation of intramural burials; slum clearance; and regular house inspections. The degree of public interest in the issue is reflected in the fact that Simon's report was carried in full in *The Times*, the *Morning Chronicle* and the *Morning Post* on 7 November and in the *Morning Herald* between the 7th and 10 November. *The Times* was unequivocal in its view, declaring in the leading article the following day, 8 November, that 'If any number of this journal ever deserved to be rescued from the usual fate of ephemeral publications and regarded as "a possession for all time" it is that of yesterday'.

Simon used the publicity brought by the epidemic to advocate reform, despite a prevaricating response from the City Commissioners, and he was supported by *The Times* and other newspapers. Improvements followed. The City Commissioners enforced slum improvement measures against landlords (including some aldermen) and by 1854 Simon could claim that only about a thousand dwellings retained cesspools.[22] The remainder were now connected to the sewers via which they emptied their contents, including cholera bacilli, into the river and hence into the water supply. Although he had some misgivings about the foul state of the river Simon was at this stage a strong adherent of the 'miasmatic' doctrine and therefore was more concerned with removing smells from dwellings than with the condition of the water supply. His views changed slowly and in step with another great Victorian reformer, William Farr.

Simon was more concerned with removing smells from dwellings than with the condition of the water supply

The Conversion of William Farr

In 1838, following one of Chadwick's campaigns, the Office of the Registrar-General was established with the task of registering births, marriages and deaths. William Farr (1807–83), who had studied medicine but never practised it, was appointed as the first compiler of abstracts (chief statistician) to the new office and quickly became the dominant influence in the organisation though in theory he was subordinate to the Registrar-General himself, a now-forgotten popular novelist called Thomas Lister who was appointed to the post because he was an active supporter of the government.[23] Farr remained in his post until 1879, becoming president of the Statistical Society in 1871. He probably gained the post through Chadwick's influence.[24]

In the years that followed, Farr used his position to campaign for better sanitation and quickly established a reputation for his skills as an advocate of reform. His *Report on the Mortality of Cholera in England, 1848–49* was described by *The Lancet* in the year of its publication (1852) as 'one of the most remarkable productions of type and pen in any age or country'.[25] He drew attention to the wide variations in mortality between different areas and particularly emphasised the high death rates recorded in London, a feature that he attributed to the conditions in which most of the population lived. In the tenth annual report, published in 1847, Farr estimated that in London at least thirty-eight people died every day as a result of poor living conditions. He went on to offer the conventional 'miasmatic' explanation for this phenomenon and to suggest that the legislature had a responsibility to introduce preventive measures:

William Farr, whose analysis of the 1866 cholera epidemic finally convinced him that infected water was the culprit. (By courtesy of the National Portrait Gallery, London)

> This disease mist, arising from the breath of two millions of people, from open sewers and cesspools, graves and slaughterhouses, is continually kept up and undergoing changes; in one season it was pervaded by Cholera, in another by Influenza; at one time it bears Smallpox, Measles, Scarlatina and Whooping Cough among your children; at another it carries fever on its wings. Like an angel of death it has hovered for centuries over London.[26]

In 1854 John Simon served with Neil Árnott and William Farr on the Committee for Scientific Enquiry into the Recent Cholera Epidemic. Farr used the data gathered by his office to draw a diagram which illustrated the relationship between the incidence of mortality from cholera and the elevation of the affected districts, using the figures compiled for the whole epidemic. His diagram revealed the incidence of mortality from cholera to be as follows:[27]

Elevation in feet	Cholera deaths per 10,000 population
0	137
15	50
25	40
35	25
45	20
55	13
65	36 (this level included the Broad Street Pump)
75	19

This clearly demonstrated that the further removed a district was from the lowest point (the Thames), the lower the mortality.[28] The most striking exception to this inverse relationship between mortality and elevation was shown by Farr's diagram to lie in the vicinity of Broad Street, the site of the pump which, according to John Snow, was supplying the locality with infected water. Despite the evident connection between the water of the Thames, the water of the pump, and the incidence of cholera, the 'miasmic' orthodoxy was at this stage so strong that the authors of the report sought an atmospheric explanation, concluding rather that:

> If the Broad Street pump did actually become a source of disease to persons dwelling at a distance, we believe that this may have depended on other organic impurities than those exclusively referred to, and may have arisen, not in its containing choleraic excrements, but simply in the fact of its impure waters having participated in the atmospheric infection of the district. . . . on the whole evidence, it seems impossible to doubt that the influences, which determine in mass the geographical distribution of 'cholera in London, belong less to the water than to the air'.[29]

The committee reached this view despite their own observations that 'in the Southwark and Vauxhall Water . . . evidence of unfiltered contamination reaches its highest degree, revealing to the microscope, not only swarms of infusorial life, but particles of undigested food referable to the discharge of human bowels'.[30] The deliberations of this Committee are a good illustration of the strength of the miasmatic doctrine at the time and, for this reason, merit further examination. The Committee undertook a detailed study of the Broad Street outbreak and observed that, on the south side of Broad Street, 48 houses out of a total of 49 were affected by cholera, while from a total of 860 persons living in the street, 90 had died, together with 25 others who worked in the street but lived elsewhere. Nothing could better illustrate the strength of the miasmic doctrine than the Committee's explanation of this:

'Evidence of unfiltered contamination reaches its highest degree, revealing to the microscope, not only swarms of infusorial life, but particles of undigested food referable to the discharge of human bowels'

'We cannot help thinking that the outbreak arose from the multitude of untrapped and imperfectly trapped gullies and ventilating shafts constantly emitting an immense amount of noxious, health-destroying, life-destroying exhalations'. They further observed that the enclosed character of the area meant that there was no wind to disperse the noxious vapours except at corners of streets and they took comfort from the fact that the incidence of deaths from cholera had been rather lower in corner houses than in others.[31]

Commenting upon Snow's conclusion that this phenomenon was due to the use of infected water from the Broad Street Pump, Simon, Farr and the rest of the Committee concluded:

The incidence of deaths from cholera had been rather lower in corner houses than in others

> In explanation of the remarkable intensity of this outbreak within very definite limits, it has been suggested by Dr Snow that the real cause of whatever was peculiar in the case lay in the general use of one particular well, situate at Broad Street in the middle of the district and having (it was imagined) its waters contaminated by the rice-water evacuations of cholera patients. After careful enquiry we see no reason to adopt this belief.[32]

The East London Epidemic

It was the failure of the East London water company to comply wholly with the requirements of the 1851 and 1852 Metropolis Water Acts, combined with the fact that its directors attempted to conceal its failure, that finally convinced Farr and others of the critical role of polluted water in the propagation of cholera. On 27 June 1866, a labourer called Hedges and his wife, living at 12 Priory Street, Bromley by Bow, both died of cholera, aged forty-six. Most of Bazalgette's system of intercepting sewers was in operation by this time but the northern low level sewer, which would eventually take the sewage from this area, had not yet been completed. The Hedges' water-closet therefore discharged into the River Lea at Bow Bridge, ½ mile below the East London Water Company's reservoir at Old Ford. The incoming tide would have carried the infected sewage back upstream towards the reservoir. This should not have mattered since the company had installed filter-beds for its new covered reservoirs and supposedly isolated these reservoirs from its older uncovered reservoirs which had pervious bottoms. Nevertheless Farr observed the degree to which the outbreak was concentrated in the area served·by the East London company and on 1 August *The Times* carried a report of the Registrar-General's weekly return of deaths from cholera which drew attention to the fact that 924 people had died in six districts served by the East London

company.[33] On the same day, upon the recommendation of the
Registrar-General's Office, notices were displayed in the affected area
advising that 'The inhabitants of the district within which cholera is
prevailing are earnestly advised not to drink any water which has not
previously been boiled' as Snow had counselled in his paper of 1854,
though the effectiveness of this advice may have been reduced by the
fact that, according to the local medical officer, Orton, temperatures
in sunlight were reaching 165 degrees Fahrenheit.[34] The engineer of
the water company, Charles Greaves, wrote to *The Times* on 2 August
1866 to refute the suggestion that contaminated water had been
allowed to enter the drinking water supply. He wrote:[35]

> the water enters the filter-beds of the company at Lea Bridge, and is
> conducted thence to their pumping establishments at Old Ford in an
> iron pipe and never sees light or risks pollution between the filter-bed
> and the consumer; and that the 'canal' alluded to by the Registrar,
> having been since 1853 disused for all purposes of supply, is only
> maintained as a drain from the filter to a lower part of the river . . . not
> a drop of unfiltered water has for several years past been supplied by
> the company for any purpose.

On 3 August Farr visited Old Ford and observed that, though
Greaves's letter to *The Times* had claimed that all its water was
filtered, two customers of the East London company, Mr Ferguson
and Mr Russell, claimed that they had found eels in their water
pipes.[36] Farr also wrote to Bazalgette in the same week about the
possibility of waste entering the water supply. Bazalgette replied:

They had found eels in their water pipes

> It is unfortunately just the locality where our main drainage works are
> not complete. The low-level sewer is constructed through the locality,
> but the pumping station at Abbey Mills will not be completed until
> next summer . . . I shall recommend the Board to erect a temporary
> pumping station at Abbey Mills to lift the sewage of this district into
> the Northern outfall sewer. This can be accomplished in about three
> weeks.[37]

In the same week that Bazalgette wrote this letter the Board
approved his proposal to realign some branches of the low level sewer
and install a temporary pumping station powered by two
20 horsepower engines to lift the sewage into the outfall.

In September twenty-nine residents supplied by the East London
company signed a 'memorial' to the Board of Trade in which they
alleged that their water supplies were being contaminated by water
from the River Lea. This occurred in November 1866[38] and led to
the appointment of Captain Tyler to report upon the matter. Tyler

examined the company's reservoirs and found evidence that they were not effectively protected from infiltration by surrounding groundwater which might itself have become contaminated. He also questioned the company's employees and discovered that on three occasions in 1866, in March, June and July, a 24-year-old carpenter had admitted water to the company's closed reservoir (from which drinking water was drawn) from an old, uncovered reservoir which was vulnerable to contamination, in clear breach of the 1851 and 1852 Metropolis Water Acts.[39] Tyler wrote, in reference to the claims of the 'memorialists':

> I am of the opinion that the allegation has been proved, and that the water of the Lea finds its way into these covered reservoirs. . . . the use of such unfiltered water so stored in an uncovered reservoir is indefensible, and was a distinct infringement of the Metropolitan Water Supply Act of 1852. . . . a case of grave suspicion exists against the water supplied by the East London company from Old Ford, and that proximity to absolute proof at which I hinted in commencing this subject, has thus been nearly reached.[40]

Tyler estimated that 4,363 deaths had occurred in July and August, of which 3,797 had been in areas supplied only by the East London company and a further 264 in an area which it shared with the New River company. Thus 93 per cent of deaths had occurred in areas supplied wholly or in part by the East London company.[41]

The Lancet took a particularly censorious view of the responsibility of the water company. Commenting upon the Board of Trade Report it wrote: 'The companies, in whose hands that supply [of water] is a monopoly, secretly infringe the law, trusting to the difficulties by which discovery is virtually rendered next to impossible. . . . greatly to be regretted that a heavy penalty has not been levied for the infraction of the law.'[42]

William Farr reached the same conclusion as Tyler and drew attention to the fact that, in most of London's parishes, the 1866 epidemic had been by far the least deadly, the marked exceptions to this trend falling in seven East End parishes, all of which were supplied by the East London company. Commenting on the figures, he wrote: 'It happened, too, that several districts in the group so heavily visited by cholera lie in the particular region which then derived no advantage from the contemplated low level sewer.' He wrote of the debate on the roles of air and water in disease propagation and gave much more favourable consideration to Snow's theory than he had in the past, using language in which his anger was barely suppressed:

Thus 93 per cent of deaths had occurred in areas supplied wholly or in part by the East London company

As the air of London is not supplied like water to its inhabitants by companies the air has had the worst of it both before Parliamentary Committees and Royal Commissions. For air no scientific witnesses have been retained, no learned counsel has pleaded; so the atmosphere has been freely charged with the propagation and the illicit diffusion of plagues of all kinds; while Father Thames, deservedly reverenced through the ages, and the water gods of London, have been loudly proclaimed immaculate and innocent. In vain did the sewers of London and of twenty towns pour their dark streams into the Thames and the Lea; their waters were assoiled [sic] from every stain by chemists who had carefully analysed specimens collected by the water companies . . . Dr Snow's theory turned the current in the direction of water, and tended to divert attention from the atmospheric doctrine . . . the theory of the East wind with cholera on its wings, assailing the East End of London, is not at all borne out by the experience of previous epidemics . . . It ignores all past experience . . . The population in London probably inhaled a few cholera corpuscles floating in the open air, and the quantity thus taken from the air would be insignificant in its effects in comparison with the quantities imbibed through the waters of the rivers or of ponds into which cholera dejections . . . had found their way and been mingled with sewage by the churning tides . . . An indifferent person would have breathed the air without any apprehension; but only a very robust scientific witness would have dared to drink a glass of the waters of the Lea at Old Ford after filtration.[43]

'The theory of the East wind with cholera on its wings, assailing the East End of London, is not at all borne out by the experience of previous epidemics'

This acceptance that cholera was primarily water-borne was a significant shift from Farr's position in the earlier outbreak of 1854 when, along with his fellow members of the Committee for Scientific Enquiries, he had explicitly rejected Snow's hypothesis. By 1866, faced by the evidence of the East London company's practices, and no doubt offended by their attempt to conceal them, Farr had clearly accepted Snow's explanation. *The Lancet* was in no doubt about the strength of Farr's case. Commenting on his report, it referred to the attempts made by water companies to argue that cholera effusions would be so diluted in water as to render them harmless but added:

We apprehend that, to an unbiased mind, the elaborate array of facts which Dr Farr has set forth with so much skill, as the result of great labour and research, will render irresistible the conclusions at which he has arrived in regard to the influence of the water-supply in the causation of the epidemic.[44]

The Conversion of John Simon

Farr's conversion to the idea that cholera epidemics were caused by water contaminated by sewage was shortly followed by that of Simon whose views by 1870 were equally unambiguous and were reported to the Privy Council in that year in the following terms:

> Not only is it now certain that the faulty water supply of a town may be the essential cause of the most terrible epidemic outbreaks of cholera, typhoid fever, dysentery and other allied disorders; but even doubts are widely entertained whether these diseases, or some of them, can possibly obtain general prevalence in a town except where the faulty water supply develop them.[45]

In the report Simon not only warmly endorsed Snow's theory but also tried to explain his own scepticism twelve years earlier as a member of the Committee for Scientific Enquiry. Of Snow he wrote:

> Dr Snow, in 1849, was not able to furnish proofs of his doctrine . . . but afterwards (and happily in great part before his premature and lamented death in 1858) distinct experiments, as well as much new collateral information, established as almost certain that his bold conjecture [i.e. that cholera was water-borne] had been substantially right.[46]

His bold conjecture had been substantially right

In the pages that followed in his 1870 Report, Simon estimated the number of lives that would have been saved in the 1848–9 and 1853–4 cholera outbreaks if steps had been taken earlier to protect the capital's water supply with effective sanitation of the kind that Bazalgette had now almost completed. He also lamented that the Act specified a fine of only £200 for contravening it. By 1874 similar views had reached the Rivers Pollution Commission which, in its sixth report on the Domestic Water Supply of Great Britain, commented favourably on the supply of well water by the Kent Water Company, adding that 'The supply of such water . . . to the Metropolis generally would be a priceless boon, and would at once confer upon it absolute immunity from epidemics of cholera'.[47]

The End of Cholera

In July 1868 Abbey Mills pumping station was commissioned (Crossness on the south side having been operating since April 1865) and from that date the sewage from both sides of the river was conveyed to the outfalls where it continued to provoke occasional complaints from neighbouring communities but without posing a threat to their health (see above, page 104ff). After 1866 there were no further epidemics of cholera or typhoid in London. The link between the construction of the intercepting sewers and the disappearance of cholera and typhoid was made either directly or implicitly by many of those concerned with public health though the 'miasmatic' doctrine survived in some quarters for many more years. In evidence to the Royal Commission of 1893–4 two chemists well known in the field of public health, Percy Frankland and E.R. Lankester, both testified that cholera and typhoid germs would be destroyed rather than propagated by sewage.

Bazalgette himself seems to have made the connection between his work and the 1866 cholera epidemic, as reflected in his apologetic correspondence with Farr (see above, page 138 and note 37) concerning the delay in lifting the low level sewage and in his attempts to alleviate the problem by building a temporary pumping station at Abbey Mills. Moreover in his address to the Institution of Civil Engineers on 14 March 1865 'On the Main Drainage of London and the Interception of the Sewage from the River Thames' the detached character of the language he used concerning the causes of cholera do not conceal his own confidence that his works had played a significant part in its elimination from the metropolis:

> although great differences of opinion existed, and continue to exist, as to the causes of the disease, yet an inspection of the houses in which deaths occurred was sufficient to show that, however occult might be the connection between death and defective drainage, the places formerly most favourable to the spread of disease became quite free from it, when afterwards properly drained.[48]

His employers, the Metropolitan Board of Works, were also in no doubt that the main drainage had made a significant contribution to the health of the Metropolis. In its *Annual Report* for 1868–9, by which time both Abbey Mills and Crossness were in full operation, the Board commented:

> A reference to the tables given in the Registrar-General's reports shows that the deaths in the Metropolis, especially in the low-lying districts, have been fewer, since the execution of the Main Drainage Works, than in previous years, which may be considered a result of the improved sanitary conditions in consequence of those works.[49]

'The deaths in the Metropolis, especially in the low-lying districts, have been fewer, since the execution of the Main Drainage Works'

The Registrar-General's report referred to is that for the year 1867 in which Farr had commented that 1867 had been the healthiest year for London since 1860, judged by the death-rate.[50] Subsequent reports confirmed the trend towards a healthier metropolis. The *Annual Report* for 1872 revealed that, in that year, the annual death rate in London was 21.5 for every 10,000 people, the lowest figure since 1850 and a lower rate than that achieved by Paris, Vienna, Berlin, Brussels, Rome or any other major European, American or Indian city, despite the fact that, with a population of 3.3 million, London was by far the largest city in the world, and urban concentration had hitherto been closely related to high death rates. After 1875 (the year in which the main drainage was finally completed with the opening of the western area drainage), the Registrar-General discontinued the practice of commenting separately upon London's death rate since it no longer differed significantly from the national average and by 1896 cholera had become so rare that it was classified as one of a number of 'exotic diseases'.[51] Even so, the very proximity of the dreaded disease continued to cause anxiety. In 1892 there was a severe outbreak on the continent, especially in Hamburg, from which port many vessels traded with London. The authorities were sufficiently concerned to commission a Parliamentary report on the subject and a committee was formed to deal with the expected epidemic. The *Illustrated London News*, in three successive issues,[52] devoted several pages and numerous pictures to the Hamburg epidemic and in the last of these it printed a picture based upon an account of its roving artist, J. Schonberg, who had 'witnessed in a shop where he called to make some purchase, a little girl drinking freely of water, the purity of which may be doubted. A few hours later he was told that this child was dead.' Some artistic licence may be allowed for but it is a telling indication of the fear that the disease still aroused. In England 135 deaths occurred from a 'disease reputed to be of the nature of cholera'.[53] The deaths were distributed across sixty-four towns, with seventeen occurring in the metropolis. Almost all the deceased were arriving passengers who had contracted the disease abroad.[54] There was no epidemic.

Bazalgette's professional contemporaries, notably Simon, may have continued to entertain some doubts concerning the aetiology of cholera, and the precise role played by the main drainage in its elimination but other contemporaries at least recognised his central role. In August 1890, less than a year before his death, Bazalgette was interviewed at his home in Wimbledon for Cassell's *Saturday Journal*. The writer of the profile began with the following paragraph: 'If the malignant spirits whom we moderns call cholera, typhus and smallpox, were one day to set out in quest of the man who had been, within the past thirty or forty years, their deadliest foe in all London, they would probably make their way to St Mary's, Wimbledon.'[55] In this confusing way it was thus recorded that the main drainage had played a critical role in banishing from the metropolis epidemics that had plagued it for over thirty years though the writer of the profile, in including smallpox and typhus (rather than typhoid) in his inventory of diseases vanquished by sanitation, reflected the fact that, even in the last decade of the nineteenth century, there was an imperfect understanding of how this had been achieved.

'Death in the Cup': a small girl in Hamburg drinking infected water during the 1892 epidemic; a few hours later the child was dead. This picture, from the *Illustrated London News*, reminds us of the fear the disease still caused. Bazalgette's system protected London from the epidemic despite official anxieties. (*Illustrated London News*)

CHAPTER SEVEN

Building the Embankments

An humble address be presented to Her Majesty, praying that she will be pleased to direct that no public offices be erected on that portion of the Thames Embankment which is reserved to the Crown, and which has been reclaimed from the river at the cost of the ratepayers of the Metropolis.
(Motion proposed by W.H. Smith, House of Commons, 8 July 1870)

As indicated in Chapter Four, the Victoria Embankment, between Westminster Bridge and Blackfriars, was conceived by Bazalgette as a vehicle for accommodating the low level sewer (the alternative being to lay it beneath the Strand). At that time the Strand was the main thoroughfare between the centre of commerce, the City, and the seat of government at Westminster. It was choked with vehicles throughout every weekday and the effect upon traffic of digging it up to lay the largest of all the sewers would have been catastrophic. Upon completion the Victoria Embankment provided an alternative route between the two centres, thus relieving the congested Strand. This chapter examines the work involved in the massive task of reclaiming 52 acres from the river to create the Victoria and Chelsea Embankments on the north side of the river and the Albert Embankment on the south side. It considers the novel construction techniques and new materials which were used for this hazardous work and the political furore which arose when the Crown Estates, with Gladstone's misguided support, tried to appropriate part of the reclaimed land for building offices, an enterprise which was frustrated by the determined opposition of W.H. Smith.

W.H. Smith who, when not selling newspapers, was protecting the Victoria Embankment from Gladstone's rapacious designs. (By courtesy of the National Portrait Gallery, London)

Paying for the Embankments

As early as 29 June 1858 the Board had recognised the advantages of

W.H. SMITH, 1825–91

Thwarted in his wish to go to Oxford, William Henry Smith was obliged to join the family business, a small newsagency founded by his grandfather in the previous century. In 1851, against the wishes of his father (also W.H. Smith), he negotiated with the London and North-Western Railway a monopoly on bookstalls at their stations and advertised on the platforms. In 1862 this was extended to all the major railway companies. The arrangement placed his newsagency in a strong position to benefit from the huge increase in newspaper readership which had followed the abolition of stamp duty in 1854 and made the business immensely profitable. In 1868 he entered Parliament as MP for Westminster and in 1877 became First Lord of the Admiralty against the wishes of the Admirals who requested a 'person of rank'. His effective reforms of naval administration led to his appointment in 1885 as Secretary for War. A devout Methodist, he gave generously to many philanthropic causes and was dubbed 'Old Morality' by *Punch*.

incorporating the northern low level sewer in an embankment and had declared its readiness to pay for its share of the work. The following year, in its Report, the Board stressed that 'it becomes of extreme urgency that an early solution of this important question should be arrived at'.[1]

After the passing of the Thames Embankment (North) Act in 1862 the Board entered into protracted negotiations with wharfingers, property owners and numerous other parties before work could begin. The passing of the Metropolitan District Railway Act, 1864, confirmed that the Embankment would accommodate the underground railway but this proved to be a source of delay since, in the words of the Board: 'The railway company's works proceeded very slowly in consequence of the difficulties of raising sufficient capital, and the Board had frequently to urge upon the company the necessity for greater expedition.'[2] Numerous references in meetings and special reports bear witness to the Board's long and sometimes impatient correspondence with the company on its slow progress.[3]

In April 1859 the Chairman of the Board, John Thwaites, had written to Metropolitan MPs drawing their attention to the inadequacy of the Board's resources to meet all its commitments, with particular reference to the prospective costs of constructing the embankments. He argued that the coal and wine duties should be assigned to the Board for these purposes.[4] These ancient duties had earlier been used for rebuilding St Paul's and other London churches after the Great Fire of 1666. In the nineteenth century they amounted to 9*d* per ton on coal brought to London by rail or sea; and 4*s* per tun on wine brought to the Port of London by sea. In 1861, 1863 and 1868 Coal and Wine Duties Acts were passed, assigning most of the proceeds of these ancient duties to the Board for the 'Thames Embankment and Metropolis Improvement Fund', for

A view of the Thames from Somerset House in 1817, before Bazalgette built the Victoria Embankment. (By courtesy of the Guildhall Library, Corporation of London)

Somerset House from Temple Gardens in 1795, before Bazalgette built the Victoria Embankment. (By courtesy of the Guildhall Library, Corporation of London)

Temple Gardens pictured in the late eighteenth century, when they opened on to the Thames. (By courtesy of the Guildhall Library, Corporation of London)

The Adelphi, bordering the Thames before Bazalgette built the Victoria Embankment. York Gate is visible to the left of the picture, now relocated to Embankment Gardens. (By courtesy of the Guildhall Library, Corporation of London)

The coffer dam being formed, behind which the Victoria Embankment would be built, 1866. (*Illustrated London News*)

construction of the embankments and for freeing bridges from tolls. The Board was also, by the Thames Embankment Acts, empowered to borrow against the security of the duties, £1,000,000 being permitted for the Victoria Embankment; £480,000 for the Albert Embankment; and £285,000 for the Chelsea Embankment.

The Victoria Embankment eventually cost £1,156,981, the Albert Embankment £1,014,525 and the Chelsea Embankment £269,591. Between them the three embankments reclaimed 52 acres from the river which were used as roads, walkways and parks.[5] Moreover the narrowing of the river which resulted from the construction of the embankments speeded the flow of water and thus the 'scouring' effect which helped to keep it clean. A close examination of the contracts and drawings prepared for the embankments reveals the complexity of the task.[6] For most of their length they were constructed within coffer dams. Piles were sunk in the bed of the river and the gaps between them were filled in with a mixture of clay and spoil. The water behind them was pumped out leaving a dry area, protected from the river, within which the embankments and their tunnels could be built. However, for the stretch of the Victoria Embankment between Westminster and Waterloo bridges boreholes revealed that solid ground was so far beneath the river bed that

Laying the foundation stone for the Victoria Embankment, 1864. Note the caissons in the background. (*Illustrated London News*)

piling would be difficult and would have to be driven so deep that damage might be done to the foundations of the bridges. For this stretch, therefore, Bazalgette specified the use of caissons. These metal chambers, like boilers without bottoms, were lowered into the riverbed at low tide. Gaps between the caissons were plugged with wooden pegs, making the barrier watertight so that excavation and building work could be carried out behind them.

New Materials

As observed in Chapter Six, the scale of the major engineering works undertaken in the early nineteenth century was such that new types of contracting organisation had to be devised to undertake them. In addition, new materials had to be found that could bear the considerable strains which would be imposed upon them by huge engineering structures. This was particularly true of the embankments which were, in effect, heavily used roads, superimposed on a honeycomb of tunnels carrying railways, water, gas and sewage, and bounded on one side by a powerful tidal river.

Early in its deliberations the Board had decided to appoint a consultant to advise on the materials which should be employed on the main drainage and associated works.[7] A particular innovation was the use of Portland cement. In the first half of the nineteenth century engineers like Telford and Brunel had used Roman cement in major civil engineering works.[8] Similar to that used by the Romans in their great works (hence the name), this material consists mostly of lime but in the late eighteenth century some engineers experimented with different processes to produce a stronger cement, especially one which could withstand immersion in water. In 1824 a Yorkshire bricklayer called Joseph Aspdin patented a technique for making a stronger cement for which he coined the name Portland cement because of its resemblance to Portland stone. The patent which Aspdin obtained in 1824 described the manufacturing process in terms that combined wordiness with lack of precision:

In the late eighteenth century some engineers experimented with different processes to produce a stronger cement

> I take a specific quantity of limestone, such as that generally used for making or repairing roads, and I take it from the roads after it is reduced to a puddle, or powder . . . I then take a specific quantity of agrillaceous earth or clay, and mix them with water . . . Then I break the said mixture into suitable lumps, and calcine them in a furnace similar to a lime kiln till the carbonic acid is entirely expelled.[9]

This process produced exceptionally strong cement. Aspdin manufactured it in his works in Wakefield from 1825, though his son William later transferred the business to Northfleet in the Medway valley in Kent, where the industry quickly became concentrated because of the ready availability of suitable chalk and clay. The new material gained acceptance very slowly because it was regarded as unreliable, if impressive. The firm of Charles Francis, manufacturers of the older (and rival) Roman cement, had little difficulty obtaining from prominent engineers a number of testimonials to the qualities of this long-established product. I.K. Brunel testified to its effectiveness in constructing the Thames Tunnel 'and many other large Works, where the quality of your cement has undergone the most severe tests'. Other endorsements were received from James Walker and Robert Stephenson for its use in buildings and railways respectively. By contrast, Portland cement's properties were untested, it was about one-and-a-half times as expensive as Roman cement and it was sensitive to errors in the production process. A small change in the mixture of materials, the temperature of the kiln or in the grinding process significantly affected the strength of the finished product in an industry where production control and quality control processes were still rudimentary.[10] Consequently, although of considerable professional interest, the new material was mostly used only in small-scale projects.

One of its characteristics was that, once hardened, it was not affected by immersion in water. Indeed there was some evidence that it actually became stronger through such immersion and that it also gained in strength over time, both of these features being very attractive to an engineer responsible for a massive engineering project whose structures would be continuously exposed to water and were expected to last indefinitely. Bazalgette therefore took the very bold step of specifying that it should be used in laying the brickwork for the sewers – the first use of the material in a large-scale public work. However, he also specified that every batch received from his suppliers should be tested for strength before it was used. He delegated this task to John Grant, one of his three assistant engineers. Percy Boulnois, one of Bazalgette's pupils, gives an account of this process which he carried out under Grant's supervision.[11] Grant later gave three papers to the Institution of Civil Engineers on the results of his experiments which were to prove critical to the future of this important material. In the words of an historian of the industry:

> The experiments of the late Mr John Grant, the engineer of the Metropolitan Board of Works in connection with the London drainage scheme of 1859, gave an impetus to the use of Portland Cement which saw many new factories spring up and originated an industry which has never flagged to this day.[12]

Grant's first paper was given to the Institution in December 1865 under the title 'Experiments on the Strength of Cement', chiefly in reference to the Portland cement used in the southern main drainage works,[13] and the degree of interest in the topic may be gauged from the fact that the discussion continued for four evenings to the exclusion of all other business. Grant introduced the subject by reminding the members that, prior to 1859, Roman cement had been used in all major civil engineering projects, with Portland cement confined mostly to the external rendering of houses and some small harbour projects on the south coast and Channel Islands where its advertised ability to withstand prolonged immersion in water had encouraged engineers to risk using it. Between January and July 1859, therefore, Grant had carried out 302 experiments on batches of Portland cement from twelve manufacturers. Some batches had been prepared neat and some with sand, and each had been immersed in water for a period of ten to fourteen days before being subjected to a crushing test. The tests revealed that, while Roman cement in these conditions broke at a pressure of about 200lb per square inch, Portland cement broke at a pressure exceeding 600lb. As a result of these experiments the material was specified for the main drainage contracts, beginning with contract number one, for the northern high level sewer, though as work progressed the specifications became more detailed and demanding, the density of the material increasing from 106 to 112lb to the bushel as the trials progressed. The following specification was inserted by Bazalgette in contract number one for the northern embankment:

> The whole of the cement for these works, and herein referred to, to be Portland cement, of the best quality, ground extremely fine, and weighing not less than 112lb to the imperial bushel. It is to be brought on to the works in a state fit for use, and is not to be used therein, until it shall have been upon the ground for three weeks at the least, nor until it has been tested by taking samples out of every tenth sack, at the least, gauging these samples in moulds, and by apparatus similar to those heretofore in use by the said Board, placing the cement at once in water, in which it is to remain for seven clear days, and testing it at the end of that time by the application of a weight or lever. All cement that shall not bear, without breaking, a weight of five hundred pounds, at the least, when subjected to this test, shall be peremptorily rejected and forthwith removed from the works.[14]

A simple machine had been devised to subject 2½ square inches of the product to breaking tests and workmen had been trained to operate the machine on site under the supervision of Grant, assisted by pupils like Boulnois. When he delivered his paper in 1865 Grant was able to report that batches from fourteen suppliers, amounting to 70,000 tons, had been subjected to 11,587 tests for the southern drainage alone. The average breaking weight had been 606.8lb and the tests had confirmed that the cement strengthened both with age and through immersion in water. After three months the strength of the product had doubled and a further strengthening was observed after twelve months.

The cement strengthened both with age and through immersion in water

In discussing Grant's paper one manufacturer, G.F. White, observed that the engineers of the Metropolitan Board were the first public officials to use testing procedures in this way. In his comments Bazalgette 'believed that great good had been done by the tests; that the manufacture of cement had been improved thereby; and that Portland cement was destined to be used to a much larger extent than it had been hitherto in engineering works'. Grant commented that testing machines had been adopted by the manufacturers for use at their works, in order to ensure that their supplies met the specification – a significant advance in the adoption of quality control procedures.

Five years later Grant gave a second paper to the Institution entitled 'Further Experiments on the Strength of Portland Cement'[15] in which he reported that, following its successful use in laying brickwork for the sewers, the Board had adopted the policy of making sewers entirely from Portland cement concrete, eliminating altogether the use of bricks. A concrete sewer measuring 4 feet by 2 feet 8 inches, costing 10s per linear foot, had been used as an alternative to a brick sewer costing 16s 6d for the same dimensions. Specifications for such sewers were now standard in the Board's contract documents. Moreover the material was being employed in much larger quantities in the construction of the embankments. The original plans for the Albert Embankment had specified brickwork for the substructure, with granite facing. Instead, after one quarter of the contract was completed, the specification was changed to substitute Portland cement for the brickwork. In all, 14,300 cubic yards of the material were used at a cost of 11s a cubic yard instead of bricks at 30s a cubic yard, though the planned granite facings were retained. Much larger quantities were subsequently used in the Victoria and Chelsea Embankments. In the words of another historian:

14,300 cubic yards of Portland cement were used at a cost of 11s a cubic yard

> Probably no event did more to set the Portland Cement Industry on its feet and demonstrate the importance and capabilities of the new material than a series of tests commenced in 1860 by John Grant, assistant engineer to the Metropolitan Board of Works.[16]

In the space of a few years, in the late 1860s, Portland cement had progressed from being a material which engineers regarded with considerable caution to one that was virtually the industry standard. The catalyst for the transition was the adoption of the material for the main drainage works and the associated testing procedures which both improved quality standards in the industry and instilled confidence in the product. Bazalgette's enterprise in adopting the new material conferred upon it an important seal of approval while his caution in establishing testing procedures of unprecedented rigour may be regarded as a significant contribution to concepts of quality control in this young industry.

Opening the Embankments

The first of the embankments to be completed was the southern one, the Albert Embankment, between Vauxhall Bridge and Westminster Bridge. Work began in July 1866 and was completed in November

Lambeth Palace adjacent to the Thames, pictured in the late eighteenth century, before Bazalgette's Albert Embankment was built. (By courtesy of the Guildhall Library, Corporation of London)

The Albert Embankment under construction, 1868. Lambeth Palace is visible in the background. (*Illustrated London News*)

Opening the Albert Embankment, November 1869. (*Illustrated London News*)

This derelict boatyard was reclaimed by Bazalgette for the Albert Embankment and is now the site of St Thomas's Hospital. (By courtesy of the Guildhall Library, Corporation of London)

St Thomas's Hospital on its new site. (By courtesy of the Guildhall Library, Corporation of London)

1869, creating an embankment almost a mile long. The main purpose of this embankment was to protect the low-lying areas in Lambeth from flooding during high tides and heavy rain, though it also provided a much-needed roadway to bypass the congested streets of the area. Part of the cost of £1,014,525 was recovered by selling 8½ acres of the reclaimed land for £105,000 to the governors of St Thomas's Hospital, recently evicted from Southwark to make way for railway works. The hospital still stands upon the land thus created. The embankment's opening ceremony on 24 November 1869 was a low-key event since the main thrust of the Board's publicity for its achievements was to focus on the opening of the more extensive and spectacular northern Victoria Embankment eight months later. The opening ceremony for the Albert Embankment was performed by the chairman of the Board, John Thwaites, Bazalgette himself, and the Board's architect, George Vulliamy. They were greeted by a band playing 'See the Conquering Hero Comes' and by a large crowd, following which Thwaites declared that the Albert Embankment was open and that Lambeth was now, in consequence, 'high and dry' and safe from flooding by the Thames.[17] Unfortunately other low-lying areas on the southern bank remained unprotected and were flooded on three occasions, in 1874, 1875 and 1877, despite the Board's constant efforts to persuade the owners of wharves and other riverside properties to bring them up to the standard required to protect the adjacent streets. In 1879, after many failed attempts, the Board secured the powers to compel the owners to undertake the necessary work and after this there were no serious floods as a result of the Thames overflowing its banks.

The Victoria Embankment was the focus of far more public interest than the Albert or Chelsea Embankments. It was larger than the other two combined. At its western end, Westminster Bridge, it lay at the heart of government and at its eastern end, Blackfriars, it provided a link to the City, the centre of finance and commerce. Bazalgette commissioned four artists' impressions of his designs which were widely reproduced, discussed and acclaimed before construction work commenced.[18] It was opened on 13 July 1870 and its formal opening was a great occasion which caused much anxiety to the contractor, George Furness. The opening had been scheduled for 25 July but the date was brought forward by almost two weeks to accommodate the reclusive Queen Victoria, still mourning Albert nine years after his death, who had been persuaded by Gladstone, the Prime Minister, to make one of her rare public appearances to open it. Furness, striving to complete the work on time, required some of his men to work on the Sabbath, the day before the opening ceremony. This incurred an unsuccessful motion of censure from Mr Shaw, a Sabbatarian member of the Metropolitan Board of Works. In the event the Queen, indulging in one of her frequent bouts of hypochondria, informed Gladstone through her private secretary Colonel Ponsonby: 'The Queen wishes me to let you know that she can make no promise; that she is already suffering much from the

Impression of the proposed Victoria Embankment, 1863. (*Illustrated London News*)

Embankment Gardens. York Gate is to the left of the picture. (*Illustrated London News*)

The Victoria Embankment under construction adjacent to Temple Gardens, February 1865. (*Illustrated London News*)

heat and that she fears it will completely exhaust her and bring on headache and neuralgia – in which case it would be quite impossible for her to open the Embankment.'[19]

Instead, the ceremony was performed by the Prince of Wales who was accompanied by five other members of the royal family, twenty-four ambassadors, virtually every Member of both Houses of Parliament and ten thousand ticket-holders who watched the event from specially erected stands. The Grenadier and Coldstream Guards provided a musical accompaniment to the sound of much cheering. *The Times* devoted its main news story to the event, commenting that it 'marked the completion of a work of which it would be difficult to speak in terms of too much praise and admiration' though, in contrast to the magnificence of the spectacle, the newspaper added that 'the shabbiness of the ill-assorted carriages of the members of the Board of Works introduced an element of the grotesque'.[20] The decorum of the occasion was further threatened by a disturbance which immediately followed the opening ceremony. In the words of *The Times* the following day: 'At this time a great mob of roughs was steadfastly bent upon pushing westward; but its progress was arrested in a masterly manner by the police and the occupants of the reserved seats spared a sudden commingling with some of the most unsavoury denizens of the least-favoured parts of London.'

The shabbiness of the Board's carriages and the behaviour of the local hooligans could not conceal the scale of the enterprise.[21] Almost

30,000,000 cubic feet of earth had been excavated, much of it being reused, and 6,000,000 cubic feet of brickwork and Portland cement concrete had been used to create the embankment. Some 650,000 cubic feet of granite had been used in building a concave river wall which was decorated at intervals with bronze mooring rings in the form of lions' heads and illuminated by cast-iron lamps, in the form of dolphins, at intervals of 70 feet. By such means over 37 acres of land had been reclaimed from what had previously been a wilderness of crumbling wharves, tenements, mud and sewage. A broad, tree-lined thoroughfare from the City to Westminster had been created, over a mile in length, and the Embankment Gardens, after some dispute (see below) provided some pleasant green spaces in a congested part of London. Besides the low-level intercepting sewer the Victoria Embankment carried service pipes for gas, water and eventually electricity and it also housed the capital's first underground railway as well as providing five landing stages for the Thames steamers at intervals along its banks. No other civil engineering project in the capital has solved so many problems simultaneously. The following year Bazalgette was made a Companion of the Bath for his services to London.

No other civil engineering project in the capital has solved so many problems simultaneously

Whose land?

The opening celebrations were performed against a background that was far from harmonious. Some 2 acres of the new embankment had been built adjacent to Crown property and, although the Metropolitan Board had purchased the squalid foreshore from the Crown for £26,375, the Commissioner of Woods and Forests, who administered the affairs of the Crown Estate, was proposing to exercise the Crown's right to build offices on the reclaimed land. No one questioned his right to do this but many questioned his tact since the Board had proposed to turn the area into riverside walks and gardens which were much needed in that part of London. Gladstone and his Chancellor, Robert Lowe, defended the decision to build on the land on the grounds that it was in the public interest to raise rents for the Crown (and hence for the government) from such a valuable property. At this time Gladstone was still cherishing the hope that he would be able to abandon the income tax that had first been imposed by Pitt during the Napoleonic wars and the possibility of a substantial windfall from Bazalgette's construction work was very attractive to him. Roy Jenkins has described Gladstone in this mood as 'a penny-pinching miser, elevating the reduction or abolition of particular taxes to the status of an ultimate achievement'.[22]

Opposition to this plan was whipped up by one of the most under-rated public figures of the nineteenth century, the statesman-stationer W.H. Smith. William Henry Smith (1825–91) had joined his father, also called W.H. Smith, in 1846 at the Strand headquarters of the newsagent's business founded by his grandfather. He transformed the business into an extremely profitable concern by securing contracts with railway companies to open bookstalls at stations. In 1868, already a very wealthy man, he had stood for Parliament as a Conservative candidate in Westminster where he defeated the philosopher John Stuart Mill. In leading the opposition to Gladstone's plans to build on the Victoria Embankment, he showed the qualities of determination and organisation that had enabled him to build a successful business and which, in 1877, led Disraeli to appoint him First Lord of the Admiralty. For this, Smith was caricatured in 'HMS Pinafore' as 'The Ruler of the Queen's Navee' but he succeeded in reforming that moribund and complacent organisation despite the opposition of senior naval officers. On the issue of the embankments Smith proved to be more than a match for Gladstone himself. On Friday 8 July 1870, five days before the embankment was opened, Smith moved in the House of Commons that: 'an humble address be presented to Her Majesty, praying that she will be pleased to direct that no public offices be erected on that portion of the Thames Embankment which is reserved to the Crown, and which has been reclaimed from the river at the cost of the ratepayers of the Metropolis.'

Smith proved to be more than a match for Gladstone himself

In opening the debate which followed Smith drew strong support for his contention that 'the public had created the land in question, and given a value to that which the government now sought to take away from them'.[23] Gladstone, in his contribution to the debate, held resolutely to the Crown's legal rights but the following Monday Smith was strongly supported by *The Times* which, in a leading article, criticised Gladstone's arguments in the most astringent terms:

> Unless the ratepayers had contributed more than £1,600,000, the worthless foreshore, where dead dogs and cats did mostly congregate, would have remained as desolate and repulsive as of yore; but their money has, it seems, made the plot now coveted worth £150,000 . . . Like Shylock he was entitled to his pound of flesh and he clutched it.[24]

Gladstone remained obdurate but W.H. Smith did not give up easily and in May 1871, as part of a concerted campaign, he organised a public meeting at St James's Hall in Piccadilly which was attended by several hundred vestrymen, ratepayers and Members of Parliament. There was much cheering of W.H. Smith and the

Metropolitan Board, much booing of the name of Gladstone and his government, and Gladstone was particularly ridiculed for claiming to represent the public interest. One speaker reminded the gathering that private owners who had owned parts of the foreshore had surrendered their rights in the public interest and that it was appropriate that the Crown should do likewise. *The Times* maintained its support, echoing in a leading article the 'demand that all the open land reclaimed from the river shall be devoted to one and the same public purpose, and be laid out as a pleasure ground for the health and recreation of the public'.[25]

Under this pressure the government finally, and ungraciously, retreated. After protracted negotiations the government agreed to hand over the land to the Board in return for a payment of £3,270 and a small piece of land which the Board owned at the foot of the proposed Northumberland Avenue. The Board was able to landscape the grounds and lay out the substantial Victoria Embankment Gardens which offer a quiet haven to the pedestrian seeking refuge from the noise of the traffic rushing past on the Embankment.[26]

In July 1871 Bazalgette began work on the Chelsea Embankment which carries the low level intercepting sewer from Battersea Bridge to Chelsea Hospital and, like the other embankments, provided a much-needed thoroughfare ¾ mile long as well as protecting from flooding the low-lying areas around Cheyne Walk. The Chelsea Embankment was opened on 9 July 1874.

Chelsea Hospital adjacent to the Thames before Bazalgette built the Chelsea Embankment. (By courtesy of the Guildhall Library, Corporation of London)

London's First Electric Light

Bazalgette's work on the Victoria Embankment had not finished with its opening. Throughout its length it was decorated with cast-iron gas lamps in the shape of dolphins at intervals of 70 feet. These remain in use and are among the few surviving structures which bear the name of the Metropolitan Board of Works in the form of its initials, MBW. In 1878, on the occasion of the Paris Exhibition, the Avenue de l'Opéra had been lighted by electricity, using the Jablochkoff system created by a Russian émigré of that name. Many visitors to the exhibition had seen the electric lighting and it was suggested to the Board of Works, in the summer of 1878, that anything Paris could do should be done better by London. Street lighting was the responsibility of the vestries except for the Victoria Embankment, for which the Board was responsible. Bazalgette, on behalf of the Board, therefore entered into negotiation with the Jablochkoff company with a view to introducing the system to London by lighting the embankment. A generator was installed close to where the embankment station now stands and came into use in December 1878. It was used first to power twenty lights but eventually the whole embankment was lit by electricity from Westminster to Blackfriars. The new lighting was an object of great curiosity, attracting considerable crowds after nightfall but the rudimentary technology which was available before the days of Edison meant that it was more expensive than gas and not very reliable, failing at unpredictable and inconvenient times. The experiment nevertheless continued until June 1884 when the Jablochkoff company went bankrupt and the embankment reverted to gas lighting.[27]

The embankments were Bazalgette's most spectacular and celebrated work though in an interview in Cassell's *Saturday Journal* in 1890, the year before his death, he put the achievement into context by commenting that 'I get most credit for the Thames Embankment, but it wasn't anything like such a job as the drainage'. Full credit for the drainage came later, after his death, with the elimination of cholera but in the meantime the embankments received the warmest praise in the columns of *The Times*: 'For the principal engineer, of course, it will be a monument of enduring fame, second to none of the great achievements that have marked the Victorian age.' Immediately after the opening of the Chelsea Embankment in July 1874 Bazalgette received a much-deserved knighthood.

'For the principal engineer, of course, it will be a monument of enduring fame'

CHAPTER EIGHT

Thoroughfares, Housing and Open Spaces

Selfish opposition is sure to be offered by every separate division of London to any large scheme designed to benefit the whole capital.

(*The Times*, 1872)

London's Traffic Problems

Shortly before the Metropolitan Board of Works took office in 1856, there appeared a report from the Parliamentary Select Committee on Metropolitan Communications.[1] The report drew attention to the fact that, in the previous forty years, the population of the metropolis had more than doubled and that to the traffic generated by this greater population had been added the effects of passengers arriving daily from the suburbs at London's new railway stations. Almost eleven million passengers were arriving annually at London Bridge, eight million at Fenchurch Street and more than three million at Waterloo. The Select Committee considered a number of radical solutions, including a 'Crystal Way' proposed by an architect called Mr W. Mosley. Mosley proposed building a railway 12 feet below street level, running from St Paul's Cathedral to Oxford Circus, with a branch to Piccadilly Circus. It would be covered by a platform surmounted by a glass enclosure (hence the name Crystal) which would accommodate a walkway with shops on either side. While recognising the visionary nature of Mosley's plan the Select Committee preferred the 'Grand Girdle Railway and Boulevard under Glass' advocated by the 'apostle of glass', Sir Joseph Paxton, MP. Having successfully employed glass to house the Great Exhibition of 1851 Paxton now intended to use the same material to solve London's transport problems. In his evidence Paxton observed that in 1854 it took less time to travel from London Bridge to

Brighton than from London Bridge to Paddington. He proposed to construct an 11½ mile railway, above ground but under glass, linking all of London's railway termini and crossing the river three times. The glass covering was to exclude London's foul air, presumably because the smoke and steam generated by the trains within the arcades was deemed more acceptable than the stench of the sewers outside as the climax of the Great Stink approached.

Although they particularly commended Paxton's plan the Select Committee also made some more mundane, and realistic, recommendations. The members suggested that all tolls on roads and bridges should be removed; that new metropolitan through routes should be constructed (preferably through poorer areas to reduce the expense and, presumably, to reduce the inconvenience to people like themselves); and that the Metropolitan Railway (later contained within the Victoria Embankment) should connect London's railway termini. They also suggested that these several tasks should be the responsibility of the 'intended Metropolitan Board of Works' – which they duly became.

New Thoroughfares

These responsibilities, along with the main drainage, fell upon Bazalgette to manage and for the Board's report for 1858–9 he prepared a comprehensive list of proposals to this end. The Board's powers to execute such schemes, however, were inadequate in several important respects. In the first place, the Board was constrained by the fact that it was, by virtue of its constitution, a coalition of vestry interests and each vestry representative was as anxious to frustrate costly schemes that did not benefit his area as he was to promote schemes that did. Since even the most ambitious street improvements benefited only a minority of vestries there was an inbuilt majority against any scheme, particularly if it was bold, ambitious and therefore costly. In addition, the City Corporation had its own agenda, appearing to favour any scheme which brought traffic, and therefore business, to the City while opposing any that did not. In a report to the Board in 1872 Bazalgette referred to: 'evidence of strong prejudice in favour of all street improvements within, or leading directly towards the City, and an equally strong objection to any which do not appear to him [Haywood, the City Engineer] to lead the traffic direct into the City'.[2]

In 1866 *The Builder* criticised the lack of 'such a comprehensive plan, or design, as has been the basis for all the great works that have been achieved in Paris during the last few years'.[3] *The Builder* praised Baron Haussmann (1809–91), who at this time was rebuilding Paris both above and below ground, as Bazalgette was doing for London.

Each vestry representative was as anxious to frustrate costly schemes that did not benefit his area as he was to promote schemes that did

Haussmann was commended for his grand vision but *The Builder* overlooked the fact that the Prefect of the Seine had the support of the authoritarian government of Napoleon III in executing his plans and did not have to concern himself with the anxieties of vestrymen. *The Times*, in a leading article, commented on 'the selfish opposition which is sure to be offered by every separate division of London to any large scheme designed to benefit the whole capital'.[4]

Little Power and Less Money

The Board also had two more technical problems, one regulatory and one financial. The regulatory problem arose from the fact that the Board had no powers of compulsory purchase to implement its street improvements. Having prepared a scheme the Board had to submit it to the Home Secretary for his approval, just as it had been required to submit the main drainage plans to Sir Benjamin Hall. The Board had been rescued from the obstructions of Sir Benjamin by the onset of the Great Stink (see Chapter Three) but ministers were under no such pressure to increase the Board's powers in relation to street improvements. Having secured ministerial approval the Board would then have to embark upon tortuous negotiations with the owners of the various properties affected by the scheme, a process that often involved the appointment of an arbitrator. After the passage of the Artisans' and Labourers' Dwellings Improvement Act of 1875 the Home Secretary introduced an additional complication by insisting that the Board could not demolish the dwellings of more than fifteen labourers without first rehousing them which, given the limited availability of nearby building land, presented the Board with almost insurmountable problems. In its *Annual Report* for 1860–1 the Board described the problems involved in creating an extension to King Street, Covent Garden (later given its own name, Garrick Street). To build this street, 140 yards in length, the Board had negotiated with eighty-eight separate claimants with leasehold, freehold or trade interests. Their original claims for compensation amounted to £164,887 but after negotiation these were reduced to £97,687.[5]

The Board's financial problem arose from the fact that most of the Board's fund-raising and borrowing powers were taken up by its commitments to the main drainage and it was therefore under pressure, in its street improvements, to make them self-financing as far as possible. Having purchased the required properties, demolished them and built the new thoroughfare the Board then leased or sold to commercial interests the space facing on to the new street, thereby recovering as much as possible of its investment. In its final report the Board enumerated the forty-two major street

The Times commented on 'the selfish opposition which is sure to be offered by every separate division of London to any large scheme designed to benefit the whole capital'

improvement schemes which it had effected and explained that the gross cost of over £12,000,000 had, by this means, been reduced to £7,437,560.[6] However, this policy made it impossible for the Board to exercise as much influence as it would have wished over the buildings erected on the land thus sold. Northumberland Avenue is a good illustration of the consequences.

Northumberland Avenue

As construction of the Victoria Embankment progressed it became clear that it would be necessary to provide better access to this new thoroughfare from the direction of Trafalgar Square. The major obstacle to this scheme was Northumberland House, the London home of the Duke of Northumberland, which stood on the south side of Trafalgar Square, with extensive gardens stretching towards the river. In 1866 the Board approached the Duke and offered to purchase the property but the Duke, who had only succeeded to the title and the property the previous year, declined on the quite reasonable grounds that he wanted to enjoy the inheritance for which he had waited so long. The Board could have applied to the Home Secretary for compulsory purchase but the Duke commanded considerable support in Parliament, much of it through sentiment since Northumberland House was the last survivor of the noble palaces that had lined the Strand, from the Savoy westwards, since the time of John of Gaunt. In 1873, following the death of the Duke, the Board approached his successor who took a more cavalier, and commercial, view of his ancestral home. He was more than happy to sell it to the Board for the enormous sum of £500,000 but this huge outlay, together with the other costs of constructing the street, put the Board under more pressure than usual to sell the adjoining land for buildings which, when completed, did not do justice to what should have been one of the noblest thoroughfares in London. Northumberland Avenue opened in 1876 and was swiftly lined with buildings whose height was out of proportion to the width of this fairly narrow street. The *Daily News* commented in 1885: 'To every eye, Northumberland Avenue is one of the saddest of thoroughfares . . . the Avenue is too high for its width or too narrow for its height.'[7] As a result of its policy of land sales the net cost of Northumberland was nothing but we live with the architectural consequences.

'To every eye, Northumberland Avenue is one of the saddest of thoroughfares'

Park Lane

In one case the Board's plans met such opposition that a distressed resident of Mayfair offered to buy them out. The Board had recognised the need for a widening of Park Lane to provide better access from Pimlico to Oxford Street. This involved turning the select residential area of Hamilton Place, which was Crown land, from a cul-de-sac into a thoroughfare. The residents were well-connected people and the Board's plans became the subject of a Parliamentary Select Committee which heard representations from three dukes, numerous nobles of lesser rank and two vestries (who, being far from Park Lane, were simply worried that they might have to help to pay for the improvements). Sir Richard Mayne, Commissioner of the Metropolitan Police, testified that 'since the opening of the Victoria Station in Pimlico'[8] traffic from that area to Marble Arch had become unmanageable and he strongly supported the proposed road widening. Despite the objections of the local nobility the Select Committee unanimously supported the Board's plans and this resulted in the passage of the Park Lane Improvements Act 1869 which gave it the authority to proceed. The Board then received a letter from a solicitor representing a 'lady resident of Park Lane' expressing 'her wish of placing at the disposal of your Board, as a free gift, the sum of fifty thousand pounds, provided that you find it practicable to suspend operations for the opening of Hamilton Place'.[9] The Board declined the offer.

St Martin in the Fields

It was more responsive to the parishioners of St Martin in the Fields who, unsurprisingly, objected to the fact that the Board's plans for creating the new Charing Cross Road involved slicing through the steps that adorn the church's fine classical portico and bricking up the portico itself. It is hard to fault the parishioners' petition which claimed that 'with the steps removed, and the front walled up, the portico would appear unmeaning, and would be an architectural monstrosity'.[10] The petitioners had made their point and Bazalgette realigned the road to spare the steps.

The parishioners' petition claimed that the portico would be an architectural monstrosity

Benefactors: Albert Grant and Leicester Square

The Board received some offers of financial assistance that it did feel able to accept. The Duke of Bedford, who owned Covent Garden, was anxious to improve access to the fruit and vegetable market and made a contribution of £15,000 towards the cost of what eventually became Garrick Street. A more altruistic and ostensibly more generous offer was made by a City financier called Albert Grant to assist the Board in developing Leicester Square, an embarrassing slum in the midst of one of London's most fashionable areas.[11] The district took its name

ALBERT GRANT, 1830–99

Born in Dublin as Abraham Gottheimer, he changed his name to Grant in 1863 and made his fortune as a 'company promoter'. An early exponent of the black art of direct mailing, he obtained names and addresses of clergymen, widows and other small investors and persuaded them to subscribe for shares in a series of doubtful enterprises in return for promises of fabulous returns, earning himself handsome commissions in the process. Schemes included the Cadiz Waterworks, the Imperial Bank of China, the Labuan Coal Company and the Emma Silver Mine. In his lifetime he raised £24,000,000 from hopeful investors, of which £20,000,000 was lost, none of it his. In 1873 he spent some of this doubtful fortune on a huge house near Kensington Palace which he used once, for a 'Bachelors Ball'. It was promptly seized by angry creditors who demolished it, sold the land and gave the main staircase to Madame Tussaud's. Grant sat as MP for Kidderminster and was bankrupted twice. In June 1877 he was the object of eighty-nine actions against him in the courts. After being made a 'hereditary Baron of the Kingdom of Italy' for unspecified philanthropic services to that newly formed nation, he insisted on being addressed as 'Baron Grant'. He died in penury in 1899, his obituary notice in the *Illustrated London News* recording that he was 'a man of agreeable presence and enthusiastic manners' whose death 'brought back to mind many an ancient adventure of his as company promoter, mineowner, millionaire and bankrupt'.

Albert Grant (born Abraham Gottheimer), whose legendary generosity with other people's money paid for the redevelopment of Leicester Square. (By courtesy of the National Portrait Gallery, London)

from Leicester House, the London home of the Earls of Leicester, which had been built in 1636. The future George II, as Prince of Wales, had taken up residence there in the eighteenth century and used it as a base from which to pursue his endless quarrels with his estranged father, George I. Later in the century it became the home of George II's son, Frederick Prince of Wales, who used it for the same purpose, setting up a court of his own to rival that of his father, now George II. In 1737, as an additional annoyance to his father, Frederick unveiled a gilded equestrian statue of George I. In 1806 Leicester House was demolished and the square became derelict. The statue was vandalised, losing its rider quite early in the process, and the horse itself was painted with spots by early graffiti artists. Numerous entrepreneurs tried to revive the fortunes of the square by constructing various vehicles for public entertainment including, in 1850, a 'Panopticon' display of scientific exhibits and, the same year, 'Mr Wylde's Great Globe' which purported to be a panoramic view of the Earth. As these descended into bankruptcy they added to the general air of decay which pervaded the square, and in 1865 a gas explosion demolished a prominent building on the northern side of the square, leaving a heap of blackened rubble. Proposals to redevelop the area were obstructed by the fact that the numerous holders of freehold and leasehold property in the square were holding out for extravagant compensation for giving up their interests in their crumbling properties. In 1873, following an approach from a group of local residents called the 'Leicester Square Defence Committee', the Master of the Rolls adjudged that the land should not be used for building, thereby greatly reducing its value. Following this judgement Albert Grant approached the principal landowner, Mr J.A. Tulk, bought out his interest and then drove harder bargains with the remaining owners. Grant offered to redevelop the square at his own expense, landscape and adorn it with four statues of distinguished former residents, and donate it to the Board's care.

In 1865 a gas explosion demolished a prominent building on the northern side of the square, leaving a heap of blackened rubble

Grant's offer to refurbish Leicester Square was timely. He spent £13,000 buying up the land and a further £15,000 developing it to a plan approved by Bazalgette and Vulliamy, the Board's architect. His gesture was described by *The Metropolitan* as 'certainly one of the most appropriate, timely and munificent gifts which could have been made to the Metropolis'.[12] The Board gladly accepted so we have Albert Grant to thank for the fact that Leicester Square remains a large open space in a crowded part of London. The statues have survived two world wars and are of Newton, Hogarth, Joshua Reynolds and the pioneering surgeon John Hunter (1728–93) who had kept his collection of 10,500 anatomical specimens in his house in the square. The statue of Shakespeare which stands above the fountain in the middle of the square also bears a tribute to Albert Grant. The square was handed over to the Board on 2 July 1874, an event which was generously covered by the press.[13] A statue of Charlie Chaplin has since been added to those given by Albert Grant.

The Board, in its final Report, was able to describe forty-two major improvements to London's thoroughfares, consisting either of new streets or streets which had been so extended or realigned as to make

Opening Queen Victoria Street, 1871. (*Illustrated London News*)

them virtually new. The best-known of these are: Shaftesbury Avenue; Southwark Street; Northumberland Avenue; Garrick Street; Queen Victoria Street; Theobalds Road; Great Eastern Street; and Charing Cross Road. To these, of course, should be added the

The eastern end of the new Queen Victoria Street, 1883. (By courtesy of the Guildhall Library, Corporation of London)

Victoria, Albert and Chelsea Embankments which, though designed for other purposes as well, provided much-needed roads in congested parts of the metropolis.

River Crossings

The Select Committee on Metropolitan Communications had recommended that one of the tasks of the Board should be to secure the abolition of tolls. When the Metropolitan Board took office in 1856 the only toll-free crossings of the Thames within the metropolis were London, Blackfriars and Westminster bridges, to which Southwark Bridge was added when the owners were bought out by the City Corporation in 1866, using funds from the City's Bridge House Trust.[14] All the other Thames bridges outside the City had been built with private capital and carried tolls. In 1869 the ever-reliable coal and wine duties were devoted to freeing from tolls bridges outside the metropolitan boundary at Kew, Kingston, Walton, Staines and Hampton Court. The Board recognised the need for more toll-free crossings and in 1876 presented a Bill which would authorise it to free the remaining bridges from tolls. The Select Committee which considered the Bill drew attention to the harmful effect of the system of tolls upon commerce and upon the labouring population. It estimated that a labourer living in the cheaper southern district and working in the north would have to pay 24s a year in tolls out of an annual wage of about £40 to £50. The Select Committee was irritated to learn that the shares of bridge companies had shot up in value when it became known that the Board might be purchasing them. Waterloo Bridge, built by John Rennie in 1817, had never made any money for its shareholders since travellers made detours to the free bridges at Blackfriars and Westminster. When the Metropolitan Board advertised its intention to introduce its Bill the value of the shares rose from £2 to £12 (though their nominal value was £100).[15]

It didn't do them much good. After the passing of the Metropolitan Toll Bridges Act in 1877, Bazalgette's survey revealed that the foundations of the bridge had been allowed to fall into a very poor condition and the bridge, which had cost £1,054,000 to build, was bought by the Board for £474,200, a further £62,705 being spent immediately, on Bazalgette's direction, on strengthening the foundations.[16] A further £98,000 was paid to free from tolls the nearby footbridge (Hungerford Bridge). The freeing of Waterloo Bridge from tolls occurred at midday on Saturday 5 October 1878 and was reported as a great event. As midday approached pedestrians obstructed the entrance to the bridge as each competed to be the last to pay the

A labourer living in the cheaper southern district and working in the north would have to pay 24s a year in tolls out of an annual wage of about £40 to £50

halfpenny toll. The toll-keepers, wearing their white aprons with huge pockets, finally stood aside, guns were fired in salute from the Surrey shore and crowds surged across the toll-free bridge.[17]

In May 1879 a more elaborate ceremony attended the freeing of the Lambeth, Chelsea, Battersea, Albert and Vauxhall bridges at a cost to the Board of £535,974. The Prince and Princess of Wales declared the bridges open and then symbolically drove over each in turn. It was a great occasion. Chelsea pensioners paraded, guns fired in salute, flotillas of boats were bedecked with flags, choirs of children sang 'God bless the Prince of Wales' and the 4-mile route was lined with flags and cheering crowds.[18] A year later a similar ceremony was enacted as the last three bridges were freed at Wandsworth, Hammersmith and Putney. These cost £223,311. Bazalgette's surveys of the structures showed that the Albert Bridge could be rendered structurally sound with expenditure of £25,367. Hammersmith, the first Thames suspension bridge, had been opened in 1827 but it was too narrow to accommodate the volume of traffic which resulted from the abolition of tolls. When Bazalgette reported that bits of it had started to fall off it was closed, widened and substantially reconstructed at a cost of £82,177.[19]

The bridges at Battersea and Putney were beyond repair. The wooden bridge at Battersea had been financed by Earl Spencer in 1772. It was demolished and replaced by Bazalgette's five-arch

Hammersmith bridge on boat race day; note the narrow entrance arch which was inadequate for the traffic which flowed across it when tolls were abolished; Bazalgette rebuilt the bridge and widened the arches. (*Illustrated London News*)

Old Battersea bridge; this was
to be replaced by Bazalgette's
iron structure. (By courtesy of
the Guildhall Library,
Corporation of London)

design, costing £112,000, which was opened by the Earl of Rosebery, chairman of the LCC, in July 1890. Putney Bridge had a longer history. Prior to 1729 there had been no bridge between London Bridge and Kingston, the long intervening stretch of the river being served by thirty-six ferries. In 1642 a bridge of boats was built between Fulham and Putney by the Parliamentarians for military purposes in the Civil War and in 1729 the site was chosen for a new wooden bridge, then called Fulham Bridge, built by a company whose shareholders included the Prime Minister, Robert Walpole. By 1880, when the bridge was freed from tolls, the bridge was too weak and too narrow for the large volumes of traffic which resulted from the abolition of tolls. The decrepit wooden bridge was replaced by Bazalgette's handsome granite bridge which cost £405,438 and was opened in May 1886. The new approaches to the bridge which Bazalgette constructed to accommodate the greater volume of traffic prompted the landlord of the Eight Bells, Fulham, to sue the Board for loss of trade. He was awarded £1,000 compensation.[20] All these bridges remain in use though Putney Bridge was widened in 1931.

The Board recognised that, while one-third of the inhabitants of the metropolis lived downstream of the City, they had no means of crossing the Thames without travelling up to London Bridge, whereas the remaining two-thirds had fourteen toll-free bridges between London Bridge and Putney. In 1878, to remedy this situation, Bazalgette produced a plan for a single-span bridge near the place where Tower Bridge now stands. Long spiral approach roads would enable pedestrian and vehicular traffic to cross the river

Old Putney Bridge, wooden and decrepit before Bazalgette replaced it with the present stone bridge. (By courtesy of the Guildhall Library, Corporation of London)

Old Putney bridge to the right awaits demolition, while Bazalgette's new bridge takes shape to the left. (*The Metropolitan*)

Four alternative designs submitted for the proposed Tower bridge. Bazalgette's design (above) was rejected in favour of a modified version of the 'bascule' design (bottom right) (*Graphic*/By courtesy of the Guildhall Library, Corporation of London)

at sufficient height to enable ships to pass below within the Pool of London. He also proposed two tunnels, one at Blackwall and one at Rotherhithe. Finally, he proposed two free ferries, one at Woolwich and the other near Greenwich. The last of these was abandoned because of objections and demands for compensation from existing ferry owners, though in 1902 the LCC built a foot-tunnel. The other proposals were eventually executed and remain in use. Even so, they encountered the sort of factional opposition with which Bazalgette was by now thoroughly familiar. The City Corporation responded to his suggestion for a crossing at the Tower by commenting that 'the need for any bridge or tunnel did not seem sufficiently proved to justify the Corporation taking part in the promotion of a scheme' while the vestry of St Olave's, on the opposite bank, complained that the bridge 'will have a prejudicial effect on the value of a large amount of property in the parish'.[21]

The City's hostile reaction may have been prompted by something more than the normal hostility that its representatives showed to initiatives of the Metropolitan Board. Sir Horace Jones, the City architect, had floated the idea of a suspension bridge across the Thames and appears to have been offended that Bazalgette had put forward his proposal without consulting him. An anonymous pamphleteer, writing as 'Aquarius', attacked Bazalgette, his bridge and the very idea of a crossing at the Tower in 1878.[22] Despite their initial misgivings the City Corporation soon adopted Bazalgette's proposal for a crossing at the Tower, though not his design. Having examined several proposals they adopted the famous 'Bascule' design by Sir Horace Jones and the engineer Sir John Wolfe Barry, which opened on 30 June 1894. In 1887 the Board obtained Parliamentary authority for the construction of Blackwall Tunnel and one of Bazalgette's, and the Board's, last official acts was to let the contracts for its construction. The works for the Woolwich Free Ferry were completed shortly after the Board handed over to the London County Council on 1 January 1889 and Bazalgette retired.

Labourers' Dwellings

The creation of new streets was frequently achieved by the demolition of large numbers of insalubrious tenements and in 1875 the Artisans' and Labourers' Dwellings Improvements Act made this another of the Board's responsibilities. The problems inherited by the Board were well described by the great philanthropist the Earl of Shaftesbury in evidence to the Royal Commission on the Housing of the Working Classes in 1884. He described a visit he had made in the 1850s to the infamous Frying Pan Alley, Holborn, which was demolished in one of the Board's improvement schemes. He told of a conversation with a woman sitting by a hole in her floor, quoting her thus: 'Look there, at that great hole; the landlord will not mend it. I have every night to sit up and watch, or my husband sits up to watch, because that hole is over a common sewer, and the rats come up, sometimes twenty at a time, and if we did not watch them they would eat the baby up.' Likewise, houses in low-lying Bermondsey had been built on makeshift piles in an island of foul water and sewage, known as 'Jacob's Island', from which the residents drew their water for washing and drinking. As a result of the Board's improvement schemes Frying Pan Alley was demolished and Bazalgette's intercepting sewer turned Bermondsey from a sewage-laden swamp into dry land with sanitary housing.[23]

> *'That hole is over a common sewer, and the rats come up, sometimes twenty at a time, and if we did not watch them they would eat the baby up'*

The Act conferred upon the Board the duty to clear away any dwellings declared by a Medical Officer of Health to be unfit for human habitation. Faced with such a request from a Medical Officer the Board was required to submit a proposed improvement plan to the Home Secretary for his approval. The Board then had to undertake the laborious and time-consuming task of checking the titles of the numerous tenants and property owners who could be relied upon to come forward with claims for compensation. The Home Secretary would then appoint an arbitrator to adjudicate on compensation claims from the property owners, a process which could itself take twelve months. The owners then had to be given three months' notice to quit.[24] As in the procedure for building new streets, noted above, this could be both time-consuming and expensive, not least since property owners could be awarded compensation for their properties as 'going concerns' even though they had been declared unfit for use. Further delays then ensued since the Board had to rehouse the displaced tenants in already overcrowded areas before work could begin. The construction of Charing Cross Road took so long, over six years, that it prompted a Parliamentary question. The delay was due to the fact that the work involved demolishing the notorious St Giles tenements at the north end of the present road. In connection with this development the Board was criticised by the coroner for Central Middlesex for causing the death of a child who had been evicted from a tenement building in the path of the road. The child and her parents, with three siblings, had moved into a room in the grandmother's house and had, said the coroner, died 'from suffocation through want of fresh air'.[25] The legislation was amended so that compensation was awarded on an 'unfit for use' basis and the problems were eased when the Board was permitted to resell land for commercial use and rehouse tenants elsewhere provided they could travel to work by workmen's trains. The legislation was certainly needed. In 1876, the year after the Act was passed, the Board received twelve representations from Medical Officers covering twenty-three schemes. The Board's annual reports gave the details of each scheme and the final report described twenty-two dwelling improvement schemes involving the demolition of 7,403 tenements and the rehousing of 38,231 people at a total cost, after land sales, of £1,500,000.[26]

The child and her parents had died 'from suffocation through want of fresh air'

Parks and Open Spaces[27]

The Metropolitan Board was also responsible for acquiring, creating or extending many of London's parks and open spaces at a time when the 'fresh air' they contained was regarded by orthodox miasmatists like Florence Nightingale as being especially important to health.[28] Battersea Park, Kennington Park, Clissold Park in Stoke Newington, Victoria Park in Hackney, Blackheath and Clapham Common were acquired, developed and sometimes extended under Bazalgette's direction. Often the Board became engaged in complex and expensive negotiations over grazing or manorial rights whose precise character was lost in medieval times. Thus the Board paid £90,000 to buy out 'grazing rights' on Hackney Downs and further sums to acquire Hampstead Heath, Kenwood and Parliament Hill Fields. The Board was negotiating to buy Epping Forest when, to its great indignation, it was made to look dilatory and parsimonious by its ancient rival the City Corporation which in 1872, in an outflanking manoeuvre, successfully promoted two Parliamentary Bills: one to give it the right to purchase the forest and one to levy a tax on grain to meet the cost. Each of the new parks had to be surveyed and assessed by Bazalgette and his engineers before being acquired and in some cases considerable work had to be done afterwards on draining and landscaping before they could be opened to the public. Ravenscourt Park and Dulwich Park were acquired and landscaped while the 63-acre Southwark Park was opened in 1869 after £99,740 had been spent clearing and landscaping the site. In the same year the 115-acre Finsbury Park was opened, £111,000 being spent by Bazalgette on draining and landscaping work. By the time the Board left office in 1889 it was managing 2,603 acres of public parks.[29]

Previous chapters have been concerned with those works for which Bazalgette is most remembered: the intercepting sewers and the embankments which housed them. Yet as this chapter has shown, he has other claims to a place in the history of London. Without the streets and bridges which he designed and constructed, Victorian London would have been overwhelmed by its traffic. The families, amounting to almost forty thousand people, who were rehoused in the dwellings that were built as a result of his street improvements probably did not know his name but many of them would not have survived if they had been obliged to remain in their rat-infested tenements. All the parks he created remain to this day in densely populated areas of modern London. The millions who use his parks, streets and bridges every day rarely speculate about how they came to be built. Without Sir Joseph Bazalgette they might never have existed at all.

CHAPTER NINE

Conclusion

Londoners who can remember the state of London and of the Thames about thirty-five years ago, before those vast undertakings of the Metropolitan Board of Works, the system of Main Drainage and the magnificent Thames Embankment, which have contributed so much to sanitary improvement and to the convenience and stateliness of this immense city, will regret the death of the able official chief engineer, Sir Joseph Bazalgette.

(Illustrated London News, 1891)

In 1889 the Metropolitan Board of Works was replaced as the metropolitan authority by the newly constituted London County Council (LCC). The members of the Metropolitan Board had been elected by vestries but with the advent of the LCC London acquired its first directly elected government. The first chairman of the LCC was the future Prime Minister, Lord Rosebery and one of his first duties was the opening of Battersea Bridge which Bazalgette had designed. Bazalgette retired when the Metropolitan Board of Works handed over to the new body and lived for only two further years in his home near Wimbledon, dying on 15 March 1891. His passing was noted with lengthy and appreciative obituaries in the national and London newspapers and in the *Proceedings* of the Institution of Civil Engineers, of which he had been President in 1883/4.

This book began by describing the critical condition of the River Thames in the hot summer of 1858 and proceeded to ask the question: Who was Joseph Bazalgette? The purpose of this examination of Bazalgette's work has been to assess his claim to a place in the ranks of nineteenth-century engineers alongside celebrities like Brunel who, not long before his death in 1859, supported Bazalgette in his application for the post of Chief Engineer to the Metropolitan Board which he occupied for the thirty-three years of its existence.[1] It would not be appropriate to labour the comparison with Brunel but a few points of reference will help to put Bazalgette's achievements in perspective. In the pages that follow

His passing was noted with lengthy and appreciative obituaries in the national and London newspapers

I will attempt to form a judgement of Bazalgette's work by reference to five criteria: the scale and complexity of the works he executed; his contribution to the developing concept of municipal management; the enterprise he showed in executing his great engineering works, especially in the use of new materials; the consequences of this for his fellow-citizens, especially for their health; and the personal qualities he needed to display.

Scale and Complexity

During the time that he held office, Bazalgette was responsible for executing well over twenty million pounds worth of works on behalf of the Metropolitan Board: a little over £4,000,000 on the main drainage; £2,500,000 on the embankments; £12,000,000 on streets; about £700,000 on strengthening and re-building bridges; about £1,500,000 (after deductions for land sales) on housing; and about £300,000 on clearing, laying out and landscaping parks. These sums mean little in 1999 but, for purposes of comparison, it may be observed that Brunel's Great Western railway cost about £8,000,000 and his SS *Great Britain* less than £200,000 so by contemporary standards Bazalgette's works were of the highest order of magnitude.

About half of the money spent on Bazalgette's works was devoted to street improvements and associated clearance of slum properties.[2] Nearly forty thousand people were moved from condemned, insanitary properties to newly built ones and, in the process, a number of celebrated London thoroughfares were created to deal with the traffic which resulted from the expansion and prosperity of Victorian London. For the same reasons all the bridges crossing the Thames were freed from tolls and Bazalgette was responsible for rebuilding or strengthening them to cope with the resulting increase in traffic. At Bazalgette's suggestion, the Woolwich Free Ferry was introduced to afford a means of crossing the Thames to the one-third of London's citizens who lived downstream of London Bridge and his work continued after his retirement and death as the tunnels he had proposed (and in the case of the Blackwall tunnel designed) were completed by his successors.

Nearly forty thousand people were moved from condemned, insanitary properties to newly built ones

Bazalgette's most conspicuous works were the Victoria, Albert and Chelsea Embankments, and it is not surprising that it was on the first of these that his monument was placed in 1901, ten years after his death. Paradoxically, his small monument, a bust set into the embankment wall beneath Charing Cross railway bridge, is dwarfed by a much larger monument to Brunel a short distance away though Brunel played no part in its design and died before work on it began. The embankments reclaimed 52 acres of land from the river which provided not only footways and parks but also much-needed thoroughfares, notably between the City and Westminster, to supplement the badly congested route from Ludgate Hill via Fleet Street and the Strand. However, although he appreciated the importance of the embankments, Bazalgette himself recognised that the main drainage was his greatest achievement. He put the work in context in his own words in his interview with Cassell's *Saturday Journal* less than a year before his death:[3]

> I get most credit for the Thames Embankment, but it wasn't anything like such a job as the drainage . . . The fall in the river isn't above three inches a mile; for sewage we want a fall of a couple of feet and that kept taking us down below the river and when we got to a certain depth we had to pump up again. It was certainly a very troublesome job. We would sometimes spend weeks in drawing out plans and then suddenly come across some railway or canal that upset everything, and we had to begin all over again. It was tremendously hard work. I was living over at Morden then and often used to drive down there from my office at twelve or one o'clock in the morning.

'I get most credit for the Thames Embankment, but it wasn't anything like such a job as the drainage'

Bazalgette was also responsible for supervising the reconstruction of the huge network of smaller sewers which had been inherited from the earlier sewers commissions and which fed into the intercepting system. The initial plans were drawn up by the vestries but they all had to be checked, often amended and finally approved by Bazalgette and his team of engineers. Each of the Metropolitan Board's *Annual Reports* from 1857 to 1888 includes an account of the sewers thus approved by Bazalgette, amounting to almost 1,200 miles of sewers. Bazalgette's work was not confined to London. Between 1858 and 1875 he produced, as a consultant, thirty-two reports on drainage works for British communities beyond the metropolis, and a further report on the drainage of communities overseas, including Budapest and Mauritius.[4]

Municipal Management

In 1991, to mark the hundredth anniversary of Bazalgette's death, the Institution of Civil Engineers organised an exhibition called 'Civil Engineering in the Victorian City' which celebrated the contribution made by Bazalgette to the development of effective municipal management through such activities as sanitary engineering, slum clearance and road-building programmes. The Metropolitan Board of Works was London's first metropolitan government and, as we have seen, its establishment did not occur

without controversy and much opposition. The idea that London
should have a metropolitan government, with powers to raise money
from all ratepayers and spend it on large projects, was fiercely
opposed by a multitude of interests, some of which were wedded to
the idea that vestries and paving boards were the appropriate
repositories of such authority while others feared that 'there was a
danger that the proposed local Parliament of forty-two members
would discuss politics instead of sewerage questions, and threaten to
overshadow the authority of the Speaker and that of the Imperial
Parliament'.[5] The original Metropolis Local Management Act had
attempted to placate both of these interest groups by giving
Parliament, in the form of the Chief Commissioner of Works, the
power to veto any significant expenditure; and by giving local
ratepayers the right to appeal against the rates levied on them by the
Board if they felt that the rates were excessive in relation to the local
benefits. The Amendment Act which Disraeli pushed through the
house in the face of the 'Great Stink' removed both of these restraints
and thereby created a more powerful body than had been intended. If
the Board had been less than highly successful in executing its great
engineering projects under Bazalgette's direction, its critics could
easily have argued that it was the nature of its authority which was at
fault and argued for a reversion to vestry government or, indeed, the
management of the metropolis from Whitehall. As it was,
controversy over the corruption of some of its officials clouded the
Board's final years[6] but the principle of metropolitan government
survived, to be inherited by the London County Council in 1889.
Bazalgette, as the Board's longest-serving and most prominent
officer, thus made an important contribution to the establishment of
the concept of representative metropolitan government. If he had
failed in the design and execution of his great works the concept of
local government for great cities would have received a possibly fatal
blow.

A New Profession and New Materials

At the time that Bazalgette was executing the main drainage works
the Civil Engineering profession was rapidly developing, as were
many of the techniques and materials used by its practitioners. The
Institution of Civil Engineers had been founded in 1818, the year
before Bazalgette's birth, with the elderly Thomas Telford becoming
its first president in 1820. Telford encouraged the practice of having
papers read to weekly meetings of the Institution. These papers were
then discussed and, from the time of James Walker's presidency
(1834–45), they were recorded in its *Proceedings*. It was on such bases

If he had failed in the design and execution of his great works the concept of local government for great cities would have received a possibly fatal blow

that the profession accumulated its knowledge and experience in these early years and by mid-century the pupillage system, from which Bazalgette had gained his own training in the service of John MacNeill, was well established. Nevertheless, at the time that Bazalgette was working there were still practitioners who had learned their trade in the most rudimentary manner such as Mr Phillips, Chief Surveyor to the Westminster Commissioners, who told the Metropolitan Sanitary Commission in 1847:

> I went to work when I was eight years old, as a bricklayer; I never had the slightest education. The little I do know I have taught myself . . . Some few months ago the members of the Institution of Civil Engineers did me the honour to elect me an Associate of that Institution.[7]

I went to work when I was eight years old, as a bricklayer; I never had the slightest education

Thomas Brassey, one of Bazalgette's principal contractors, had been apprenticed to a land surveyor. It was upon such experience that Bazalgette frequently depended to execute his plans and he later played his full part in advancing the professionalism of civil engineering. He took on pupils as he had himself been taken on by John MacNeill; he presented numerous papers on his work; and he encouraged his officers, notably John Grant, to do likewise. In the circumstances it is not surprising that, in choosing contractors, he preferred to work with those who had done good work for him in the past even if their prices were a little higher, though as we have seen this caused him some embarrassment in his choice of Furness for the northern reservoir.[8]

Bazalgette's decision to use Portland cement in the construction of the intercepting sewers and the Albert Embankment mark him out as a pioneer in the use of this material and in the development of effective quality control techniques in this young industry. Bazalgette's decision to use it for the first time in a major civil engineering project may be regarded as bold. He was also generous enough to give John Grant most of the credit for the work that Grant had carried out under Bazalgette's direction:

> The improved manufacture of Portland cement up to the present time has been promoted by the careful experiments of Mr Grant. Portland cement concrete could now be used with advantage and safety where brickwork and stonework were previously used, thus effecting a large economy in engineering works.[9]

The manufacturer G.F. White, who had advocated the use of the material in a paper presented at the Institution in May 1852,[10] observed in the discussion of Grant's first paper that the Board's engineers had been the first to use effective testing procedures on the product.[11] The material became a standard for the industry, which it remains to this day. Bazalgette's decision to give Grant a central role in experimenting with the new material confirms that the earlier skirmish over pipe sewers had not blinded him to Grant's qualities as an engineer (see Chapter 4, page 67).

The End of Cholera Epidemics

The most startling phrase from the quotation in the Introduction (page 3) is the claim that Bazalgette probably 'saved more lives than any single Victorian public official'. A comparison of Bazalgette's work with that of other Victorian figures such as Edwin Chadwick and Florence Nightingale is unlikely to generate any satisfactory quantitative assessment of such a claim. However, a century after his death there is no longer any serious doubt that the elimination of cholera and other epidemics from the metropolis was caused by the fact that the main drainage, when completed, played a major part in protecting the water supply from cholera, typhoid and other water-borne infections: a fact of which his successors, who now manage the system he created, are fully aware.[12]

The main drainage played a major part in protecting the water supply from cholera, typhoid and other water-borne infections

Nevertheless, at the time of Bazalgette's death in 1891, many well-qualified authorities failed to recognise the clarity of the link between epidemics and infected water, persisting in the belief that a 'miasma' of foul air was the cause, despite mounting evidence to the contrary. The convictions of Edwin Chadwick and the early scepticism of figures like John Simon and William Farr have already been noted but there could be no better illustration of the reluctance to abandon the miasmatic explanation of infection than the experience of Hamburg, whose severe cholera epidemic in 1892 caused some anxiety in London, despite the fact that twenty-five years had passed since London's last epidemic. In the 1860s and 1870s Hamburg's drainage system had been rebuilt on the advice of an Englishman, William Lindley, who based his design on that of London. However, the system suffered from two serious defects. As late as the 1890s about twenty thousand inhabitants were left unconnected to the system, their waste being stored in leaking cesspools similar to those which had caused such problems in London in the 1840s. The second defect concerned the means of sewage disposal. It was emptied, in its raw state, into the River Elbe where tidal conditions ensured that it flowed up and down the city's shoreline, much of it entering the city's canals, whence it could make its way into other watercourses. In 1885 a zoologist published an article entitled 'The Fauna of the Hamburg Water Main' in which he identified sixty species of organisms, while several contemporaries reported finding eels and fish in the water mains.[13] The situation invites comparison with the London of the 'Great Stink' and with the condition of the East London company's water supply in the 1866 outbreak.[14]

A further comparison with London of the 1860s is to be found in the scepticism with which the Hamburg city authorities greeted the idea that infected water was the cause of cholera epidemics. In 1883 the Prussian scientist Robert Koch had visited Calcutta and succeeded in isolating and identifying the cholera bacillus. He returned to Prussia to be fêted and honoured by the Emperor and, when cholera broke out in Hamburg in 1892, the Prussian government gave him what amounted to dictatorial powers in the face of an outbreak in which recorded mortality rates were twice the levels recorded in London's worst outbreak of 1849. Nevertheless Koch encountered the same scepticism that had greeted Snow's hypothesis. The newspaper *Hamburger Fremdenblatt* scorned the idea that the bacillus caused the disease. At the same time the Burgomeister complained that during the 1892 outbreak 'it was the Imperial Health Office and Professor Koch who ran things here'.

The anxiety felt in London at the proximity of the 1892 outbreak was justified by precedent. The previous epidemics, including that of 1866, were all believed to have entered through major ports and the authorities were sufficiently alarmed to commission a report on the subject.[15] There was no epidemic and, at the very least, it may be argued that Bazalgette's now complete main drainage system saved the metropolis from the epidemic that devastated Hamburg, killing 8,605 people in a city one-seventh the size of London. If the epidemic had struck London to the same degree that it struck Hamburg, the deaths in the metropolis would have exceeded those of the four previous epidemics combined.

Bazalgette's now complete main drainage system saved the metropolis from the epidemic that devastated Hamburg, killing 8,605 people in a city one-seventh the size of London

Personal Qualities

Bazalgette's laconic description[16] of the difficulties that he overcame in designing and constructing the main drainage draws attention to an aspect of his character which is frequently glimpsed in his public statements and writings: a dogged patience that carried him through many controversies. He was not an entrepreneur in the heroic mould like Brunel. Unlike Brunel he did not have to raise the money for his great works, this being left to the Metropolitan Board. His brief period as an independent consultant during the Railway Mania led to a breakdown in his health and a year's recuperation was required before he became a public servant as assistant surveyor to the Metropolitan Sewers Commission.[17] Bazalgette had the considerable advantage of working within the framework of an organisation, the Metropolitan Board of Works, whose authority over the governance of the metropolis had been won after many battles waged by others.

On the other hand, Bazalgette often had to demonstrate heroic patience when dealing with or placating politicians, vestrymen and Board members. These qualities of detachment were evident during the battles over the position of the outfalls which preceded the 'Great Stink' of 1858 and, particularly, during the later disputes with Captain Calver over the shoals which had supposedly been formed in the vicinity of the outfalls as the result of sewage deposits. During the dispute Bazalgette had been subjected to some hostile criticism of a personal nature[18] but when an independent enquiry upheld the Board's view against those of Captain Calver Bazalgette contented himself with observing that 'Captain Calver's imaginary sewage zone in the lower reaches of the river can have no existence'. It is hard to imagine Brunel showing such restraint.

It is hard to imagine Brunel showing such restraint

Only once did Bazalgette allow his objectivity to be seriously compromised, during the 'pipe sewer' controversy which occurred during the time that he was working as Engineer to the Sewers Commission and in which he showed himself rather too anxious to be loyal to the organisation which employed him. Following the controversy over Bazalgette's thoroughly biased report, of which John Thwaites was highly critical in his account of the episode,[19] the Metropolitan Commissioners asked their five district engineers to report on their pipe sewers, including those that Bazalgette had criticised in his report. None of the five supported Bazalgette directly though some were muted in their criticism of the report of their superior. John Grant, however, was less inhibited, commenting that: 'Had the former examination been as full, and accompanied by similar explanations, the diffusion of a considerable amount of error would have been prevented, and the benefits of good drainage immensely extended.'[20]

This was harsh criticism from a subordinate and there followed an exchange of correspondence in which Bazalgette tried to excuse any errors on the grounds that he had had to prepare his reports in great haste, while Grant continued to press his criticism. The exchanges ended with Bazalgette implying that he was considering suing Grant. It says much for both men that Bazalgette later appointed Grant as one of his principal assistants at the Metropolitan Board, gave him responsibility for the critical experiments with Portland cement and gave Grant full credit for the work and for the 'large economy in engineering works' which it helped to achieve.

A Victorian patriarch:
Sir Joseph and Lady Bazalgette
with their children and
grandchildren in 1890, a year
before Sir Joseph's death.
(Derek Bazalgette)

Bazalgette also enjoyed a harmonious relationship with Thwaites, despite the earlier disagreement and the predictions of *The Observer*.[21] It is hard to imagine the more flamboyant Brunel making such a ready accommodation.

Bazalgette's obituary in the *Proceedings* of the Institution of Civil Engineers summarises the personal qualities that enabled him to carry out his great work in the face of difficulties that others had found insurmountable: 'Although of small stature and somewhat delicate health, he possessed great energy and strength of will, which enabled him to combat and surmount the difficulties, often considerable, of his responsible public post. He had in later years often suffered seriously from asthma.'[22] Although in his public work Bazalgette appears to have been notably calm and objective in the face of errors and difficulties, these qualities were perhaps not so evident in his private life, his great-grandson having recorded that 'he was small, very asthmatic, and probably rather irascible'.[23]

Bazalgette's achievements are certainly comparable with those of Brunel in their scale, their complexity, their use of new materials and their effects on his fellow citizens. If he had lived a year longer

Bazalgette could have observed the Hamburg epidemic, confident in the knowledge that his intercepting system would protect London, despite the anxiety that it occasioned among the politicians. He worked within the framework of an emerging concept of local administration to which his great works helped to give authority, dealing calmly and effectively with problems that had driven his predecessor at the Sewers Commission, Frank Forster, to an early grave. Bazalgette may not be in the heroic tradition of Brunel as an 'Engineering Knight Errant'[24] but his patience and persistence in the face of difficulties which had defeated others were heroic and certainly earn him the 'niche in the temple of fame' proposed for him by Sir Harry Haward, comptroller and historian of the LCC.[25]

The Bazalgette family thrived. The picture on page 189 was taken on 20 April 1890, a year before Sir Joseph's death, with some of his children and grandchildren. Many of his descendants (of whom over thirty are living) have achieved distinction themselves in many different fields. Sir Joseph's son Edward was himself a distinguished civil engineer. His great-grandson Derek Bazalgette followed the example of Joseph's father and entered the Royal Navy, reaching the rank of Rear Admiral and being made a Companion of the Bath like Sir Joseph before him. Another great-grandson died an early, heroic death. Ian Willoughby Bazalgette was born in Calgary, Alberta. He joined the Royal Air Force in 1941 and became a bomber pilot. By 1943 he had completed thirty operations and been awarded the Distinguished Flying Cross when he arranged to be posted to the Pathfinders, an elite force which flew in ahead of the main forces to mark the targets for the bombers that followed. On 4 August 1944, as the battle of Normandy was raging, Squadron Leader Ian Bazalgette attacked a V1 rocket site near Paris. It had been attacked on the previous two days and the defences were ready. Ian Bazalgette flew through a wall of anti-aircraft gunfire to mark the target and emerged with a badly damaged plane and two injured crew members. Having ordered the remaining crew members to strap him into his seat and bale out themselves, he diverted his plunging aircraft away from the French village of Senates and struggled to save the lives of his two remaining injured crewmen by attempting to make an emergency landing in a field. The plane exploded on landing and all three on board were killed instantly. Squadron Leader Bazalgette had given his own life in saving others. He was awarded a posthumous Victoria Cross whose citation concluded: 'His heroic sacrifice marked the climax of a long career of operations against the enemy. He always chose the more dangerous and exacting roles. His courage and devotion to duty were beyond praise.' Sir Joseph's great-great-grandson, Peter Bazalgette, is a familiar name to those who

Ian Willoughby Bazalgette, whose heroism in Normandy in 1944 saved the lives of many others and earned him a posthumous Victoria Cross.

watch the television programmes of his production company Bazal Productions, including 'Food and Drink', 'Changing Rooms' and 'Ground Force'.

Perhaps the last word on Sir Joseph Bazalgette should be left to the obituarist of *The Times* whose tribute was generous in length and sentiment and which recorded both the enduring character of his works and their very great contribution to the welfare of London's citizens:

> When the New Zealander comes to London, a thousand years hence, to sketch the ruins of St Paul's, the magnificent solidity and the faultless symmetry of the great granite blocks which form the wall of the Thames Embankment will still remain to testify that, in the reign of Victoria, 'jerry-building' was not quite universal. Of the great sewer that runs beneath Londoners know, as a rule, nothing, though the Registrar-General could tell them that its existence has added some twenty years to their chance of life.[26]

Notes

ICE refers to the Institution of Civil Engineers.

Preface

1. *The Times*, 9 July 1855.
2. Letter to the author from Dr Walker, 4 November 1997.

Introduction

1. Sir William Cubitt (1785–1861); civil engineer; inventor of self-regulating windmill sails (1807) and the treadmill (1818); F.R.S. (1830); constructed the Oxford and Liverpool Junction canals; Cardiff and Middlesbrough Docks; the South-Eastern Railway; consulting engineer to other railway works in Britain and France and to the Berlin waterworks; President, ICE, 1850, 1851; not to be confused with his contemporary, also William Cubitt (1791–1863), builder and Lord Mayor of London.
2. See the Metropolitan Board of Works, *Annual Report* (1888), pp. 40–50, 97, held in the Metropolitan Archives, for an account of these works.
3. J. Doxat, *The Living Thames, the Restoration of a Great Tidal River*, (Hutchinson Benham, 1977).
4. R. Porter, *London, a Social History* (Hamish Hamilton, 1994), p. 91.
5. Cassell's *Saturday Journal*, 30 August 1890, pp. 1160–1: 'Representative Men at Home; Sir Joseph Bazalgette, CB, at Wimbledon'.
6. Ibid.
7. ICE, *Minutes of Proceedings* (1890–1), vol. 105, pt III, pp. 106–7.
8. *Almanach Cévenol* (1970), pp. 169–76: Archives Départementales, Mende, France.
9. Lease dated 25 June 1287, held in the Departmental Archives.
10. An account of the Bazalgette family compiled by Jean Bazalgette, Cardet, Gard, from family records and others held in the Lozère archives, France.
11. Jean-Louis Bazalgette's will, in the possession of the Bazalgette family.
12. R.D. Gwynn, *Huguenot Heritage* (Routledge & Kegan Paul, 1985), p. 71.
13. This, and other information about Jean-Louis and Joseph Bazalgette (see below) is extracted from papers in the Royal Archives (RA) which are quoted with the gracious permission of Her Majesty the Queen.
14. Later William IV.
15. Coutts Bank archives.
16. Royal Archives, box 7/32, *Proceedings of the Commissioners*.
17. Royal Archives, box 7/34, p. 56 and box 7/32, p. 205.
18. A copy of the letter, held in the Royal Archives, was shown to the author by Jean-Louis' descendant, Peter Bazalgette; RA 31726.
19. 'Letters of Denization and Acts of Naturalisation for Aliens in England and Ireland, 1701–1800', Guildhall Library.
20. Particulars of sale of the estate sold on the death of Jean-Louis, Surrey County Record Office.
21. Jean-Louis Bazalgette's will in the possession of the Bazalgette family.
22. W.R. O'Byrne, *Naval Biographical Dictionary* (John Murray, 1849), p. 59.
23. ICE, *Minutes of Proceedings* (1891), vol. 105, pp. 302–8: Bazalgette's obituary.
24. ICE, *Minutes of Proceedings* (1837–40), vol. 1, p. 41: 'On Reclaiming Land from the Sea, with Plans Illustrative of Works in Loughs Swilly and Foyle'.
25. J.W. Bazalgette's Graduate Membership Certificate, ICE.
26. J.W. Bazalgette's Transfer to Membership Certificate, ICE.
27. *Men of the Time* (George Routledge, 1887): Joseph Bazalgette.
28. *The Builder*, 4 December 1852, p. 773.
29. L.T.C. Rolt, *Victorian Engineering* (Penguin, 1970), pp. 145–6.

30. H.P. Boulnois, *Reminiscences of a Municipal Engineer* (St Bride's Press, 1920), pp. 29, 31.
31. Ibid., p. 29.
32. Bazalgette's will, at Somerset House, shows that the estate was valued at £155,747 upon his death (1891) but this valuation was revised to £184,431 in 1901.
33. Newcomen Society, *Transactions* (1986–7), vol. 58: Dr Denis Smith, discussion of paper.
34. See Chapter Two, page 54 for an account of Forster's untimely death.
35. Sir Harry Haward, *The LCC from Within* (Chapman and Hall, 1932), p. 5.
36. See ICE Name Index for details.
37. ICE, *Minutes of Proceedings* (1840), vol. 1.
38. ICE, *Minutes of Proceedings* (1864–5), vol. 24.
39. See for example ICE, *Minutes of Proceedings*, vol. 19, p. 42; vol. 37, p. 152; and vol. 54, p. 32.
40. ICE Archives, Ref. 1865 BAZ RDT manuscript volume, pp. 489 et seq.
41. ICE Archives; Octavo tract; vol. 307.
42. For this information I am indebted to Geoff Facer, City Engineer (drainage).
43. Perhaps this was unwise: in October 1869 Bazalgette was absent from work for a week owing to ill health; see p. 90, n. 21.
44. ICE Archives, B867 BAZ RDT, pp. 454–511.
45. Ibid. pp. 454, 459.
46. The episode is chronicled in the Royal Archives; ref. MOH 10/520–556 and MOH LB I, p. 428.
47. ICE Archives, B872 BAZ RDT pp. 28–9; Bazalgette's reply is not recorded.
48. ICE Archives, B872 BAZ RDT, p. 260.
49. ICE Archives, B890 BAZ CLR, p. 462: proof of Sir Joseph Bazalgette.
50. Ibid., p. 153: Sir Joseph Bazalgette's evidence.

Chapter One

1. 'Quondam' writing in *The Builder*, 19 February 1853.
2. *The Builder*, 18 July 1844, pp. 350–1.
3. C. Lucas, 'Essay on Waters' (London, 1756), vol. 1, p. 127.
4. Samuel Leigh, *Leigh's New Picture of London* (London, 1818), p. 33, Metropolitan Archives.
5. John Britton, *The Original Picture of London, Enlarged and Improved* (London, 1826), p. 22.
6. See *Memorials of London Life of the 13th and 14th Century*, ed. H.T. Riley, p. 14, Guildhall Library; also *History of the Water Supply of London from the Creation of Man* (Adam Gladstone, 1884), Guildhall Library pamphlet.
7. See A. Hardy, 'Water and the Search for Public Health in London in the Eighteenth and Nineteenth Century', *Journal of Medical History* (1984), vol. 28, pp. 250–82.
8. An account of the circumstances in which Wright wrote the pamphlet is found in *The Guildhall Miscellany*, Guildhall Library, no. 2, February 1953, pp. 31–4.
9. *The Dolphin* (T. Butcher, London, 1828), p. 61.
10. *Parliamentary Papers* (1828), vol. 8, p. 4.
11. *Household Words*, 13 April 1850.
12. *Parliamentary Papers* (1828), vol. ix, p. 149.
13. *The Builder*, 19 February 1853, p. 119.
14. *Parliamentary Papers* (1884), vol. 41, p. ix: Historical Note.
15. Trench and Hillman, *London under London* (John Murray, 1984), p. 39.
16. J. Hollingshead, *Underground London*, 1862, Guildhall Library.
17. *The Builder*, 16 August 1884, p. 215.
18. L.B. Wood, *The Restoration of the Tidal Thames* (Adam Hilger Press, 1982), p. 18.
19. *Parliamentary Papers* (1828), vol. 9, pp. 61–2, 122–3, 168.
20. R. Fitter, *London's Natural History* (Collins, 1945), p. 82.
21. E. Chadwick, *Report on the Sanitary Condition of the Labouring Population of Great Britain, 1842* (Edinburgh University Press edition, 1965), p. 351.
22. *Memorials of London Life*, ed. H.T. Riley, p. 295, Metropolitan Archives.
23. Trench and Hillman, *London Under London*, p. 60.
24. Ibid., p. 61.
25. R.C. Middlemass, *London's Main Drainage: Historical Background* (Thames Water, 1975), p. 1.
26. John Thwaites, *A Sketch of the History and Prospects of the Metropolitan Drainage Question*, 1855, p. 7.
27. *Analytical Index to the Remembrancia, 1579–1664* (Corporation of London, 1878), p. 330, Guildhall Library.
28. Ibid., p. 482.
29. Ibid., p. 483.
30. ICE, *Minutes of Proceedings* (1864–5), vol. 24, p. 281.
31. *Parliamentary Papers* (1844), vol. 17, q. 5891: evidence of Joseph Quick.

Chapter Two

1. *Parliamentary Papers* (1840), vol. 11, q. 3452: Cubitt's evidence to the Select Committee on the Health of Towns.
2. M.W. Flinn, *Introduction to Chadwick's Report* (Edinburgh University Press edition, 1965), p. 43.

3. J. Simon, *English Sanitary Institutions* (1897), p. 187, note, Metropolitan Archives.

4. Flinn, *Introduction to Chadwick's Report*, p. 52.

5. Chadwick, *Report on the Sanitary Condition of the Labouring Population*, p. 410.

6. Ibid., p. 387.

7. Ibid., p. 127.

8. *Parliamentary Papers* (1844), vol. 17: First Report of the Commissioners, p. 150.

9. Ibid., p. 170.

10. R.C. Middlemass, *London's Main Drainage: Historical Background* (Thames Water, 1975), p. 1.

11. Chadwick, *Report on the Sanitary Condition of the Labouring Population*, p. 117.

12. H. Jephson, *The Sanitary Evolution of London* (Fisher Unwin, 1907), p. 104.

13. A. Faulkner, *The Grand Junction Canal* (W.H. Walker, 1993), p. 195.

14. *Parliamentary Papers* (1834), vol. 15, pp. 602, 612–15.

15. H. Gavin, *Sanitary Ramblings* (January, 1848), p. 75, Metropolitan Archives.

16. Ibid., p. 80.

17. A.B. Hopkins, *The Boroughs of the Metropolis* (Bemrose, 1900).

18. I. Neil, *Joseph Bramah: a Century of Invention* (David & Charles, 1968), p. 30.

19. L. Wright, *Clean and Decent* (Routledge, 1980), p. 78.

20. *Parliamentary Papers* (1844), vol. 18, q. 181.

21. *Parliamentary Papers* (1884), vol. 41, p. xi.

22. Dr J. Strang (City Chamberlain, Glasgow): 'On Water Supply to Great Towns', *Journal of the Statistical Society* (June, 1859), p. 233:

23. *Parliamentary Papers* (1857), vol. 36, p. 4, n. 3.

24. G. Best, *Mid-Victorian Britain, 1851–75* (Weidenfeld & Nicolson, 1971), p. 23.

25. J. Hollis and A. Seddon, *The Changing Population of the London Boroughs* (Stat. series no. 5, 1985), O.N.S. Library.

26. One of the Commissioners was the ageing Duke of Wellington; there is no record that he ever attended a meeting.

27. Middlemass, *London's Main Drainage*, p. 1.

28. *Parliamentary Papers* (1840), vol. 11, q. 3452.

29. *Parliamentary Papers* (1834), vol. 15, pp. 371–5.

30. *Parliamentary Papers* (1839), vol. 5, p. 161.

31. Benjamin Hawes is better remembered as Under-Secretary for War during the Crimean War and as a formidable obstacle to Florence Nightingale's attempts to reform the army medical services. He married I.K. Brunel's sister.

32. *Commons Journal* (1839), vol. xciv: the Bill received its first and only reading on 1 August.

33. *Parliamentary Papers* (1844), vol. 3, p. 591.

34. *Parliamentary Papers* (1847), vol. 2, p. 473.

35. So called because the Bill was prompted by alarm at the approach of a second epidemic whose progress across Europe was being anxiously watched. It reached Britain in 1848.

36. *Parliamentary Papers* (1847–8), vol. 32, p. 3.

37. *Parliamentary Papers* (1845), vol. 18.

38. S.E. Finer, *The Life and Times of Sir Edwin Chadwick* (Methuen, 1952), p. 356.

39. Sir George Humphreys, *The Main Drainage of London* (LCC, 1930), p. 10.

40. *Parliamentary Papers* (1884), vol. 41, p. xiii.

41. ICE, *Minutes of Proceedings* (1864–5), vol. 24, pp. 283, 287.

42. Metropolitan Board of Works, *Annual Report* (1888), p. 3.

43. Gavin, *Sanitary Ramblings*, p. 75.

44. British Library 8776h., 28/29: Reports of the Metropolitan Commissions of Sewers.

45. Ibid.

46. Ibid.

47. The controversy is described in John Thwaites, *A Sketch of the History and Prospects of the Metropolitan Drainage Question* (Ash and Flint, 1855), p. 9, Metropolitan Archives.

48. Better remembered as a railway engineer and designer, with his father George, of The Rocket.

49. *The Times*, 16 March, 1850, p. 7, cols 1–4.

50. See Hansard, 16 May 1851 and 29 July 1851.

51. *Civil Engineer and Architect's Journal* (1852), vol. 15, p. 160.

52. ICE, *Minutes of Proceedings* (1852–3), vol. 12, p. 158.

53. See Chapter Five for an examination of these schemes.

54. *Plans for Metropolitan Drainage, 1848–65*, Metropolitan Archives.

55. *Parliamentary Papers* (1852–3), vol. 36: Bazalgette's evidence, 10 June 1853.

56. Thwaites, *A Sketch of the History and Prospects*, p. 11.

57. Ibid., p. 13.

58. Ibid.

59. See the quotation from Humphreys above, p. 49.

Chapter Three

1. *The Times*, 20 March 1855, p. 9.

2. Ibid.

3. R. Porter, *London, a Social History* (Hamish Hamilton, 1994), p. 243.

4. See *Quarterly Review* (1850), vol. 88, p. 455.

5. Hansard, 3rd Series, vol. 137, cols 703–7: Sir Benjamin Hall's speech, 16 March 1855.

6. *The Times*, 7 November 1854, p. 7.
7. A. Briggs, *Victorian Cities* (Pelican, 1968), p. 376.
8. Ibid., p. 20.
9. Chadwick to Macvey Napier, 11 October 1842.
10. *The Economist*, May 1848.
11. *Morning Chronicle*, 29 April 1848.
12. J. Toulmin Smith, *Government by Commissions, Illegal and Pernicious* (Henry Sweet, 1849), p. 340.
13. *Eclectic Review*, August 1850, p. 146.
14. ICE, *Minutes of Proceedings* (1852–3), vol. 12, pp. 70–1.
15. *Parliamentary Papers* (1854), vol. 26, p. xxxviii.
16. C. Gibbon and R.W. Bell, *History of the LCC* (1939), pp. 22–3.
17. Such anxieties, and the reluctance to confer any real authority on the Board in this first Act, echo similar worries over the activities of the GLC in the twentieth century.
18. H. Jephson, *The Sanitary Evolution of London* (Fisher Unwin, 1907), p. 96.
19. Frederick Boase (ed.), *Modern English Biography* (Frank Cass, 1868), p. 782.
20. *The Elector*, 13 June 1857.
21. Metropolitan Board of Works, *Minutes of Proceedings* (1856), pp. 5, 7.
22. Ibid., p. 35.
23. *The Observer*, 6 January 1856, p. 5.
24. This controversy is reflected in numerous Parliamentary enquiries; *Parliamentary Papers* (1844), vol. 17; (1847–8), vol. 32; (1852), vol. 19.
25. Metropolitan Board of Works, *Minutes of Proceedings* (1856), p. 96 (southern drainage) and p. 200 (northern drainage).
26. Metropolitan Board of Works, *Printed Papers*, vol. 1 no. 10, Metropolitan Archives.
27. Humphreys, *Main Drainage*, p. 11.
28. *Parliamentary Papers* (1884), vol. 41: Minutes of evidence 6491.
29. Ibid., pp. xvi–xvii.
30. *Illustrated London News*, 30 December 1856, p. 605.
31. *The Builder*, 8 November 1856, p. 609.
32. Metropolitan Board of Works, *Annual Report* (1856–7), p. 7.
33. Ibid., p. 5.
34. *Parliamentary Papers* (1884), vol. 41, pp. xvii–xx.
35. *Parliamentary Papers* (1857, Second Session), vol. 41, p. 4: correspondence respecting the state of the Thames.
36. Metropolitan Board of Works, *Annual Report* (1857–8), pp. 5–6.
37. Ibid., p. 7.
38. Hansard, 11 June 1858, 3rd Series, vol. 150.
39. Hansard (1857–8), vol. 151, cols 27–8.
40. G. Weightman and S. Humphries, *The Making of Modern London, 1815–1914* (Sidgwick & Jackson, 1983), p. 161.
41. Metropolitan Board of Works, *Minutes of Proceedings* (2 June 1858), p. 383: the motion was rescinded on 29 June, after the Parliamentary debate had concluded.
42. Hansard (1857–8), vol. 151, col. 39.
43. Ibid., col. 23.
44. *The Times*, 21 July 1858, p. 9, col. 2.
45. *Journal of Public Health and Sanitary Review* (1858), vol. iv, p. 142.
46. Hansard (1858), vol. 151, cols 2156–7.
47. Ibid., col. 2075.
48. G. Clifton, *Professionalism, Patronage and Public Service in Victorian London: the Staff of the Metropolitan Board of Works, 1856–86* (Athlone Press, 1992), p. 24.

Chapter Four

1. *The Builder*, 30 April 1859, p. 292.
2. These details are taken from the *Annual Reports* of the Metropolitan Board of Works, 1860–88, which are available in the Metropolitan Archives or Guildhall Library and from Bazalgette's paper given in 1865 to the ICE (ICE, *Minutes of Proceedings* (1864–5), vol. 24, pp. 280–358); further details from J.E. Worth and W.S. Crimp in ICE, *Minutes of Proceedings* (1897), vol. 129.
3. Staffordshire Blue bricks, made for the main drainage, are still used today for heavy duty work.
4. Metropolitan Board of Works, *Annual Report* (1856–7), p. 7. The eventual cost was £4,107,277.
5. Metropolitan Board of Works, *Minutes*, 15 May 1863, pp. 466–7; 5 June, pp. 534–45. The *Annual Report* (1863–4), Appendix C, p. 70, contains further details.
6. *Parliamentary Papers* (1863), vol. 50; Metropolitan Board of Works, *Annual Report* (1861–2), pp. 1–2.
7. Metropolitan Board of Works, *Annual Report* (1858–9), p.7.
8. ICE, *Minutes of Proceedings* (1864–5), vol. 24, p. 313.
9. *A History of the Society of Medical Officers of Health* (Society of Medical Officers of Health, 1906), p. 36.
10. ICE, *Minutes of Proceedings* (1864–5), vol. 24, p. 314.
11. Metropolitan Board of Works, *Annual Report* (1860–1): Engineer's Report, p. 23.
12. For Bazalgette's monthly reports see Metropolitan Board of Works, Documents 2321 et seq.
13. Metropolitan Board of Works, Document 2503, Metropolitan Archives.

14. Ibid., p. 5.
15. Metropolitan Board of Works, Document 2429a, Metropolitan Archives.
16. *Parliamentary Papers* (1889), vol. 29.
17. Metropolitan Board of Works, Document 2521/5: northern middle level contract.
18. See Bazalgette's monthly reports for 1861; Metropolitan Board of Works, Document 2321, Metropolitan Archives.
19. *Parliamentary Papers* (1889), vol. 29; Bazalgette's evidence to the Commission, given on 10 July 1888, is on pp. 321–2 of the Commissioners' Report.
20. The interview is quoted in Chapter Nine, p. 183.
21. Metropolitan Board of Works, *Minutes*, 29 October 1869, p. 1118; 5 November, p. 1139; 10 December, p. 1264.
22. Metropolitan Board of Works, *Minutes*, 27 November 1863, p. 1070.
23. *Clerkenwell News*, 11 November 1863, p. 2.
24. Ibid., 18 November 1863, p. 2.
25. Metropolitan Board of Works, *Miscellaneous Reports*, no. 13, p. 5, Metropolitan Archives.
26. An account of Bazalgette's enquiries, with relevant correspondence, is included in Metropolitan Board of Works, *Minutes*, 30 December 1864, pp. 1291–302.
27. Metropolitan Board of Works, *Miscellaneous Reports*, no. 11, 24 November 1863.
28. Metropolitan Board of Works, *Miscellaneous Reports*, no. 13, p. 7.
29. *Illustrated London News*, 19 February 1859, p. 173.
30. *The Observer*, 14 April 1861, p. 5.
31. *City Press*, 14 September 1861, p. 4.
32. *Marylebone Mercury*, 2 February 1861, p. 2; 9 March 1861, p. 2; 12 October 1861, p. 2.
33. *The Observer*, 6 July 1862, p. 3.
34. *Marylebone Mercury*, 30 July 1864, p. 2.
35. Metropolitan Board of Works, *Minutes*, 28 April 1865, p. 512.
36. *City Press*, 20 May 1865 p. 2.
37. *The Builder*, 8 April 1865, pp. 238–9, contains a detailed account of the event.
38. Metropolitan Board of Works, *Minutes*, 3 April 1868, p. 879.
39. Metropolitan Board of Works, *Minutes*, 1868, pp. 879, 956, 1026 et seq.
40. *The Builder*, 22 August 1868, p. 627, contains an account of the visits.
41. Metropolitan Board of Works, *Annual Report* (1863–4), p. 13.
42. Metropolitan Board of Works, *Annual Report* (1888), pp. 16–19, gives an account of these works.
43. Metropolitan Board of Works, *Printed Papers*, vol. 1, no. 10, Metropolitan Archives.
44. ICE, *Minutes of Proceedings* (1864–5), vol. 24, pp. 292–3.
45. *The Builder*, 17 August 1867, p. 614.
46. Metropolitan Board of Works, *Miscellaneous Reports*, no. 23.
47. Metropolitan Board of Works, *Annual Report* (1865–6), p. 17.
48. *Parliamentary Papers* (1868–9), vol. 50, p. 475.
49. *Parliamentary Papers* (1870), vol. 11.
50. Metropolitan Board of Works, *Annual Report* (1875), pp. 20–1.
51. *Parliamentary Papers* (1884), vol. 41, p. xxxiv.
52. *The Times*, 12 December 1877, p. 8, col. 1.
53. *The Times*, 18 December 1877, p. 7, col. 6.
54. See *The Times*, 4 September 1878, p. 7, col. 4, for the earliest account, with extensive coverage on the days that followed.
55. *Saturday Review*, 5 October 1878, pp. 423–4.
56. *Parliamentary Papers* (1884), vol. 62; *Papers Relating to the Pollution of the River Thames* contains Wigner's report; see *The Times*, 24 October 1878, p. 7, col. 6.
57. Metropolitan Board of Works, *Annual Report* (1880), p. 21.
58. Metropolitan Board of Works, *Annual Report* (1878–9); Bazalgette's *Report*, p. 135.
59. *Parliamentary Papers* (1884), vol. 41, p. lxvii: conclusion 4.
60. Hansard, vol. 151, 1858, col. 2157; see also Chapter Three, p. 75.
61. Metropolitan Board of Works, *Annual Report* (1881), p. 20 and (1882), p. 6.
62. *Parliamentary Papers* (1884–5), vol. 31; *Royal Commission on Metropolitan Sewage Discharge*, p. lxvi.
63. *The Times*, 30 November 1885, p. 9, col. 4.
64. *Pall Mall Gazette*, 7 January 1886, p. 11.
65. Metropolitan Board of Works, *Minutes*, 14 January 1887, and 24 July 1888.
66. Metropolitan Board of Works, *Minutes*, 26 March 1886, pp. 613–17.
67. For an account of these works see Metropolitan Board of Works, *Annual Report* (1888), pp. 26–7.
68. The remaining five vessels, *Barking, Binnie, Barrow, Burns* and *Belvedere*, arrived between 1887 and 1895; see LCC, *Annual Report* (1913).
69. See above, p. 103, for this reference.
70. D. Owen, *The Government of Victorian London* (Belknap, 1982), p. 73.
71. See *Water Pollution Research, Technical Paper no. 11*: 'Effects of Polluting Discharges on the Thames Estuary' (HMSO, 1964), pp. 96 et seq. for a later assessment of the problem.
72. For the details that follow I am indebted to Graham Pilkington, Operations Manager, Beckton catchment, Thames Water Utilities and his staff.

Chapter Five

1. Chadwick, *Report on the Sanitary Condition of the Labouring Population*, p. 118.
2. J.T. Way, 'Composition and Money Value of Guano', *Journal of the Royal Agricultural Society of England* (1850), vol. 10, pp. 313–79.
3. *The Times*, 7 November 1859, p. 6.
4. *The Builder*, 8 November, 1862, p. 800. See also the article by Baron Liebig and Alderman J.J. Mechi, 'The sewage of towns', *Farmer's Magazine* (1860), 3rd Series, 17, pp. 163–5.
5. *The Builder*, 4 December 1875, p. 1073.
6. *The Builder*, 21 October 1843, p. 444.
7. *Farmers' Magazine* (1848), 2nd Series, 17, p. 219: report of monthly discussion.
8. *The Builder*, 3 June 1848, p. 273 and 24 June 1848, p. 309.
9. *Parliamentary Papers* (1852), vol. 19, p. 144: minutes of information.
10. *The Builder*, 20 August 1870, pp. 662–3.
11. *Parliamentary Papers* (1852), session 2, vol. 20, p. 93; and (1852–3), vol. 26, q. 2022.
12. *Farmer's Magazine* (1860), vol. 17, pp. 254–5.
13. *Parliamentary Papers* (1862), vol. 14, p. 91: appendix: Second Report.
14. Ibid., p. xv.
15. Metropolitan Board of Works, *Minutes of Proceedings* (1856), p. 108.
16. *The Observer*, 20 April 1856, p. 6.
17. Metropolitan Board of Works, *Minutes of Proceedings* (1856), p. 548.
18. See above, Chapter Three, pp. 66–76.
19. Metropolitan Board of Works, *Minutes of Proceedings* (1859), pp. 354–5.
20. *The Builder*, 17 September 1859, p. 619.
21. Metropolitan Board of Works, *Annual Report* (1859–60), p. 11.
22. Ibid.
23. Ibid., p. 12.
24. *Parliamentary Papers* (1865), vol. 8, p. 58, qq. 1601–5.
25. Metropolitan Board of Works, *Minutes of Proceedings* (1862), p. 10.
26. Metropolitan Board of Works, Document 967, 1 January 1862, pp. 441–4, Metropolitan Archives.
27. *Parliamentary Papers* (1864), vol. 14, p. iii.
28. Ibid., qq. 4785–9.
29. Ibid., p. v.
30. Metropolitan Board of Works, *Minutes of Proceedings* (1865), p. 367.
31. *The Times*, 16 November 1864, p. 8, col. 5.
32. Baron Liebig, *Letters on the Subject of the Utilisation of the Metropolitan Sewage Addressed to the Lord Mayor of London* (London, 1865), p. 13.
33. *The Builder*, 18 February 1865, p. 120.
34. *The Times*, 2 March 1865, p. 8, col. 6.
35. Readers may recall that, a century later, Maplin Sands was proposed by Edward Heath's government as the site for the third London airport.
36. *Parliamentary Papers* (1865), vol. 8, minute 1681; *Parliamentary Papers* (1864), vol. 8, pp. 423–39 describes the scheme.
37. *Parliamentary Papers* (1864), vol. 14, p. 641.
38. *City Press*, 19 November 1864.
39. Metropolitan Board of Works, *Minutes of Proceedings* (1865), p. 263, and *Annual Report* (1864–5), pp. 115 and 119, articles 1, 4 and 24.
40. Metropolitan Board of Works, *Annual Reports* (1865–6), p. 22; and (1866–7), p. 20.
41. For a contemporary account of the schemes see *Farmer's Magazine* (1868), 3rd Series, 33, pp. 438–40; and J.C. Morton, *Experience with 300,000 tons of London Sewage at the Lodge Farm, Barking* (London, 1868).
42. Metropolitan Board of Works, *Annual Report* (1867–8), p. 13.
43. W. Hope, 'The use and abuse of town sewage', *Journal of the Society of Arts* (1869–70), 18, p. 302.
44. Metropolitan Board of Works, *Annual Report* (1870–1), p. 36.
45. Metropolitan Board of Works, *Annual Report* (1888), p. 21.
46. Metropolitan Board of Works, *Minutes of Proceedings* (1865), pp. 515, 819, 1249–52 and 1409.
47. Metropolitan Board of Works, *Minutes of Proceedings* (1871), pp. 135–6.
48. Metropolitan Board of Works, *Annual Report* (1873), pp. 18–19.
49. A. Voelcker, 'On the composition and practical value of several samples of native guano prepared by the ABC sewage process of the Native Guano Company', *Journal of the Royal Agricultural Society of England* (1870), 2nd Series, 6, pp. 415–25.
50. ICE, *Minutes of Proceedings* (1877), vol. 48, p. 158.
51. *The Builder*, 19 May 1877, p. 493.
52. *The Builder*, 15 June 1872, p. 469.
53. *Parliamentary Papers* (1876), vol. 38, p. xii, conclusions 6 and 7.
54. *The Metropolitan*, 24 February 1877, pp. 120–1.
55. *The Builder*, 10 April 1875, p. 331.
56. J.C. Wylie, *Fertility from Town Waste* (Edinburgh, 1955), p. 25.
57. Department of the Environment, *Code of Practice for the Agricultural Use of Sewage Sludge* (1989).
58. Dr T. Evans, 'The management of water and wastewater solids for the 21st century: a global

perspective' (World Economic Forum, Washington DC, June 1994); and interview with Dr Evans at Little Marlow, 25 September 1996.

59. *Australian Capital Territory Future Water Supply Strategy* (1994), pp. 15–16.

Chapter Six

1. ICE, *Minutes of Proceedings* (1864–5), vol. 24, p. 285: Joseph Bazalgette.
2. C. Creighton, *A History of Epidemics in Britain* (Cambridge University Press, 1894), p. 858.
3. The disease remains a familiar horror in refugee camps and similar sites with inadequate sanitation.
4. *The Lancet*, 12 November 1831, p. 216.
5. Ibid., 22 October 1853, pp. 393–4.
6. *The Times*, 12 September 1849, p. 3, cols 3–4; 13 September, p. 4, cols 2–3.
7. Florence Nightingale, *Notes on Nursing* (Harrison, 1859, facsimile reprint), p. 16.
8. *The Builder*, 18 July 1844, pp. 350–1.
9. *Parliamentary Papers* (1846), vol. 10, p. 651.
10. Doulton later became a member of the Metropolitan Board of Works. The company continues in business to this day producing high quality dinner services.
11. *The Builder*, 1 February 1890, pp. 78–9.
12. *Parliamentary Papers* (1844), vol. 17, p. 50.
13. *Parliamentary Papers* (1850), vol. 21, p. 543: Report of the General Board of Health on the Epidemic Cholera of 1848 and 1849.
14. For example, *On the Communication of Cholera by Impure Thames Water* (1854), p. 365; and *Drainage and Water Supply in Connection with the Public Health* (1858), pp. 161, 189; Wellcome Institute Library.
15. J. Snow, *Medical Times and Gazette*, 1858, p. 191.
16. J. Snow, *On Cholera* (Wade Hampton Frost, New York, 1936), pp. 124, 110.
17. J. Snow, 'Cholera and the Water Supply in the Southern Districts of London', *British Medical Journal* (1857), vol. 2, p. 864.
18. *Report of the Health of London Association on the Sanitary Condition of the Metropolis, 1847*, p. viii.
19. Guildhall Papers, MS Minutes, Sewers Commission lxxxiii, 529–36.
20. *The Times*, 10 October 1849 p. 5, col. 4.
21. J. Simon, 'First Annual Report' in *Reports Relating to the Sanitary Condition of the City of London* (1854), p. 9, Metropolitan Archives.
22. MS Minutes, Sewers Commission lxxxix, f. 1010, Metropolitan Archives.
23. One is tempted to compare him with Jeffrey Archer.

24. An account of the events leading to Farr's appointment is given in S.E. Finer, *The Life and Times of Sir Edwin Chadwick* (Methuen, 1952), p. 143.
25. *The Lancet*, 13 March 1852, p. 268.
26. Tenth Annual Report of the Registrar-General, 1847, p. xvii.
27. *Parliamentary Papers* (1854–5), vol. 21, p. 16; see also pp. 26–31 for the Committee's explanations.
28. Ibid., p. 48.
29. Ibid.
30. Ibid., p. 47
31. Ibid., pp. 155–61: Appendix 4: Report on Golden Square.
32. Ibid. p. 52.
33. *The Times*, 1 August 1866, p. 11.
34. *Parliamentary Papers* (1867), vol. 37, pp. 295–6 and 294: Ninth report of the Medical Officer to the Privy Council, Appendix 7f.
35. *The Times*, 2 August 1866, p. 10.
36. *Parliamentary Papers* (1867–8), vol. 37, p. 95: Narrative of Proceedings at the General Register Office during the Cholera Epidemic of 1866.
37. Ibid., p. 117.
38. Ibid., p. 102.
39. Ibid., Greaves's evidence.
40. *Parliamentary Papers* (1867), vol. 58: Report of Captain Tyler to the Board of Trade, in Regard to the East London Waterworks Company, pp. 6, 8 and 20.
41. Ibid., pp. 14–15.
42. *The Lancet*, 2 November 1867.
43. *Parliamentary Papers* (1867–8), vol. 37, pp. 79–80.
44. *The Lancet*, 15 August 1867.
45. *Parliamentary Papers* (1870), vol. 38, p. 21: Twelfth Annual Report of the Medical Officer to the Privy Council.
46. Ibid., p. 22.
47. *Parliamentary Papers* (1874), vol. 33, pp. 624–5.
48. ICE, *Minutes of Proceedings* (1864–5), vol. 24, p. 285.
49. Metropolitan Board of Works, *Annual Report* (1868–9), p. 11.
50. *Parliamentary Papers* (1868–9), vol. 16, p. liii: Thirtieth Annual Report of the Registrar-General.
51. *Parliamentary Papers* (1896), vol. 37: Supplement to 24th Report of the Local Government Board, 1894–5, p. v.
52. *Illustrated London News*, 10, 17 and 24 September 1892.
53. *Parliamentary Papers* (1894), vol. 40, pp. vii–ix.
54. An account of the Hamburg epidemic may be found in R.J. Evans, *Death in Hamburg: Society and Politics in the Cholera Years, 1830–1910* (Pelican, 1987).

55. Cassell's *Saturday Journal*, 30 August 1890,
     pp. 1160–1: Representative Men at Home: Sir
     Joseph Bazalgette, CB, at Wimbledon.

Chapter Seven

1. Metropolitan Board of Works, *Annual Report*
    (1859–60), p. 3.
2. Metropolitan Board of Works, *Annual Report*
    (1888), p. 29.
3. For example, Metropolitan Board of Works, *Minutes*
    (1868), p. 1191; and (1869), p. 94; also
    Miscellaneous Reports, no. 31, pp. 1–20,
    Metropolitan Archives.
4. Metropolitan Board of Works, *Annual Report*
    (1858–9), pp. 6–11, includes a copy of Thwaites's
    letter.
5. Metropolitan Board of Works, *Annual Report*
    (1888), pp. 30–3; also ICE, *Minutes of Proceedings*
    (1877–8), vol. 54: 'The Victoria, Albert and
    Chelsea Embankments of the River Thames', paper
    by Edward Bazalgette, Sir Joseph's son.
6. Metropolitan Board of Works, Documents 2422 et
    seq. (contracts); 2530 et seq. (drawings); see also
    Edward Bazalgette's paper on the embankments in
    ICE, *Minutes of Proceedings* (1877–8), vol. 54.
7. Thus on 9, 16 and 23 November 1858 the Main
    Drainage Committee corresponded with Lewis
    Thompson and Dr Richardson, both of Newcastle,
    with a view to securing their services. There is no
    record of the advice they gave. Metropolitan Board
    of Works, Document 965, Metropolitan Archives.
8. A.J. Francis, *The Cement Industry, 1796–1914*
    (David & Charles, 1977), p. 12.
9. Quoted in A.C. Davis, *A Hundred Years of Portland
    Cement, 1824–1924* (Concrete Publications Ltd,
    1924), pp. 35 and 37.
10. For an account of the development of Portland
    cement see Francis, *The Cement Industry*, ch. 8; also
    Davis, *A Hundred Years of Portland Cement*.
11. H.P. Boulnois, *Reminiscences of a Municipal Engineer*
    (St Bride's Press, 1920), p. 29.
12. Davis, *A Hundred Years of Portland Cement*, page xix.
13. ICE, *Minutes of Proceedings* (1865–6), vol. 25,
    pp. 66–159.
14. Metropolitan Board of Works, Documents 2431/1:
    Thames Embankment, Middlesex Side, contract no.
    1, clause 45, 27 October 1863.
15. The details that follow are taken from ICE, *Minutes
    of Proceedings* (1870–1), 32, pp. 266–328.
16. Francis, *The Cement Industry*, p. 132.
17. The event was described in the *Illustrated London
    News*, 4 December 1869, p. 567.

18. Three of the artists' impressions are shown in the
    colour plate section.
19. P. Guedalla (ed.), *The Queen and Mr Gladstone*
    (Hodder & Stoughton, 1933), p. 233.
20. *The Times*, 14 July 1870, p. 10.
21. Details are given in ICE, *Minutes of Proceedings*
    (1877–8), vol. 54, pp. 1 et seq.
22. Roy Jenkins, *Gladstone* (Papermac, 1996), p. 375.
23. Hansard, 3rd series, vol. 202, col. 1753, 8 July
    1870.
24. *The Times*, 11 July 1870, p. 9.
25. *The Times*, 14 April 1871, p. 7.
26. Metropolitan Board of Works, *Annual Report*
    (1873), p. 20, gives details of the final settlement.
27. Metropolitan Board of Works, *Annual Reports* for
    1879, 1880 and 1888 recount the history of the
    experiment.

Chapter Eight

1. *Parliamentary Papers* (1854–5), vol. 10, contains the
    report in full and includes the plans for the schemes
    of Mosley, Paxton and others.
2. Report to the Metropolitan Board of Works, British
    Library catalogue, 8229.99.30.
3. *The Builder*, 1 December 1866, p. 877.
4. *The Times*, 26 January 1872, p. 9.
5. Metropolitan Board of Works, *Annual Report*
    (1860–1), p. 14.
6. Metropolitan Board of Works, *Annual Report*
    (1888), p. 43.
7. *Daily News*, 14 December 1885, p. 7.
8. *Parliamentary Papers* (1865), vol. 8, contains a full
    account of the enquiry.
9. Metropolitan Board of Works, *Minutes of Proceedings*,
    24 September 1869.
10. Metropolitan Board of Works, *Minutes of Proceedings*,
    24 November 1876.
11. T. Taylor, *Leicester Square* (Bickers & Son, 1874) and
    J. Hollingshead, *The Story of Leicester Square* (Simkin
    Marshall, 1892) both contain accounts of the
    history of the square.
12. *The Metropolitan*, 24 January 1874.
13. The *Illustrated London News*, 4 July 1874, contains
    an illustrated account.
14. The funds, paradoxically, originated in bridge tolls
    in the reign of Edward I; a farthing for pedestrians
    and a penny for horse and rider.
15. *Parliamentary Papers* (1877), vol. 14: the Committee
    gave the company secretary, William Clarke, a hard
    time on the matter of the share price.
16. The costs are recorded in the Board's *Annual Report*
    (1888), pp. 48–51.

17. The scene was described in the *Daily Chronicle* and *Clerkenwell News*, 7 October 1878.
18. Vividly described and illustrated in the *Illustrated London News*, 31 May, 1879.
19. Hammersmith Bridge was closed to cars and lorries for repairs in 1997 and reopened in 1998.
20. C.J. Feret, *Fulham Old and New* (Leadenhall Press, 1952), tells the history of the bridge.
21. Metropolitan Board of Works, *Annual Report* (1888), p. 52; and *Minutes of Proceedings*, 22 March 1878.
22. All described in 'Aquarius', *The Tower High Level Bridge, an Imperial Question* (Spon, 1878), Guildhall Library.
23. Metropolitan Board of Works, *Annual Report* (1888), p. 7, and *Parliamentary Papers* (1884–5), vols 30 and 31, describe the conditions.
24. The process is described in *Parliamentary Papers* (1881), vol. 7.
25. Reported in the *Daily News*, 19 August 1878, p. 5.
26. Metropolitan Board of Works, *Annual Report* (1888), pp. 45 et seq.
27. Metropolitan Board of Works, *Annual Report* (1888), pp. 57 et seq., describe the Board's work in creating parks.
28. See Chapter Six for a discussion of the issue.
29. Metropolitan Board of Works, *Annual Report* (1888), p. 146.

Chapter Nine

1. See above, Chapter Three, p. 66.
2. Metropolitan Board of Works, *Annual Report* (1888), pp. 30 et seq. summarises the information referred to in the following paragraphs.
3. Cassell's *Saturday Journal*, 30 August 1890, p. 1160.
4. See the Introduction for details of this work.
5. Hansard, 3rd series, vol. 137, col. 726, 16 March 1855; see Chapter Three for a summary of these debates, notably pp. 64 et seq.
6. See *Parliamentary Papers* (1889), vol. 29: 'Royal

Commission Appointed to Inquire into Certain Matters Connected with the Metropolitan Board of Works' for an account. Neither Bazalgette nor any of his staff were criticised in the report.
7. *Parliamentary Papers* (1847–8), vol. 32A, p. 42.
8. See above, Chapter Four, p. 90: 'The Odessa Contract'.
9. ICE, *Minutes of Proceedings* (1870–1), vol. 32, p. 314.
10. ICE, *Minutes of Proceedings* (1851–2), vol. 11, pp. 478 et seq.
11. ICE, *Minutes of Proceedings* (1865–6), vol. 25, pp. 66 et seq.
12. When I asked the young engineer who manages the Beckton incineration plant how she describes her job to others she replied 'I prevent cholera epidemics'.
13. R.J. Evans, *Death in Hamburg* (Clarendon Press, 1987), p. 149 gives details and references.
14. See above Chapter Six, pp. 137 et seq.
15. *Parliamentary Papers* (1894), vol. 40.
16. In Cassell's *Saturday Journal*, 30 August 1890; see p. 183.
17. See the Introduction, page 9.
18. See Chapter Four, p. 103.
19. Thwaites, *A Sketch of the History and Prospects*, pp. 15–17.
20. *Parliamentary Papers* (1854–5), vol. 53, p. 33.
21. See Chapter Three, p. 66, for an account of this episode.
22. ICE, *Minutes of Proceedings* (1891), vol. 105, p. 308.
23. Newcomen Society, *Transactions* (1986–7), vol. 58, p. 111; Rear Admiral Derek Bazalgette in discussion of paper by Dr Denis Smith. The reference to Sir Joseph's irascibility is the closest thing to an anecdote about him that I have been able to find.
24. A. Vaughan, *Isambard Kingdom Brunel: Engineering Knight Errant* (John Murray, 1991).
25. Sir Harry Haward, *The LCC from Within* (Chapman & Hall, 1932), p. 5.
26. *The Times*, Monday 16 March 1891, p. 4: obituary of Sir Joseph Bazalgette.

Bibliography

Parliamentary publications

Parliamentary Papers
1828 vol. viii, vol. ix
1830–1 vol. xiv
1834 vol. xv, vol.li
1836 vol. xx
1837 vol. xxv
1839 vol. xx
1840 vol. xi
1843 vol. xxi
1844 vol. iii, vol. xvii, vol. xviii
1845 vol.v, vol.xviii
1846 vol. x, vol. xliii
1847 vol.i, vol. ii
1847–8 vol.iv, vol. xxxii
1849 vol. iv, vol. xxiv
1850 vol. xxi, vol. xxii, vol. xxxiii
1851 vol. xv, vol. xxiii, vol. xlviii
1852 vol xix and (session 2) vol.xx
1852–3 vol.xxvi, vol. xxxvi, vol. xcvi
1854 vol. xxvi, vol. xxxv, vol. lxi
1854–5 vol. xx, vol. xxi, vol. xlv, vol. liii
1856 vol. lii, vol. liii
1857 (Second Session) vol. xxxvi, vol. xli

1857–8 vol. iii, vol. xxiii, vol. xxxii, vol. xlviii
1860 vol. xx, vol. xxix
1861 vol. xviii
1862 vol.xiv
1863 vol. i
1864 vol.xiv
1865 vol. viii, vol.xxvii
1867 vol. ix, vol. xxxvii, vol. lviii
1867–8 vol. xxxvii, vol. lv
1868–9 vol. xvi, vol. xxxiii, vol. l
1870 vol. xi, vol. xxxviii
1874 vol. xxxi, vol. xxxiii
1875 vol. xviii
1876 vol.xxxviii
1878–9 vol.xiii
1884 vol. xli, vol. lii, vol. lxi, vol. lxii
1884–5 vol.xxxi
1889 vol. xxix
1892 vol. xxiv
1893–4 vol. xl
1894 vol. xl
1896 vol. xxxvii
Hansard, Third Series, 1848; 1851; 1855; 1857–8; 1858

Records of the Metropolitan Commissioners of Sewers

BL 8776 h. 28 & 29 Metropolitan Commissions of Sewers Records
MS Minutes Sewers Commission lxxxiii 529–36, Guildhall collection

Records of the Metropolitan Board of Works

Metropolitan Board of Works Annual Reports, 1856/7–1888 (the final Report, of 1888, contains a brief account of the Board's work throughout its existence); bound volumes are available in different formats in the Guildhall Library and in the Metropolitan Archives, the latter having most of the volumes on open shelves
Metropolitan Board of Works Minutes of Proceedings, 19 December 1855 to 15 March 1889; available in bound volumes, on open shelves, in the Metropolitan Archives
Metropolitan Board of Works Miscellaneous Reports available from the archives of the Metropolitan Archives
Metropolitan Board of Works Printed Papers and Presented Papers also available from the archives of the Metropolitan Archives

Institution of Civil Engineers

J.W. Bazalgette's Graduate Membership Certificate, ICE
Institution of Civil Engineers *Minutes of Proceedings*; numerous volumes have been referred to, notably vol. 1 (1837–40)

which contains an account of early reclamation work undertaken by Bazalgette in Northern Ireland; vol. 24 (1864–5) which contaions Bazalgette's own account of the main drainage work; vols 32 (1870–1), 41 (1874–5), 54 (1878) and 62 (1880) which contain papers on the use of Portland cement; vols 32 (1871) and 48 (1877) which deal with the subject of the use of sewage as manure; vol. 105 (1891) which contains Bazalgette's obituary; vol. 129 (1897) which gives an account of the effects of the precipitation works; and vol. 204 (1916–17) which contains an account by Sir George Humphreys of Bazalgette's work and later developments.

Bazalgette's own papers, donated to the Institution by his great-grandson Rear-Admiral Derek Bazalgette, are filed in the Institution's archives in bound quarto and octavo volumes under the reference BAZ, together with the year in which the work was undertaken e.g. 1882 BAZ.

Books and pamphlets published in London unless stated otherwise

Ackernecht, E.H. *A Short History of Medicine* (Baltimore, Johns Hopkins University Press, 1982)

Adamson, J. and Hudson, L. (eds), *The London Town Miscellania* (Alexius Press, 1992)

Anonymous pamphlet, *Engineers and Officials* (Metropolitan Archives, 1856)

Baldwin Latham, J. *A Lecture on the Sewage Difficulty* (Spon, 1867)

Beckett, D. *Brunel's Britain* (David & Charles, 1980)

Bellamy, C. *Administering Central-Local Relations, 1871–1919* (Manchester University Press, 1988)

Bentham, J. *Constitutional Code, Volume 1 of Collected Works* (Oxford Clarendon Press, 1983)

Best, G. *Mid-Victorian Britain 1851–75* (Weidenfeld & Nicolson, 1971)

Binnie, G.M. (ed.), *Early Victorian Water Engineers* (Thomas Telford Press, 1981)

Boulnois, H.P. *Reminiscences of a Municipal Engineer* (St Brides Press, 1920)

Boulnois, H.P. *The Municipal and Sanitary Engineer's Handbook* (Spon, 1883)

Briggs, A. *Victorian Cities* (Pelican, 1968)

Briggs, A. *Victorian People* (Pelican, 1955)

Britton, John *The Original Picture of London, Enlarged and Improved* (Longman, 1832)

Brundage, A. *England's 'Prussian Minister' Edwin Chadwick and the Politics of Government Growth, 1834–54* (Penn State University Press, 1988)

Buchanan, R. *The Engineers: a History of the Engineering Profession in Britain* (Kingsley, 1989)

Budd, W. *Memorandum on Asiatic Cholera, its Mode of Spreading and its Prevention* (Bristol, J. Wright & Co., 1866)

Budd, W. *Typhoid Fever, Its Nature, Mode of Spreading and Prevention* (Longmans Green, 1873)

Bynum, W.F. *Science and the Practice of Medicine in the Nineteenth Century* (Cambridge University Press, 1994)

Bynum, W.F. and Porter, R. (eds), *Living and Dying in London* (Wellcome Medical History Supplement no. 11, 1991)

Cannadine, D. and Reeder, D. (eds), *Essays in Urban History by H.J. Dyos* (Cambridge University Press, 1982)

Cannadine, D. and Dyos, H.J. (eds), *Exploring the Urban Past* (Cambridge University Press, 1982)

Chadwick, E. *Papers Read Before the Statistical Society of Manchester* (Charles Knight, 1846)

Chadwick, E. *Report on the Sanitary Condition of the Labouring Population of Great Britain* (1842; Edinburgh University Press edition, 1965)

Cherry, S. *Medical Services and the Hospital in Britain, 1860–1939* (Cambridge University Press, 1996)

Church, R. (ed.), *The Dynamics of Victorian Business* (Allen & Unwin, 1980)

Clifton, G. *Professionalism, Patronage and Public Service in Victorian London: the Staff of the Metropolitan Board of Works, 1856–86* (Athlone Press, 1992)

Copland, J. (ed.), *A Dictionary of Practical Medicine* (Longmans Green, 1844–58)

Corfield, W.H. *A digest of facts relating to the treatment and utilisation of sewage* (Macmillan, 1871)

Creaton, H. (ed.), *Bibliography of Printed Works on London History to 1939* (Library Association, 1994)

Creighton, C. *A History of Epidemics in Britain* (Oxford University Press, 1894)

Cruickshank, D. and Burton, N. *Life in the Georgian City* (Viking, 1990)

Daunton, M.J. 'Health and Housing in Victorian London' in Bynum & Porter (eds)

Daunton, M.J. *House and Home in the Victorian City* (Edward Arnold, 1983)

Davis, A.C. *A Hundred Years of Portland Cement, 1824–1924* (Concrete Publications, 1924)

Davies, E. *The Story of the LCC* (Labour Publishing Co., 1925)

Davis, J. *Reforming London* (Clarendon Press, 1988)

Denton, J. Bailey *The Sewage Question* (Spon, 1871)

Dexter, J.T. *The Government of London* (Stanford, 1875)

Dicey, A.V. *Law and Public Opinion during the 19th Century* (Macmillan, 1914)

Dickinson, H.W. *Water Supply of Greater London* (Newcomen Society, 1954)

Doxat, J. *The Living Thames* (Hutchinson Benham, 1977)

Dyos, H.J. & Wolff, M. (eds), *The Victorian City, Image and Realities* (Routledge & Kegan Paul, 1973)

Evans, R. *The fabrication of Virtue: English Prison Architecture, 1750–1840* (Cambridge University Press, 1982)

Evans, R.J. *Death in Hamburg Society and Politics in the Cholera Years, 1830–1910* (Pelican, 1987)

Eyler, J.M *Victorian Social Medicine: the Ideas and Methods of William Farr* (Baltimore, Johns Hopkins University Press, 1979)

Eyles, D. *Royal Doulton, 1815–1965* (Hutchinson, 1965)

Farr, W. *Vital Statistics, ed. Noel Humphreys* (The Sanitary Institute, 1885)

Faulkner, A. *The Grand Junction Canal* (W.H. Walker, 1993)

Finer, S.E. *The Life and Times of Sir Edwin Chadwick* (Methuen, 1952)

Firth, J.F.B. *London Government and How to Reform it* (Cassell, Petter, 1882)

Firth, J.F.B. *Municipal London, or London Government as it is* (Longmans, Green, 1876)

Firth, J.F.B. *Reform of London Government and of City Guilds* (Swann, Lowrey 1888)

Fitter, R. *London's Natural History* (Glasgow, Collins, 1945)

Flinn, M.W. *Introduction to Chadwick's Report* (Edinburgh University Press edition, 1965)

Floud, R. and McCloskey, D. (eds), *The Economic History of Britain since 1700* (Cambridge University Press, 1994))

Fortescue, S.E.D. *People and Places* (Great and Little Bookham, Fortescue, 1978)

Fraser, Sir William *London Self-Governed* (Francis Harvey, 1866)

Frazer, W.M. *Duncan of Liverpool. Being an Account of the Work of Dr W.H. Duncan, M.O.H. of Liverpool, 1847–63* (Hamish Hamilton, 1947)

Frazer, W.M. *A History of English Public Health, 1834–1939* (Bailliere, Tindall & Cox, 1950)

Gavin, H. *Sanitary Ramblings* (John Churchill, 1848)

General Board of Health Report, 1850, quoted in Binnie, G.M. (ed.), *The Supply of Water to the Metropolis in 'Early Victorian Water Engineers'* (Thomas Telford Press, 1981)

Gibbon, G. and Bell, R.W. *History of the LCC* (Macmillan, 1939)

Gwynn, R.D. *Huguenot Heritage* (Routledge & Kegan Paul, 1985)

Hamlin, C. 'State Medicine in Great Britain' in Porter, D. (ed.), *The History of Public Health and the Modern State* (Editions Rodopi, 1994)

Hardy, A. *The Epidemic Streets* (Oxford University Press, 1993)

Harris, P. *London and its Government* (Dent, 1913)

Haward, Sir Harry *The LCC from within* (Chapman & Hall, 1932)

Hennock, E. *Fit and Proper Persons: Ideal and Reality in Mid-Victorian Government* (Edward Arnold, 1973)

History of the Society of Medical Officers of Health (Society of Medical Officers of Health, 1906)

Hodgkinson, R. (ed.), *Public Health in the Victorian Age* (Gregg (Wellcome), 1973)

Hollis, J. and Seddon, A. *The Changing Population of the London Boroughs*, Statistical Series no. 5 (OPCS, 1985)

Hopkins, A.B. *The Boroughs of the Metropolis* (Bemrose, 1900)

Humphreys, Sir George *The Main Drainage of London* (LCC, 1930)

Jefferys, J.B. *The Story of the Engineers* (Lawrence & Wishart, 1945)

Jenks, L.H. *The Migration of British Capital to 1875* (New York, Knopf, 1927; Nelson facsimile reprint, 1971)

Jephson, H. *The Sanitary Evolution of London* (Fisher Unwin, 1907)

Kirby, R.S. *et al. Engineering in History* (Dover publications, 1990)

Kuhn, T.S. *The Structure of Scientific Revolutions* (Chicago University Press, 1962)

Kynaston, D. *The City of London, 1815–90* (Chatto & Windus, 1994)

Lambert, R.J. *Sir John Simon* (McGibbon & Kee, 1963)

Leigh, S. *Leigh's New Picture of London* (Samuel Leigh, 1818)

Letheby, H. *Report on the Sanitary Condition of the City of London* (Metropolitan Archives, 1872–3)

Lewis, R.A. *Sir Edwin Chadwick and the Public Health Movement* (Longmans, 1952)

Lucas, C. *Essay on Waters* (London, 1756, vol. 1)

Luckin, W. *Pollution and Control: a Social History of the Thames in the 19th Century* (Adam Hilger, 1986)

Luckin, W. *Urban Disease and Mortality in Nineteenth-Century England* (Batsford Academic, 1984)

MacDonagh, O. *Early Victorian Government 1830–70* (Weidenfeld & Nicolson, 1977)

McCulloch, J.R. *A Statistical Account of the British Empire* (OPCS library)

MacLeod, R. (ed.), *Government and Expertise: Specialists, Administrators and Professionals, 1860–1919* (Cambridge University Press, 1988)

McNeil, I. *Joseph Bramah: a Century of Invention* (David & Charles, 1968)

Magner, L.N. *A History of Medicine* (Marcel Dekker, 1992)

Mayhew, H. *London Labour and the London Poor* (1851; Penguin Classics reprint)

Metropolitan Board of Works (Argos Publishing Company, 1888) – reprint of six articles (including one by Edwin Chadwick) on the circumstances which led to the appointment of a Royal Commission to investigate the Board

Middlemass, R.K. *The Master Builders* (Hutchinson, 1963)

Midwinter, E.C. *Seminar Studies in History Victorian Social Reform* (Longman, 1968)

Mitchell, B.R. and Deane, P. *Abstract of British Historical Statistics* (Cambridge University Press, 1962)

Morris, R.J. and Rodger, R. *The Victorian City, a Reader in British Urban History, 1820–1914* (Longman, 1993)

Nightingale, Florence *Notes on Nursing* (Harrison, 1859, facsimile reprint)

Olsen, D.J. *The Growth of Victorian London* (Batsford, 1984)

Owen, D. *The Government of Victorian London* (Belknap, 1982)

Pelling, M. *Cholera, Fever and English Medicine, 1825–65* (Oxford University Press 1978)

Penrose, E.T. *The Theory of the Growth of the Firm* (Oxford University Press, 1959)

Perkin, H. *The Rise of Professional Society; England since 1880* (Routledge, 1989)

Peterson, M.J. *The Medical Profession in Mid-Victorian London* (Berkeley, 1978)

Pollard, S. *The Genesis of Modern Management* (Edward Arnold, 1965)

Port, M.H. *Imperial London Civil Government Building in London, 1851–1915* (Yale University Press, 1995)

Porter, D. (ed.), *The History of Public Health and the Modern State* (Editions Rodopi, 1994)

Porter, R. *London, a Social History* (Hamish Hamilton, 1994)

Porter, R. *Disease, Medicine and Society in England, 1550–1860* (Cambridge University Press, 1995)

Riley, H.T. (ed.), *Memorials of London Life* (Longmans, Green, 1868)

Robson, W.A. *The Government and Misgovernment of London* (Allen & Unwin, 1939)

Rolt, L.T.C. *Isambard Kingdom Brunel* (Pelican, 1970)

Rolt, L.T.C. *Thomas Telford* (Pelican, 1979)

Rolt, L.T.C. *Victorian Engineering* (Penguin, 1970)

Rosen, G. *The History of Public Health* (M.D. Publications, 1958)

Sheldrake, J. *Modern Local Government* (Dartmouth, 1992)

Simon, J. *English Sanitary Institutions* (Cassell, 2nd edn, 1897)

Simon, J. *First Annual Report, published in Reports Relating to the Sanitary Condition of the City of London* (John Parker & Son, 1854)

Simon, J. *Report to Local Board of Health of Croydon with Regard to the Causes of Illness Recently Prevailing in That Town* (J. & A. Churchill, 1877)

Smiles, Singer, C. (ed.), *A History of Technology* (Oxford, Clarendon Press, 1958)

Smiles, Samuel, *The Life of Thomas Telford* (John Murray, 1867)

Smiles, Samuel, *Lives of the Engineers* (John Murray, 1904)

Smith, E. *Victorian Farnham* (Phillimore, 1971)

Smith, F.B. *The People's Health, 1830–1910* (Croom Helm, 1979)

Stamp, G. *The Changing Metropolis* (Viking, 1984)

Statistical Abstract for London (LCC, vol. 1, 1897, 6)

Summerson, J. *The London Building World of the 1860s* (Thames & Hudson, 1973)

Sutherland, G. (ed.), *Studies of the Growth of Nineteenth-Century Government* (Routledge & Kegan Paul, 1972)

Tames, R. (ed.), *Documents of the Industrial Revolution* (Hutchinson, 1971)

Thompson, F.M.L. (ed.), *Cambridge Social History of Britain, 1750–1950* (Cambridge University Press, 1990)

Thwaites, J. *A Sketch of the History and Prospects of the Metropolitan Drainage Question* (Ash & Flint, 1855)

Toulmin Smith, J. *Government by Commissions, Illegal and Pernicious* (Henry Sweet, 1849)

Toulmin Smith, J. *The Metropolis Local Management Act* (Henry Sweet, 1857)

Trench, R. and Hillman, E. *London Under London* (John Murray, 1984)

Trevelyan, G.M. *English Social History* (Longman, 1942)

The Triumphant Bore, A Celebration of Marc Brunel's Tunnel (ICE Publications)

Vaughan, A. *Isambard Kingdom Brunel* (John Murray, 1991)

Walvin, J. *Victorian Values* (Andre Deutsch, 1987)

Watson, J.G. *The Civils* (Thomas Telford Press, 1988)

Watson, T. *Lectures on the Principles and Practice of Physic* (Philadelphia, Lea & Blanchard, 1847)

Weightman, G. and Humphries, S. *The Making of Modern London, 1815–1914* (Sidgwick & Jackson, 1983)
Weston, G. *The Civils: the Story of the Institution of Civil Engineers* (Thomas Telford, 1988)
Wohl, A.S. *Endangered Lives: Public Health in Victorian Britain* (Methuen, 1984)
Wood, L.B. *The Restoration of the Tidal Thames* (Adam Hilger Press, 1982)
Woods, R. and Woodward, J. (eds), *Urban Disease and Mortality in Nineteenth-Century England* (Batsford, 1984)
Woodward, Sir Llewelyn *The Age of Reform, 1815–70* (Clarendon, 1962)
Wright, T. *The Dolphin* (London, T. Butcher, 1828, reprinted by Guildhall Library)
Wright, L. *Clean and Decent* (Routledge, 1980)
Wynn-Hammond, C. *Towns* (Batsard, 1976)
Young, K. and Garside, P.L. *Metropolitan London – Politics and Urban Change, 1837–1981* (Edward Arnold, 1982)

Journals, magazines, newspapers and reports
Arnott, N. and Kay, J. 1837–8, vol. 5 p. 70 'Report on the Physical Causes of Fever in the Metropolis, which might be removed by Proper Sanatory (sic.) Measures', in *Fourth Annual Report of the Poor Law Commissioners*
Bonar, J. and Macrosty, H. 'Annals of the Royal Statistical Society, 1834–1934', *British Medical Journal*, April 1867 and January 1894
The Builder has frequently been referred to, with the following editions yielding particularly valuable material: 21 October 1843; 13 and 18 July, 30 November 1844; 13 September, 4 October and 1 November 1845; 7 March 1846; 18 December 1847; 22 January, 18 March, 3 June, 24 June, 15 July, 26 August, 29 September and 7 October 1848; 6 October 1849; 19 October 1850; 25 January, 8 February, 22 March, 21 June and 5 July 1851; 3 January and 4 and 18 December 1852; 19 February, 5 November and 17 December 1853; 14 and 28 January, 4 March, 1, 8, 15 and 22 April 1854; 13 January 1855; 23 February, 29 March, 3 May, 12 and 26 July, 2 and 16 August, 27 September, 4 and 11 October, 8 and 29 November, 6, 13 and 27 December 1856; 3 and 17 October 1857; 20 March, 17 April, 15 May, 3, 10 and 24 July, 25 September, 9 October, 27 November 1858; 1 January, 30 April, 14 May, 13 August, 17 September, 10 December 1859; 12 May, 23 June and 7 July and 27 October 1860; 25 May 1861; 18 January, 15 February, 8 and 15 November, 1862; 14 February, 9 May, 25 July, 1 and 15 August, 12 September 1863; 7 May, 9, 16 and 30 July, 6 August, 17 September, 22 and 29 October, 6 November 1864; 14 January, 18 February and 8 April 1865; 17 August 1867; 22 August and 26 September 1868; 3 April, 10 July, 6 October, 11 and 25 December 1869; 29 January, 20 August and 29 October 1870; 28 January 1871; 15 June 1872; 31 May and 2 August 1873; 10 April, 7 August and 4 December 1875; 22 April and 25 November 1876; 19 May 1877; 16 February, 4 May, 20 July, 3 August, 26 October and 7 December 1878; 15 November 1879; 22 May 1880; 30 April and 3 September 1881; 12 January, 6 and 16 August, 11 October 1884; 22 August and 28 November 1885; 20 March and 3 April 1886; 9 April, 17 and 24 December, 1887; 13 April 1889; 1 February 1890; 21 March 1891
Cassell's Saturday Journal, August 1890
Chadwick, E. 'London Centralised', *Contemporary Review*, June 1884
City Press: 19 June 1858; 14 September 1861; 4 April 1863; 19 November 1864; 20 May 1865; 16 July 1870; 24 July 1878
Civil Engineer and Architect's Journal, 1852, vol. 15
Clerkenwell News, 11 and 18 November 1863
Contemporary Review: 1873, 1875, 1882
Dracup, S.B. 'Water Supply in Great Britain, a Brief History in Six Parts', in *British Water Supply*, January–June 1973
Dunbabin, J. 'Local Government Reform: the Nineteenth Century and After', *Historical Journal*, October 1977
Echo, 27 August 1878
Eclectic Review, August 1850
Economist, May 1848
Edinburgh Review: 1849, 1850 and 1875
Elector: 13 June and 5 August 1857
Eyler, J.M. 'William Farr on the Cholera: the Sanitarian's Disease Theory and the Statistician's Method', *Journal of the History of Medicine*, vol. 28, April 1973
Farr, W. 'Influence of Elevation on the Fatality of Cholera', *Journal of the Statistical Society*, vol. 15, June 1852
Fraser's Magazine: vol. 36, 1847; vol. 38, 1848
Galton, Capt. D. 'Paper on Metropolitan Sewage, given at R.S.A.', February 1885
Goddard, N. '"A Mine of Wealth"? The Victorians and the Agricultural Value of Sewage', *Journal of Historical Geography*, 22, 3 (1996)
Guildhall Miscellany, Guildhall Library, no. 2, February 1953

Hamlin, C. 'Edwin Chadwick and the Engineers, 1842–54 Systems and Antisystems in the Pipe-and-Brick Sewers War', *Technology and Culture*, xxiii, 1992

Hamlin, C. 'Muddling in Bumbledon', in *Victorian Studies*, 32, (1), 1988/9

Hamlin, C. 'Predisposing Causes and Public Health in Early Nineteenth-Century Medical Thought', *Social History of Medicine*, 5, (1992) pp. 55 and 48

Hardy, A. 'Diagnosis, Death and Diet the Case of London, 1750–1909', *Journal of Interdisciplinary History*, 18, 1988

Hardy, A. 'The Medical Response to Epidemic Disease During the Long Eighteenth Century', in *Epidemic Disease in London*, Centre for Metropolitan History Working Papers no. 1, 1993

Hardy, A. 'Water and the Search for Public Health in London in the Eighteenth and Nineteenth Centuries', *Medical History*, 28, 1984

Hennock, E.P. 'Urban Sanitary Reform a Generation Before Chadwick', *Economic History Review*, vol. 10, 1957, no. 1

Hornet, The, 1870

Household Words: 13 April, 29 June and 10 August 1850

Illustrated London News: 13 December 1856; 24 July and 22 August 1858; 19 February, 12 March, 19 May and 27 August 1859; 30 November 1861; 21 May 1864

Institution of Junior Engineers Record of Transactions, vol. vii, 1896–7

Journal of Public Health & Sanitary Review: 1855 and 1858

Jones, E.C. and Falkus, M. 'Urban Improvements and the English Economy in the Seventeenth and Eighteenth Century', *Research in Economic History*, iv, 1979

Journal of the Huguenot Society, vol. 27

Lambert, R.J. 'A Victorian National Health Service: State Vaccination 1855–71', *Historical Journal*, vol. V, 1962, no. 1

Lancet, The: 12 November 1831; 7 July and 9 August, 1849; 13 March, 1852, 22 October 1853; 13 February, 1858; 2 November 1867; 15 August, 1868

Lewis, R.A. 'Edwin Chadwick and the Railway Labourers', *Economic History Review*, 2nd Series, vol. iii, no. 1, 1950

Loudon, I. 'The Origins and Growth of the Dispensary Movement in England,' *Bulletin of the History of Medicine*, 55, 1981

Luckin, W. 'The Final Catastrophe – Cholera in London, 1866', *Medical History*, vol. 21, 1977

MacDonagh, O. 'The Nineteenth-Century Revolution in Government a Re-appraisal' *Historical Journal*, 1, 1958

Maiwald, K. 'An Index of Building Costs in the United Kingdom, 1845–1938', *Economic History Review*, 2nd series, vol. vii, 2

Marylebone Mercury: April 1859, February, March, October, 1861; July 1864; April 1865; August 1870

Matossian, M.K. 'Death in London, 1750–1909', *Journal of Interdisciplinary History*, 16, 1985

McKeown, T. and Record, R.G. 'Reasons for the Decline of Mortality in England & Wales during the Nineteenth Century', *Population Studies*, 1962–3, vol. 16

Metropolitan: May, 1872; April, 1873; February 1877; March, 1880

Morning Chronicle, April 1848

Mukhopadhyay, A.J. 'The Politics of London Water', *London Journal*, 1, 1975

Observer: January, March, April and November, 1856; September 1858; April 1861; July 1862

Pall Mall Gazette: May 1872, January 1886

Porter, D. and Clifton, C. 'Patronage, Professional Values and Victorian Public Works: Engineering and Contracting the Thames Embankment', *Victorian Studies*, 31, 1988

Punch, July, 1857

Quarterly Review: 1842, 1843, 1850, 1851

Saturday Review: October 1878; June 1879

Singer, D. 'Sir John Pringle and his Circle', *Annals of Science*, vi, 1948

Smith D. 'Sir Joseph William Bazalgette, 1819–91', *Newcomen Society Transactions*, vol. 58, 1986–7

Snow, J. 'Cholera and the Water Supply in the Southern Districts of London', *British Medical Journal*, 1857, vol. 2

Snow, J. *Medical Times and Gazette*, 1858

South London News: January, February, March and May 1857

Strang, J. 'On Water Supply to Great Towns', *Journal of the Statistical Society*, June 1859

Tait's Edinburgh Magazine, vol. 9, 1842

The Times: 12, 13 and 26 September, 10 and 26 October 1849; 16 March 1850; 6 September, 7 November 1854; 20 March, 9 July 1855; 21 July 1858; 7 November 1859; 16 November 1864; 2 March 1865; 1 and 2 August 1866; 5 October 1869; 9 August 1870; 12 and 18 December 1877; 4 September 1878; 20 November 1885

Weare, K.M. 'Engineering Ethics History, Professionalism and Contemporary Cases', *Louvain Studies*, 13 (1988)

Westminster Review, vol. 54, 1856

Index